advanced

Gold

teacher's book

Sally Burgess

with Richard Acklam

Longman

Pearson Education Limited
Edinburgh Gate
Harlow
Essex CM20 2JE
England
and Associated Companies throughout the world.
www.longman-elt.com

First published 2001

ISBN 0 582 33799 2

Set in 9/12 Frutiger

Prepared for the Publishers by Stenton Associates

Printed in Spain by Graficas Estella

Acknowledgements

We are grateful to the following for permission to reprint and record copyright material:

Atlantic Syndication Partners (Previously Solo Syndications) for extracts from the articles 'Cold Comfort' by Hazel Knowles in *Daily Mail* 29 August 1995, 'A funny thing happened ...' by Sue Carpenter in *Daily Mail Weekend* 27 January 1996 and 'I'm Proud of my Dad ...' by Lester Middlehurst in *Daily Mail* 26 January 1998; BBC Worldwide for extracts from *The Hitchhiker's Guide to the Galaxy* by Douglas Adams, © Completely Unexpected Productions Ltd 1979; EMI Music Publishing/IMP for songwords 'Dr Heckyll and Mr Jive' from the album *Cargo* by Men at Work; Gruner & Jahr for adapted extracts from the articles 'Work: the daily grind we can't do without' by Windsor Chorlton in *Focus* 1995, '... Wacky future of sport' by Chris Hulme in *Focus* January 1995 and an extract from an article by Paul Simpson in *Focus* October 1998; Independent Newspapers Ltd for extracts from the articles 'Girl Wonder a Real Good Sport' by Keith Elliott in *The Independent* 30 May 1996, and an adapted extract from the article 'Athletics: the enduring allure of the one-to-one challenge' by Mike Robottom in *The Independent* 31 May 1997 and 'Wherefore art thou hip, Mr. Shakespeare?' by Lucy Ward in *The Independent on Sunday* 24 July 1997; IMP for

the songwords 'When You Dream' Words and Music by Ed Robertson and Steven Page © 1998 Treat Baker Music/WB Music Corp, USA. Warner/Chappell Music Ltd, London W6 8BS. Lyrics reproduced by permission of IMP Ltd; Microsoft Corporation for an extract from *The Road Ahead* by Bill Gates Copyright © 1995 by William H. Gates III; News International Syndication, 'Four years ago, Max Valentin buried a £100,000 owl' by Christopher Hadley, in *The Sunday Times Magazine* 8 November 1997 © Christopher Hadley/Times Newspapers Limited 1997 and an extract from the article 'Relative Values' by Sue Fox in *Sunday Times Magazine* 4 October 1998 © Times Newspapers Ltd 1998; the author's agent Mayday Management for extract from *Pole to Pole* by Michael Palin BBC, 1992; Realworld Music Ltd for songwords to 'I Don't Remember' from the album *Peter Gabriel* by Peter Gabriel; Sony Music Publishing for songwords to 'Missing' by Ben Watts/Tracey Thorn; Random House UK Ltd for an adapted extract from *Illustrated Catwatching* by Desmond Morris and Reader's Digest Association for the article 'Nation Shall Speak Unto Nation' from 'Did You Know?' in *Reader's Digest* (1990).

Sample OMR sheets are reproduced by permission of the University of Cambridge Local Examination Syndicate.

Contents

Introduction

Profile of an *Advanced Gold* student

The students with whom you will be using **Advanced Gold** will for the most part be preparing for the **Certificate in Advanced English (CAE)** examination. CAE is intended for students who want a qualification which indicates that their English is at an advanced level either for work or study purposes. They may also be taking CAE because they ultimately intend to take the **Cambridge Certificate of Proficiency in English (CPE)** examination. A CAE course provides such students with a means of developing the skills for this and other high-level examinations. Your students may have successfully taken the **First Certificate in English (FCE)** examination, though this is not a requirement for CAE.

A typical *Advanced Gold* student will already use many of the structures of English fluently and will be able to respond appropriately to a wide range of both predictable and unforeseen situations quite naturally. They will have a growing awareness of the ways in which register affects their choices of grammatical structures and vocabulary. They will be able to express opinions, take part in discussions, etc., and adjust their language according to the social situation in which they find themselves. They will also be able to produce a variety of written texts showing sensitivity to register considerations. Their reading ability will be moving towards a level where they are able to enjoy reading a wide range of both factual and fictional material that they have chosen themselves.

Preparing for CAE

What the typical student will need to succeed in the CAE examination is further refinement and development of all the skills and abilities outlined above, in addition to specific exam strategies and techniques.

Grammar

Students at this level will need to revise, refine and extend their knowledge of grammar encountered at lower levels. In addition, they will need to acquire a command of a range of more sophisticated grammatical structures that befit the advanced learner and user.

Vocabulary

Success at CAE level depends crucially on students expanding their knowledge of vocabulary and refining their understanding of words already acquired. This involves their learning to make distinctions in meaning, connotation, collocation and grammatical constraints between groups of words, and extending lexical sets to include a wider range of subtly distinct items. A further important area of word knowledge essential for CAE is an understanding of word formation and of the meanings and grammatical functions of the full range of affixes. Spelling also often requires attention.

Pronunciation

CAE students often have very clear and intelligible pronunciation but still require some remedial work. They may, for example, have a good command of the individual sounds of English but may still experience difficulty with stress and intonation.

The skills

In terms of reading and listening skills, CAE students will need to be able to listen to or read a text and find the main ideas, distinguishing these from secondary ideas. They should be able to listen or read for gist, as well as extract specific information or detail. The ability to recognise attitude and opinion is also a requirement at this level. In the case of reading, students will also need to learn to identify structure within the text, and to work out what different pronouns, etc. are referring to, and to work out the meaning of unknown words or infer their meaning from context. **CAE Paper 1: Reading** includes up to 3000 words of reading material, plus questions, to be covered in one hour and fifteen minutes. This means that most students will need to increase their reading speed.

In terms of writing, students will need to learn to produce texts of approximately 250 words. Writing successfully at CAE level involves paying careful attention to task input material, generating ideas, organising these ideas, and writing in substantively error-free English. CAE writing tasks demand that students address the requirements of specific audiences, and demonstrate knowledge of the layout conventions, style and register constraints of a number of genres, including articles, reports, reviews, competition entries, leaflets, information sheets, contributions to brochures, letters, personal notes and messages.

Students will need as much speaking practice as possible. By the time they take the CAE examination, their spoken English should be fluent and accurate. Their pronunciation should be clear and intelligible and they should be able to use a wide range of structures and vocabulary in speech to express their ideas, attitudes and opinions. In addition, they should be able to interact in a comfortable and natural manner with the other candidate and the examiner.

Features of the *Advanced Gold* course

The *Advanced Gold* course is made up of the **Advanced Gold Coursebook** and cassettes, the **Advanced Gold Exam Maximiser** and cassettes and free CDs, and this **Advanced Gold Teacher's Book**.

Advanced Gold Coursebook

General features

The *Advanced Gold Coursebook* offers progressive preparation for CAE through fifteen graded units. There are **Review** pages, each of which includes at least one exam-style exercise, to revise the language taught. These Review pages occur at the end of all units except 5, 10 and 15. These three units are followed by **Progress checks** designed to test students' knowledge of the language presented in the previous five units. The Progress checks include **Paper 3 (English in Use)** exam-format tasks covering all six parts of Paper 3.

In addition to the units themselves, at the back of the *Advanced Gold Coursebook* you will find a **Writing reference**, a **Grammar reference**, a **Language index** and **Communication activities**. The Writing reference provides model answers for the genres tested in **Paper 2 (Writing)**. These are annotated with 'dos and don'ts'. In addition, the Writing reference includes useful expressions for each genre. The Grammar reference is a mini-grammar, covering the advanced grammar points presented in the units.

Each unit in the *Advanced Gold Coursebook* provides an integrated package containing the presentation and practice of grammar and vocabulary, as well as reading, listening, speaking and writing development activities, all linked to a theme. A feature of each unit is an **Exam focus** section, which presents and practises the techniques required for a specific task in one of the five papers in the CAE examination. Additional exam training tasks in each unit lead into these Exam focus sections by gradually building up the necessary

exam skills. Particular problem areas of grammar and vocabulary are dealt with in regular **Watch Out!** sections.

Grammar

The *Advanced Gold Coursebook* includes in each unit two major grammar elements. The first of these are **Grammar check** sections, in which grammatical areas students have met before are reviewed and practised. These sections also fulfil the role of laying a foundation for the **Grammar plus** sections, in which students' knowledge and command of the language is extended to cover advanced grammar points that they may not have met formally prior to using *Advanced Gold*.

In both Grammar check and Grammar plus sections, structures are taken from authentic texts used in the unit, presented through error analysis or through matching rules to examples. Each grammar presentation is followed by a number of controlled practice activities, both spoken and written, and then by freer practice activities, in which students have a further opportunity to put the structures to use in either speech or writing. The Grammar plus sections are cross-referenced to the Grammar reference at the back of the *Advanced Gold Coursebook*, and the Grammar check sections are cross-referenced to the *Advanced Gold Exam Maximiser*. If, after working through a Grammar check section in class, students require more practice or revision of a point, you should direct them to the exercises in the *Advanced Gold Exam Maximiser*, either setting these for independent study or working through them in class.

Vocabulary

Throughout the *Advanced Gold* course, students will be encouraged to thoroughly exploit the authentic texts used for reading practice as sources of vocabulary. The majority of reading texts are followed by vocabulary activities to help students derive meaning from context. In addition, each unit contains two or more topic-related vocabulary sections, many of which contain exercises labelled with the symbol shown here. In these exercises, students use their dictionaries to find information on pronunciation, word formation, meaning, word grammar and collocation. Once again, freer practice activities in which students make use of vocabulary in speech or writing normally follow.

Pronunciation

The *Advanced Gold Coursebook* includes regular exercises focussing on stress and intonation.

Reading

Authentic texts from a range of sources (newspapers, magazines, reference books, etc.) are used to develop reading skills. Many texts are accompanied by photographs or illustrations, which can be used as a means of generating interest in the text and getting students to predict what the text will be about. Students read to get a general idea of the text, answering a specific question or questions the first time they read, for example, about how far predictions they have made on the basis of the illustration or title are accurate. They then go on to read for more detailed information or to distinguish main from subsidiary ideas, or to recognise text structure, attitude, etc. There is also regular practice with working out the meaning of unknown words. Activities practising these sub-skills reflect the task types used in the actual exam.

Listening

Again, a range of sources is used for listening texts, and the recordings offer students practice with a variety of accents. Pre-listening tasks help students predict what they will hear. Activities provide practice in listening for specific information, for gist and for inferring through tasks which reflect the **Paper 4** listening tasks. There is a gradual build-up in terms of difficulty of text and task as the course progresses.

Songs are another feature of the listening component of the course. The songs are related to the theme of each unit and provide a motivating use of authentic material.

Writing

Writing activities in each unit provide practice with the genres students are expected to produce in the exam itself (articles, reports, reviews, competition entries, leaflets, information sheets, contributions to brochures, letters, personal notes and messages). Many writing sections focus on the analysis of sample answers or texts of the same type. In all writing sections, students are encouraged to plan their work and to produce more than one draft, discussing their work with another student. Penultimate drafts are also frequently discussed with others, who help with editing and error correction (spelling, grammar and vocabulary; task demands, style and layout).

Speaking

The Grammar check and Grammar plus sections, as well as the vocabulary, reading, listening and writing activities above, will involve students in speaking practice through pair and group work. In addition, specific speaking activities in each unit give students the opportunity to discuss issues open-class or in pairs or groups, and to take part in role-plays. As well as these speaking activities, many of the units in the *Advanced Gold Coursebook* contain a communication activity, in which students work in pairs. These are information gap activities in which each student looks at different information. Where **Paper 5 (Speaking)** is the object of exam training, or is the Exam focus for the unit, specific speaking practice for each part of the test is provided. Particular attention is paid to the language needed to manage the interaction in Paper 5.

Exam focus

Each unit contains at least one Exam focus section, which provides information about an exam task and a procedure to adopt for that task. These sections complete the progressive exam training for each exam task in earlier units. By working through the Exam focus sections, students become familiar with the exam itself, and develop appropriate strategies for dealing with each of the task types, so that they approach the final exam with confidence.

Watch Out! boxes

The Watch Out! sections are designed to pick up on errors that are common to CAE students from a range of language backgrounds. They are typically language points that arise from a Grammar plus section.

Grammar reference

Each Grammar plus section is cross-referenced to the Grammar reference, but students will also make use of this section in their revision in the lead-up to the exam itself.

Writing reference

Like the Grammar reference, this section can be referred to regularly as you work through the units with your class and meet the genres tested in CAE Paper 2 (Writing). Once again, this element will also be a crucial component in students' revision immediately prior to the exam.

Advanced Gold Exam Maximiser

Each of the fifteen units corresponds thematically to the *Advanced Gold Coursebook*, and contains exercises specifically designed to recycle the grammar and vocabulary presented in the coursebook. All such exercises are cross-referenced to the relevant sections in the *Advanced Gold Coursebook*.

A feature of the *Advanced Gold Exam Maximiser* is an explicit focus on exam strategies. Each unit contains a number of tasks, like those in the exam itself, accompanying information on the task, and a series of strategies to apply. **Hot tips!** throughout the *Advanced Gold Exam Maximiser* are designed to give students pointers on how to get extra marks or to avoid losing marks in specific papers and tasks. Learner training sections extend the development of exam strategies. In the final units of the *Advanced Gold Exam Maximiser*, students practise timing their answers and transferring them to sample answer sheets. There is also a complete **Practice exam** at the back of the *Advanced Gold Exam Maximiser*, which can be done in the lead-up to the exam itself. *CAE Practice Tests Plus 2* can be used in the weeks prior to the exam.

The *Advanced Gold Exam Maximiser* makes extensive use of annotated sample answers and is accompanied by cassettes with Paper 4 (Listening) material and simulated Paper 5 (Speaking) tasks. Students have the opportunity to evaluate these sample answers and simulated tasks themselves.

Using the *Advanced Gold Exam Maximiser*

The *Advanced Gold Exam Maximiser* can be used in class in tandem with the *Advanced Gold Coursebook* as a means of providing immediate follow-up work on specific grammar or vocabulary and key exam practice. Alternatively, students can do the appropriate exercises at home.

Another way of organising your CAE programme is to start by working through the *Advanced Gold Coursebook*, and then go on to use the *Advanced Gold Exam Maximiser* for intensive exam preparation in the term prior to students' taking the exam.

Students preparing for the exam independently can also use the *Advanced Gold Exam Maximiser*, though it is advisable for them to have access to the *Advanced Gold Coursebook* as well.

Advanced Gold Teacher's Book

The third element in the *Advanced Gold* course is the *Advanced Gold Teacher's Book*. This provides suggestions about how to use the material in the *Advanced Gold Coursebook* to best advantage, and answers to all exercises (including line references for reading tasks, and a **Tapescript** in which key passages are highlighted). **Extra activities** and **Alternative procedures** are also included in the teaching notes, as is an indication of any **Advance preparation** you will need to make before doing the activities in the unit with your class.

An important element in the *Advanced Gold Teacher's Book* is **Background information** relevant to many of the texts and images used in the *Advanced Gold Coursebook*. An innovative feature of these sections is cross-referencing to websites in which additional background information can be found. Teachers can simply give students the website addresses and then in a subsequent class ask what information students found there. Alternatively, teachers can visit the sites themselves and prepare one or two questions to give students a reason for exploring the site. By regularly accessing these sites, teachers and students alike will raise their awareness of the Internet as a resource for language teaching and learning.

At the back of the *Advanced Gold Teacher's Book* there is a bank of fifteen tests, including twelve **Unit tests**. These provide a quick and convenient means of testing your students after they have completed the **Unit review** pages in the *Advanced Gold Coursebook*. The tests are multiple choice and can be marked very quickly and easily by either teachers or students, using the **Answer key** provided. They can be done in class in under 30 minutes. In the bank of tests you will also find three **Progress tests** to be done when students have completed the Progress checks at the end of Units 5, 10 and 15. These tests include exam tasks from Papers 1 (Reading), 2 (Writing) and 3 (English in Use). Each Progress test should take approximately one hour to complete. Answer keys for these tests are also provided.

If class time is short, students can be asked to do the tests outside class.

Teaching methodology

Marking written work

Throughout the *Advanced Gold Coursebook*, students are encouraged to develop the ability to edit and evaluate their own and other students' work. Nevertheless, final versions of written work will usually be marked by the teacher.

Teach your students the correction code which follows. Encourage them to use it when correcting one another's written work, and use it yourself.

vf	= verb form e.g. *My father always play tennis on Saturdays.*
vt	= verb tense e.g. *Last year I have visited Italy.*
ww	= wrong word e.g. *We arrived to the airport half an hour late.*
wo	= word order e.g. *I go usually to the beach in the summer.*
g	= grammar e.g. *Why you not tell me you were Spanish?*
sp	= spelling e.g. *I'm really looking forward to my hollidays.*

```
p      = punctuation
         e.g. Do you come here often.
?      = meaning or handwriting unclear
         e.g. I was very happy to see my brother next
         weekend.
/      = missing word
         e.g. I went to / United States.
```

Write in the correct form wherever you feel the error is one involving language beyond the scope of a CAE student. Add a short comment on layout and task achievement as appropriate.

Give back work marked up with the code and tell students that you will collect their work again after they have tried to correct their errors. Initially, this error-correction phase should be done in class so that you can supervise students and provide help where necessary. Make sure that they keep a record of their errors and make a note yourself of any errors that are common to many of your students.

During the early stages of the course it is probably unnecessary to grade students' written work. As the course progresses you should begin to grade. Provide global grades, e.g. Unsatisfactory, Satisfactory, Good or Excellent, but base your assessment on the following: use of vocabulary; use of grammar; spelling and punctuation; task achievement. Continue to use the correction code and to comment on students' work briefly throughout the course.

Dealing with speaking tasks

Avoid 'assessing' students when they are doing fluency activities in the *Advanced Gold Coursebook*. Unobtrusively monitor speaking activities, noting errors to go through with the whole class after the activity. During these feedback sessions, do not say who made the errors.

During controlled practice, immediately correct basic errors and encourage students to correct themselves and one another. If these errors occur while students are engaged in fluency activities, mention them in the feedback session at the end.

Towards the end of the course, you may choose to do practice Paper 5 tests with your students. Evaluate these for grammar and vocabulary, discourse management, pronunciation and interactive communication.

Recycling and revision

Advanced Gold provides many opportunities to revise and recycle language presented. Each unit of the *Advanced Gold Coursebook* concludes with a Review page or a Progress check; the *Advanced Gold Exam Maximiser* offers a range of activities to recycle language from the *Advanced Gold Coursebook*, as well as a complete practice exam; this *Advanced Gold Teacher's Book* includes revision tests for all fifteen units. The *CAE Practice Tests Plus 2* can be used in the weeks immediately prior to the exam itself.

Advance preparation

▊ (Optional) Compile a collection of dictionaries (monolingual and bilingual) to bring to class for **Vocabulary 2** on page 8.

▊ Ask students to bring one or two grammar reference books to class for **Grammar check 2** on page 13. Alternatively, compile a collection to bring to class yourself.

▊ Ask students to bring some of their recent written work to class for **Grammar check 4** on page 13.

Reading p.6

▶ **Paper 1 Part 3** (multiple choice)

1 Students discuss the items in pairs, and then open-class.

2 Focus attention on the photographs. Students work individually before checking their answers with a partner and then open-class.

ANSWER

The photograph of the girl with the hoops is described in lines 21–27.

3 (p.7) Read through the suggested procedure with the class.

ALTERNATIVE PROCEDURE: read the first part containing the information about Paper 1, Part 3 (P1, Pt3) and ask students to discuss in pairs how they would approach this part of Paper 1. Students discuss their approaches open-class and compare them with the suggested procedure.

Draw attention to the **Remember** section. Ask students for any examples of vocabulary that reveals the author's attitude from the first two paragraphs of the Cirque du Soleil text.

POSSIBLE ANSWERS

The author seems to feel very positive about the circus. Evidence: ' … well, one of the greatest shows on earth' (lines 2–3); 'Easily as compelling, if not more so … ' (line 21).

4 Lead the class through the suggested procedure, enforcing the time limit on the first step.

ANSWERS

1 D (lines 5–14)   2 D (lines 21–27)   3 D (lines 45–58)
4 C (lines 66–71)   5 C (lines 76–77)   6 B (lines 81–85)
7 C (Evidence: entire paragraph 3; paragraph 4 'has captured the imagination of audiences around the world'.)

5 Discuss the question open-class.

BACKGROUND INFORMATION: Cirque du Soleil (French = 'Circus of the Sun') is an alternative circus organisation founded in Montreal, Canada in 1984. Cirque du Soleil began as a small group of travelling performers and now employs about 2000 people worldwide. They run training programmes in circus skills for young people, especially for those who are considered to be 'at risk'. Cirque du Soleil has established relationships with a number of charitable organisations, including Oxfam. One per cent of box-office revenue is allocated to social action. Members of the troupe are recruited from all over the world by talent scouts visiting circus schools and athletics and sporting events. A feature film of their show *Alegría* was made in 1999. It may be available on video. More information can be found on the website at: http://www.cirquedusoleil.com/en/.

*FURTHER PRACTICE: **Advanced Gold Exam Maximiser** pp.8–9.*

Vocabulary: deducing from context and choosing a dictionary p.8

1 Ask students how they normally go about working out the meaning of unfamiliar words. Do Question 1, *awestruck*, with the whole class. [Adjective. Ask students what expression they would have on their faces if they were 'awestruck'; in monolingual classes accept translation equivalents. Clue to meaning: reaction to the multiple talents of the performers. Meaning: very surprised and impressed. The *Longman Dictionary of Contemporary English* (LDOCE) has: 'feeling extremely impressed by the importance, difficulty, or seriousness of someone or something'.

Students work individually on the other words before comparing their answers with a partner.

2   Students check their answers with the dictionary definitions on page 215 of the *Advanced Gold Coursebook*.

3   Students discuss the questions in groups and report back to the whole class. Draw students' attention to the information provided in the LDOCE entries:
• British and American pronunciation (all);
• word class (all);
• word having more than one meaning (e.g. *gasp*);
• meanings explained in clear language (all);
• examples (all);
• derived words shown without definition (e.g. *haunting*);
• grammar codes (e.g. *gasp*, *penchant*, *twirl*);
• labels showing style, region, origin (e.g. *penchant*).

ALTERNATIVE PROCEDURE: form groups of four and give each group two dictionaries from the collection you have compiled for this class. Ask them to compare the information provided in the two dictionaries with that provided in the LDOCE entries. Ask what they like/dislike about the dictionaries. Ask them to discuss Questions 1 and 4 from Exercise 3 and report back to the rest of the class.

FURTHER PRACTICE: Advanced Gold Exam Maximiser p.10.

Grammar plus: verb patterns (1) p.8

Focus attention on the sentences from the text. They are taken from lines 12–14, lines 69–71 and lines 18–19 respectively.

1   Students work individually, reading through the information on verb patterns and deciding if the verbs in the example sentences are transitive, intransitive or if they can be both. Check answers open-class.

ANSWERS

see = both   *use* = transitive   *stride* = intransitive

2   Students work individually before comparing answers in pairs and then checking answers open-class.

ALTERNATIVE PROCEDURE: if students still have copies of the dictionaries used in Vocabulary 3 above, they can check answers in the dictionaries.

ANSWERS

transitive: *invite   want   surprise*
transitive with two objects: *send   make; describe explain* (both with prepositional object)
intransitive: *wait   sit   happen   sleep   fall*
transitive and intransitive: *burn   pull   lose   start   eat shut   wake   warn   spoil*

3   Students work individually before checking answers open-class.

ANSWERS

1 the car   2 food   4 cigarettes

4   (p.9) Students work individually before checking answers open-class.

ANSWERS

1 a) correct   b) incorrect (i.e. very unnatural in contemporary British English)
2 a) correct   b) incorrect
3 neither (*Do you need to borrow some money/to borrow some money from me?*)
4 a) correct   b) incorrect (i.e. very unusual word order in contemporary British English)
5 both correct
6 a) incorrect   b) correct
7 a) correct   b) incorrect
8 both correct
There are no easy 'rules' that can be learned. It is better to learn what kind of pattern follows each verb. Students can help themselves do this by recording dictionary information about verb patterns with each new verb they learn.

5   Make it clear that students should try to test each other with their sentences. They can therefore write sentences that are NOT correct. Students work individually and then with a partner. Each pair then reads their sentences to the whole class.

Point out to students that there is a **Grammar reference** at the back of the *Advanced Gold Coursebook* (pp.192–198). Explain that they can use this to revise and check grammar points. Tell them to read through 14.1–14.6 of the section on **Verb patterns** on page 197.

FURTHER PRACTICE: Advanced Gold Exam Maximiser p.10.

Listening: elena lev p.9

▶ **Paper 4 Part 3** (sentence completion)

Point out to students that the **P4, Pt3** means Paper 4, Part 3 of the *Certificate of Advanced English* exam.

1 Students discuss the photograph and questions in pairs.

2 Focus attention on the two summary questions. Play the cassette once straight through. Elicit answers open-class.

ANSWERS

1 She enjoys it. She has lots of friends and she says it's a very rich life with opportunities to travel and learn languages.
2 She loves her daughter and is proud and protective of her. She says she will always be there to help her.

3 Students work in pairs and then compare answers open-class.

4 Play the cassette for a second time. Students answer individually before comparing answers with a partner. Check answers by playing the cassette again, pausing and replaying the underlined sections of the **Tapescript** on page 111.

ALTERNATIVE PROCEDURE: distribute photocopies of the **Tapescript** on page 111. Students listen again, following the **Tapescript** and correcting their own work. Do a final check open-class.

5 Students discuss the questions in pairs, and then open-class.

Vocabulary: word formation (suffixes) p.10

1 Elicit answers to the questions open-class.

ANSWER

All the words are nouns. The suffix *-ity* is a noun suffix. (In monolingual classes, ask students what the equivalent suffix is in their L1.)

2 1 Students work in pairs before comparing answers open-class.

ANSWERS

al'terna**tive** (noun)   'op**tion** (noun)
succ'ess**ful** (adjective)   responsi'bil**ity** (noun)

'organ**ism** (noun)   'weak**ness** (noun)
'count**able** (adjective)   'brown**ish** (adjective)
'modern**ise** (verb)   en'joy**ment** (noun)
de'lic**ious** (adjective)   'leg**al** (adjective)

2 Students work individually before comparing answers in pairs. Read the words aloud while students check their answers.

ALTERNATIVE PROCEDURE: students check answers in their dictionaries and then individuals read the words aloud.

3 Students work in pairs before checking answers open-class.

ANSWERS

nouns from adjectives: *-ity   -ness*
nouns from verbs: *-ive* (also adjectives from verbs/nouns), *-ion   -ment*
an adjective meaning 'can be done': *-able*
an adjective less precise: *-ish*
verbs from adjectives: *-ise* (US and most other varieties *-ize*)

Watch Out!   *responsible*

Explain to students that these boxes occur throughout the *Advanced Gold Coursebook* and are intended to draw attention to areas of grammar and vocabulary that cause problems for students of many different language backgrounds.

Read the two sentences aloud. Students discuss them in pairs. Check answers open-class or by asking students to use their dictionaries.

ANSWERS

Sentence 1 means that he is a very sensible person who is able to make good decisions and can be trusted.
Sentence 2 means that he is the person with the duty of making all the financial decisions.
Sentence 1 describes a personal quality, whereas Sentence 2 describes the nature of someone's position in a company.

N.B. The LDOCE has a number of other meanings, among which are: 1 'having done or been the cause of esp. something bad; guilty: *Who's responsible for this terrible mess?*' and 4 '(of a job) needing a trustworthy person to do it: *She holds a very responsible position in the firm.*' You may wish to discuss these with students.

ALTERNATIVE PROCEDURE: put these two definitions on the board and ask students to match the sentences to them.
a) having a duty to be in charge of or to look after someone or something;
b) sensible and able to make good judgments so that you can be trusted.

ANSWERS

a 2   b 1

4   Students work in groups of four before reporting back to the whole class.

POSSIBLE ANSWERS

explosive   representative   negotiation   fixation
regretful   careful   hostility   credibility   criticism
Buddhism   sadness   warm-heartedness   manageable
washable   pinkish   youngish   privatise   Americanise
resentment   argument   precious   atrocious   regal
loyal

N.B. More examples can be found in the **Word formation** appendix at the back of the LDOCE.

5   Students work individually before checking answers open-class.

ANSWERS

1 forgivable   2 donation   3 outrageous   4 refusal
5 forgetfulness   6 standardise   7 productive
8 mid-thirtyish   9 hopeful

6   Students work in pairs.

ALTERNATIVE PROCEDURE: if your class enjoys games, set up two teams. Each team chooses a pair of representatives and works with them to prepare the conversation. Each pair then performs their conversation for the rest of the class who keep track of the score.

Exam focus p.10

Paper 5 Speaking: Part 1 (introduction)

Explain that in each unit of the *Advanced Gold Coursebook* there is an **Exam focus** section providing information on and practice with a specific part of each of the five papers in the *Certificate of Advanced English* exam.

Read the exam information aloud to the class.

1   (p.11) Students work in pairs before checking answers open-class.

ANSWERS

1   So where were you brought up ~~from~~ originally?
2   Tell me a little about your family. Do you have many brothers and sisters? What are they like?
3   ✓
4   Do you have a particular reason for learning English or is it just out of general interest?
5   ✓
6   Do you have much of an idea of what you'll be doing over the next few years?

2   Play the cassette and elicit students' opinions about the candidates.

COMMENTS ON THE CANDIDATES

Candidate 1 Brita Carlsson: She is lively, chatty and interested. Although she has a noticeable foreign accent she has good clear pronunciation. She would get top marks on the basis of this part of Paper 5.

Candidate 2 Marco Natoli: Sounds dull and is unwilling to answer in more than monosyllables. He also has a stronger foreign accent than Brita. Marco would not pass Paper 5 on the basis of what we have here.

3   Ask students to work in pairs. Play the cassette or read the **Tapescript** on page 112 aloud to the class.

ALTERNATIVE PROCEDURE: form groups of three. Give copies of the **Tapescript** to one student in each group. The student with the **Tapescript** then interviews the other two students. They then change roles.

FURTHER PRACTICE: *Advanced Gold Exam Maximiser* **p.12.**

English in Use p.11

▶ Paper 3 Part 3 (error correction, extra word)

1   Read the exam information aloud to the class.

2   Set a one-minute time limit for the reading task. Students work individually before comparing their answers in pairs.

SUGGESTED ANSWERS

He only wore white linen clothes; he refused to have any black cattle on his farm and only had white horses; he lectured a fox that had been caught killing his poultry rather than having it killed; he was a vegetarian and wouldn't wear anything produced by an animal.

3   Students work individually.

4   Students compare answers in pairs before checking open-class.

ANSWERS

1 the   2 even   3 ✓   4 although   5 him   6 ✓   7 if
8 been   9 ✓   10 of   11 up   12 have   13 which
14 ✓   15 than   16 ✓

FURTHER PRACTICE: *Advanced Gold Exam Maximiser p.13.*

Listening: modern 'art'? p.12

1   Focus attention on the photographs of the works of art. Get individual students to describe them. The rest of the class listen and say which picture is being described.

BACKGROUND INFORMATION: if the class is interested, give them the following background information about the artists.

The first photograph shows a pile of bricks exhibited at the Tate Gallery in London.

The second photograph is of John Baldessari's 1966–68 'No Ideas have entered this work'. Baldessari is an American Conceptual artist born in California in 1931. He burned all the work he had done between 1953 and 1966.

The third photograph shows the 'Wrapped Reichstag'. This was a project undertaken by Bulgarian artist Christo and his artistic collaborator Jeanne-Claude between 1971 and 1995. Christo, who is famous for wrapping landscapes and buildings, worked with Jeanne-Claude to wrap the Reichstag in Berlin in shiny paper. The project was filmed and there are a number of places on the Internet where still and video images of the wrapping of the building can be viewed. One of the better ones is: http://prelectur.stanford.edu/lecturers/christo.

The fourth photograph shows the performance art creation 'The Maybe'. Actor Tilda Swinton spent seven days sleeping in a glass case, first at the Serpentine Gallery in London in 1995 and then at the Museo Barraceo in Rome in 1996.

2   Play the cassette. Elicit answers open-class.

ANSWERS

The picture of the bricks and the bed in the glass case.

3   Students read the questions through, answering as many as they can before listening to the cassette for the second time. Check the answers by playing the cassette, pausing and replaying the passages that have been highlighted in the **Tapescript** on page 112.

ANSWERS

1   at the weekend
2   They had lunch and a chat.
3   recent modern art
4   The Tate Gallery paid thousands of pounds for them.
5   the way it was described in the catalogue
6   They might be playing a joke on them.
7   to try new things and experiment
8   sceptical

4   Play the cassette a third time while students note down the expressions.

ANSWERS

1   I just can't understand how
2   it amazes me how
3   Don't you think it's incredible that

5   Students discuss the questions in groups and then report back to the whole class.

ALTERNATIVE PROCEDURE: discuss the questions open-class.

6   Students work in groups discussing the works of art. Ask them to appoint a representative and to report their discussion to the whole class.

ALTERNATIVE PROCEDURE: discuss the works of art open-class.

BACKGROUND INFORMATION: if the class is interested, give them the following background information about the pictures.

Pablo Picasso, who was born in Málaga, Spain, in 1881, went to live in Paris in 1901. He was initially influenced by the Post-Impressionists and painted a number of portraits of people living in the streets of Paris using blue as the dominant colour. The second of the two paintings, 'Boy with a Pipe', is from this 'Blue Period'. The first work, 'Man with a Pipe', was made after Picasso had evolved the style known as 'Analytic Cubism', and had begun to experiment with collage.

FURTHER PRACTICE: *Advanced Gold Exam Maximiser p.11.*

Grammar check: overview p.13

1   Students work individually before comparing answers in pairs, and then open-class.

ANSWERS

1 I **know** that she wants to be on her own tonight.

2 We **never go** out to restaurants any more.

3 Where are **the** car keys? I had them a minute ago.

4 This computer game is a lot ~~more~~ cheaper than the last one you bought.

5 If I'd ~~have~~ seen him, I'd have invited him to the party.

6 Unless you work a bit harder, **you'll** fail your exams. OR If you work a bit harder, you won't fail your exams.

7 They were really helpful and gave us lots of information~~s~~.

8 We considered **going** to the new French restaurant, but it was too expensive.

9 My dad won't let me ~~to~~ stay overnight at John's house.

10 I really wish I **had** more time.

11 He went rock-climbing despite ~~of~~ his fear of heights.

12 They might **have** decided to go to the circus after all. OR They might decide~~d~~ to go to the circus after all.

13 Sarah's new boyfriend is **very** nice. She's very lucky.

14 Last night I dreamt I was being **chased** by this huge black dog.

15 Could you tell me whether **there is** another train to London tonight?

16 She's the girl **whose** brother I went to school with.

17 He apologised for **being** late.

18 We're having the front of the house **painted** next week.

19 They've been living here **for** at least 30 years.

20 I can't get used to **starting** work so early.

21 He's ~~a~~ such a terrible liar that no-one ever believes him.

2 1 Tell students not to worry if they had difficulty with more than two of the sentences as most of these areas will be revised in the **Grammar check** sections of the *Advanced Gold Coursebook*. Students work in groups comparing the sentences they had difficulty with and agreeing to look at another two sentences each.

2 Students work in pairs and then check answers open-class. Accept terminology to describe the areas other than that used in the suggested answers (categories taken from *First Certificate Gold*).

SUGGESTED ANSWERS

1 verb tenses: present simple versus continuous

2 adverbs of frequency: position   3 the article

4 comparison   5 conditionals   6 conditionals

7 countable and uncountable nouns

8 gerunds and infinitives

9 words that cause confusion: *make   let   allow*

10 hypothetical meaning   11 linking words

12 modal verbs   13 modifiers and intensifiers

14 passives   15 questions

16 relative clauses and pronouns

17 gerunds and infinitives

18 *to have something done*

19 verb tenses: present perfect   20 *used to/would*

21 words that cause confusion: *so/such*

3 Use the grammar books you and/or the students have brought to class. Allot each pair one or two areas of grammar to research. Give each member of the pair a different grammar reference to look at. Students work individually, researching their answers and preparing to explain what they have learnt to a partner.

4 Students work with the same partner. Ask more confident students to tell the whole class what they learnt.

ALTERNATIVE PROCEDURE: if you do not have enough grammar reference books for the whole class, set this as an out-of-class activity. Make a note of which students are responsible for researching each area.

3 Students discuss their answers in pairs, and then open-class.

4 Ask what students do with the mistakes that teachers mark on their written work. Emphasise the importance of their keeping a Grammar Checklist with typical mistakes classified according to grammar area and accompanied by an example of the correct form. Point out these features in the model Grammar Checklist.

Students work individually, starting or adding to a Grammar Checklist based on mistakes in the recent written work they have brought to class.

Tell students you will expect them to keep their Grammar Checklist up to date and to refer to it when revising their written work for you.

Writing: drafting p.14

▶ Paper 2 Part1 (compulsory)

1 Draw students' attention to the **Writing reference** on pages 200–214 of the *Advanced Gold Coursebook*. Tell them to study the Part 1 task and answer on pages 200–202.

Students then discuss the TRUE(T)/FALSE(F) statements in pairs before checking open-class.

ANSWERS

1 T (Paragraph 1 clearly states the purpose of the letter. The areas of complaint are then specified in the penultimate paragraph.)
2 F (It is a formal letter, but not excessively so.)
3 T (It is 208 words rather than 200.)
4 T (e.g. 'The most serious of our complaints is that … '; 'Aside from being extremely expensive, it was closed … ')
5 T (*on behalf of*, *compensation*, *cramped*, *forced*)
6 T (Paragraph 1 identifies the writer and states the reason for writing.
Paragraph 2 is about complaints related to payment.
Paragraph 3 is about the quality of the accommodation and facilities.
Paragraph 4 states what future action will be taken.)
7 T (*Furthermore, If this were not enough … , Another problem was … , Aside from being … , Finally*)

2 1 Focus attention on the task. Students work individually, underlining key words before comparing answers in pairs.

SUGGESTED ANSWERS

given tickets   world famous circus   disappointed
thank you note to friends
without going into what you weren't happy about
letter of complaint   management of circus
highlighting various points   not happy about   letter
advert   comments   using information   note [50 words]
letter complaint [200 words]   use own words

2 Turn to the **Useful language** box on page 202 of the **Writing reference** in the *Advanced Gold Coursebook*. Students study the expressions for letters of complaint, all of which could be used here.

3 (p.15) Students read the letter and then in pairs discuss other linking words that could be used before comparing their answers with the rest of the class.

OTHER LINKING WORDS

First of all: To begin with   Firstly   In the first place
Secondly: In the second place
Furthermore: What's more   Moreover
Finally: Lastly

4 Students work together discussing the two plans.

SUGGESTED CHANGE

The second point of the letter plan should be changed as there is no mention in the task of children. The note plan is fine.

5 Students work individually, completing the note and letter. When they have finished, read the checklist aloud to them, allowing time for them to look at their work again and answer the questions. Allow time for students to revise their work if they have not been able to answer 'yes' to all the checklist questions.

6 Students work in pairs, reading and editing one another's note and letter.

FURTHER PRACTICE: **Advanced Gold Exam Maximiser pp.14–15.**

Speaking: storytelling p.16

1 Focus attention on the pictures and elicit the words *a weaver   cloth   a loom   a procession*. Students work in pairs, putting the pictures in order.

ANSWERS

Picture 2: The emperor changing into a new selection of finery, looking at himself in the mirror, surrounded by fawning courtiers.

Picture 1: The emperor on his throne, surrounded by his retinue, listening to the weavers describing the wonderful cloth they can make and its magical powers.

Picture 5: The weavers with their loom, pretending to weave, and the emperor, who has gone to see how they are getting on, looking on with a bewildered expression on his face.

Picture 4: The emperor in his underwear, with the two weavers, who have pretended to dress him in his new suit and who are telling him how wonderful he looks.

Picture 3: The emperor walking naked in the street procession, and the boy pointing as he says, 'But the emperor has nothing on.'

2 Students work in pairs, telling their stories.

3 Play the cassette. Ask students for examples of similarities and discrepancies between their stories and the one on the cassette.

4 Students discuss the questions in groups.

SUGGESTED ANSWERS

N.B. Accept students' interpretations first.
- Vanity makes us stupid and gullible.
- Most of us are afraid of telling those who hold power what we really think.
- Powerful people are often insulated from reality.
- Physical beauty is an illusion.

5   Set the writing task for homework.

Unit 1 review p.17

Unit reviews can be done in class, set for homework, or a combination of the two.

ANSWERS

1   If students all have the same L1, accept translation equivalents. The suggested answers are taken from the LDOCE.
a) *meshes* verb (intransitive) 'fits together suitably' *Their characters just don't mesh*
b) *spellbinding* adjective 'holding the compete attention; fascinating' *a spellbinding performance*
c) *swooping* verb (intransitive) 'moving down suddenly and steeply, esp. to attack'
d) *honed* verb (transitive) 'sharpened' *a finely honed wit*.

2   1 ✓
2 Shaun proposed ~~a wedding~~ to me last night. I didn't know what to say.
3 ✓
4 ✓
5 You surprised **me** when you said you were leaving at the end of the week.
6 I wonder if you could suggest a good grammar book.
OR I wonder if you could suggest a good grammar book **to me**.
7 ✓
8 He still owes **us/me (money)** for his share of the holiday we had together last year.

3

VERB	NOUN	ADJECTIVE
to alternate	alternative	alternate/alternative
to opt	option	optional
to succeed	success	successful/unsuccessful
to enjoy	enjoyment	enjoyable
to weaken	weakness	weak/weakened
to count	count	countable/ uncountable/countless
–	responsibility	responsible
to modernise	modernisation	modern

4   1 had   2 to   3 last   4 are   5 as   6 as   7 them   8 least   9 Despite   10 can   11 a   12 times   13 along   14 the   15 if

UNIT
2 It takes all sorts

Advance preparation

▌ Remind students to bring dictionaries to class for the **Vocabulary** exercises on page 22. Alternatively, bring a class set of dictionaries yourself.

▌ (Optional) Ask students to bring grammar reference books or copies of *First Certificate Gold Coursebook* to class for the **Grammar check** on page 26.

Listening: an alien? p.18

1 Focus attention on the photograph. Elicit and accept answers from students open-class.

2 Students listen, discuss answers with a partner and then compare open-class.

ANSWERS

The man in the dressing gown with his arms folded is Arthur Dent. The 'man' in the striped blazer is Ford Prefect. Arthur is trying to stop his house being demolished and is sitting in front of a bulldozer when his friend Ford Prefect comes to visit him. The man on the bulldozer is a local council officer.

3 Students read the statements individually. If they can decide on answers before listening to the recording again, encourage them to do so. Play the recording again while students answer individually. They then compare answers, first in pairs and then open-class. Insist on justifications for answers and replay relevant sections of the recording where necessary.

ANSWERS

1 F   2 T   3 F   4 T   5 T   6 F   7 F   8 F   9 T   10 T
(For justifications, see underlining in the **Tapescript** on page 113.)

4 Focus attention on the quotation and the dictionary entry. Ask students what information the entry provides about the word *sarcasm* (ANSWER: two pronunciations; noun class = uncountable; definition; collocation; example).

Students discuss the questions in groups, appointing a representative to report their discussion to the rest of the class.

ALTERNATIVE PROCEDURE: discuss the questions open-class.

BACKGROUND INFORMATION: The photograph is taken from the film of the cult humorous novel *The Hitchhiker's Guide to the Galaxy* by Douglas Adams. In the novel, Arthur Dent is rescued from Earth moments before it is obliterated to make room for a cosmic freeway. Dent is left to hitchhike round the universe, wearing a dressing gown and accompanied by his pal Ford Prefect,* who is a researcher for *The Hitchhiker's Guide to the Galaxy*. Prefect has been living on Earth for fifteen years, posing as an out-of-work actor. The two have all sorts of amusing adventures as they hitchhike through space. The book came out in 1979 and was enormously popular among young people in the UK and elsewhere in the English-speaking world. It was serialised on radio and later made into a TV series. Both cassettes of the radio series and videos of the TV series are available. There is also an interactive website officially associated with the book at: http://www.h2g2.com. [* The Ford Prefect is a car that was popular in the 1950s.]

Vocabulary: adverbs of manner p.18

1 Students work individually before checking their answers while listening to the recording. Go through the answers open-class.

ANSWERS

1 broadly   2 guiltily   3 wildly   4 distractedly

2 (p.19) Students work in pairs before comparing answers open-class.

SUGGESTED ANSWERS

1 sweetly   2 abruptly; suddenly
3 hysterically; manically   4 longingly; intently

3 Students work individually before comparing their answers with a partner and then checking open-class.

ANSWERS

laugh helplessly; uneasily
dress neatly; elegantly
listen attentively; patiently
bitterly; sincerely **regret** (N.B. word order)
behave irresponsibly; abominably
change drastically; imperceptibly
know intuitively; intimately

4   Students work in pairs writing sentences.

POSSIBLE ANSWERS

She laughed uneasily when Inspector Millington asked her
    where she had been on the night the jewels went
    missing.
Alex always dressed elegantly, even if it was only to go out
    to buy a paper on Sunday morning.
The children listened attentively as their grandfather began
    to tell them one of his famous ghost stories.
'I sincerely regret to inform you that we see no option but
    to take legal action,' the letter ended.
Aunt Agnes told Edward that he would not be having any
    ice cream for dessert, as he had behaved abominably all
    morning.
She had changed imperceptibly from the bubbly young girl
    he had known twenty years earlier to the rather silent
    woman with whom he shared his life.
She knew intuitively that she would not succeed in
    convincing him, but she tried as hard as she could.

EXTRA ACTIVITY: Pairs exchange sentences. They write short
    stories continuing from the sentences with the adverb of
    manner. Ask each pair to read one of their stories aloud to
    the rest of the class.

EXAMPLE

He laughed uneasily when his sister joked that she and her
entire family might come and live with him. He knew that
things were not going well between her and Brian and
worried that perhaps she was thinking of leaving him.
Where would she possibly go with three small children?
Tim's large house with its three spare bedrooms was the
obvious choice. But he loved his solitude. What on earth
would he say to her if she seriously asked him to help them
out?

Speaking: p.19

1   Focus attention on the picture and discuss the
questions open-class.

2   Students work in groups, appointing a representative to
report their discussion to the rest of the class.

Reading: p.19

▶ Paper 1 Part 4 (multiple matching)

1 & 2   Students work individually before comparing their
answers with a partner and checking on p.215 of the
Advanced Gold Coursebook.

3   Students work in pairs and then in groups, appointing a
representative to report their methods to the whole class.

4   (p.20) Focus attention on the photograph and the
section headings in the text or write them up on the board.
Ask students which of the headings the photograph shows.
Students work in pairs before sharing their answers open-
class.

ALTERNATIVE PROCEDURE: discuss the questions open-class.

5   Students work individually. Enforce the time limit,
telling them when two-and-a-half and four minutes have
passed.

6   (p.21) Go through the rubric and the procedure with
the class. Students work individually before comparing their
answers in pairs and open-class.

ANSWERS

N.B. Where more than one extract is a match, answers can
be in any order. Here they are in the same order as the
extracts.
1 F line 166   2 C lines 74–75   3 C lines 97–99
4 D lines 115–116   5 F line 164   6 B lines 42–43
7 D lines 121–124   8 E lines 135–139   9 D lines 127–128
10 B line 65   11 C line 85   12 E line 153
13 A line 26   14 E line 162   15 B lines 42–43
16 A lines 26–31   17 F lines 176–179
18 E lines 140–144   19 D lines 118–120
20 F lines 180–182 & 189   21 B lines 36–38 & 56–58
22 A lines 15–16

7   1 & 2 If your students are from different cultural
backgrounds, form groups in which different cultures are

represented. Students discuss the questions in groups before reporting back to the rest of the class.

In classes where students are all from the same cultural background, discuss the questions open-class, focussing on regional differences.

FURTHER PRACTICE: **Advanced Gold Exam Maximiser pp.16–17.**

Vocabulary: words with similar meaning p.22

1   Students work in pairs before checking their answers open-class.

ANSWERS

1 **to commiserate** to express your sympathy for someone who is unhappy about something

2 **a premonition** a strange and unexplainable feeling that something, especially something unpleasant, is going to happen

3 **to inflame** to make someone's feelings of anger, excitement etc much stronger

4 **to terminate** if something terminates, or if you terminate it, it ends

5 **to soothe** to make someone feel calmer and less anxious, upset or angry

6 **an assembly** a group of people who have gathered together for a particular purpose

7 **to sanction** to officially accept or allow something

8 **a password** a secret word or phrase that someone has to speak before they are allowed to enter a place such as a military camp

2   Students work in groups of three before checking their answers in a dictionary, and then open-class.

ALTERNATIVE PROCEDURE: if time is short, make each group responsible for checking only one group of words in their dictionaries. They then report their findings to the other members of the class, who take notes on the differences in meaning.

ANSWERS

1 **to celebrate** to show that an event or occasion is important by doing something special or enjoyable: *It's Dad's birthday and we're going out for a meal to celebrate.*
to commemorate to do something to show that you remember and respect someone important or an important event in the past: *a parade to commemorate the town's bicentenary*

to honour to treat someone with special respect: *our honoured guests this evening*

2 **a spirit** an inner part of someone that includes their thoughts and feelings, and is thought of as making them what they are: *His spirit was untameable.*
a phantom a frightening and unclear image, especially of a dead person: *The phantom hound loomed suddenly out of the mist.*
a ghost the spirit of a dead person that some people think they can feel or see in a place: *The ghosts of past landlords are said to haunt this pub.*

3 **to douse** to put out a fire by pouring water on it: *It took hundreds of litres of water to douse the flames.*
to extinguish *formal* to make a fire or light stop burning or shining: *Please extinguish all cigarettes.*
to smother to make a fire stop burning by preventing air from reaching it: *Kitchen fires are often best smothered with a damp cloth.*

4 **to originate** to have the idea for something and start it: *Who originated the present complaints procedures?*
to initiate *formal* to arrange for something important to start, such as an official process or a new plan: *The plaintiffs initiated court proceedings in order to recover their debts.*
to conceive to think of a new idea, plan etc and develop it in your mind: *Scientists first conceived the idea of the atomic bomb in the 1930s.*

5 **to startle** to make someone suddenly surprised or slightly shocked: *You startled me! I didn't hear you come in.*
to alarm to make people very worried about a possible danger: *Her high temperature alarmed the doctors.*
to frighten to make someone feel afraid: *Don't stand so near the edge, you're frightening me!*

6 **a rebellion** active opposition to someone in authority: *a rebellion by right-wing members of the party*
an insurrection an attempt by a large group of people within a country to take control using force and violence: *an armed insurrection against the party in power*
a mutiny a situation in which people, especially sailors or soldiers, refuse to obey the person who is in charge of them, and try to take control for themselves: *There was already talk of mutiny among the crew.*

7 **to ban** to say that something must not be done, seen, used etc: *Smoking is banned in the building.*
to outlaw to completely stop something by making it illegal or socially unacceptable: *Certain countries have outlawed the sale of alcohol.*
to prohibit to officially stop an activity by making it illegal or against the rules: *Smoking is strictly prohibited inside the factory.*

8   **a symbol** a picture or shape that has a particular meaning or represents an idea: *The dove is a symbol of peace.*
a sign a picture, shape etc that has a particular meaning: *For some reason the computer can't display the dollar sign.*
a logo a small design that is the official sign of a company or organization

3   Students work individually before checking their answers open-class.

ANSWERS

1 prohibited   2 conceived   3 smothered   4 mutiny
5 symbol   6 ghost   7 startled   8 honoured

FURTHER PRACTICE: Advanced Gold Exam Maximiser p.19.

Speaking: p.22

▶ Paper 5 Part 2

1   Read the exam information aloud to the class.

2   Students work in pairs, before comparing their answers with the rest of the class.

SUGGESTED ANSWERS

Possible key vocabulary	Possible useful expressions
coloured lights	On the one hand …
dancing wildly	In both photographs …
absolutely packed	One important difference
dance the night away	between the photographs
blowing out candles	is …
surrounded by her friends	The two photographs are
three cheers	similar in that they both
singing 'Happy Birthday'	show …

3   Students do the task in pairs. Monitor and choose a good pair to repeat the task for the rest of the class.

FURTHER PRACTICE: Advanced Gold Exam Maximiser p.18.

Grammar plus: noun phrases p.23

1   Read the information on noun phrases aloud to the class. Students study the example and the uses of noun phrases. They work on the matching exercise individually before checking their answers in pairs and then open-class.

ANSWERS

2 c)   3 g)   4 j)   5 a)   6 h)   7 d)   8 e)   9 f)   10 i)

2   Play each pair of sentences, allowing students time to repeat and discuss the meanings with a partner. Check the answers open-class.

ANSWERS

1   That's <u>Simon's</u> brother. (NOT my, Tom's, Sandra's, etc. brother); That's Simon's <u>brother</u>. (NOT his cousin, uncle, son, etc.)
2   Do you have a <u>book</u> about indoor plants? (rather than a tape or a CD-rom); Do you have a book about <u>indoor plants</u>? (rather than a book about gardens, etc.)
3   I'd like to buy my girlfriend a <u>gold</u> ring. (rather than a silver, platinum, etc. ring); I'd like to buy my girlfriend a gold <u>ring</u>. (rather than a necklace, bracelet, pair of earrings, etc.)
4   I love <u>goat's</u> cheese. (but I don't like other cheeses); I love goat's <u>cheese</u>. (but I don't like goat's milk)

3   Students work individually before checking answers open-class.

ANSWERS

1   Susan's hair needs cutting.
2   ✓
3   There is an excellent **shoe** shop in the high street.
4   ✓
5   We need an **18-year**-old girl to play this part.
6   Tom was involved in a minor **car** accident at the weekend.
7   ✓

4   Students work individually before comparing answers with a partner and then checking open-class.

ANSWERS

1   There was a three-hour delay at the airport in Rome for/due to technical reasons.
2   He has a 100-year-old Williamson oil painting/oil painting by Williamson in his study.
3   She has been a maths teacher at a local secondary school for 25 years.
4   We did a 20-mile walk for a children's charity at the weekend.
5   They had a three-course meal with a bottle of wine for under £35.
6   A 13-year-old girl was awarded a gold medal for bravery by the mayor.

FURTHER PRACTICE: *Advanced Gold Exam Maximiser* **p.21.**

Refer students to the **Grammar reference** on p.194 of the *Advanced Gold Coursebook*.

Watch Out! *containers*

Students work in pairs before checking answers open-class.

> **ANSWERS**
>
> 1 **wine glass** = a glass of the size and type normally used for drinking wine.
> 2 **a glass of wine** = a glass with wine in it.

English in Use p.24

▶ Paper 3 Part 6 (gapped text)

1 Read the exam information aloud to the class. Go through the procedure step by step, reading the instructions aloud and then pausing for the students to action them.

1 Set a one-minute time limit for this gist reading. Check answers open-class.

> **ANSWERS**
>
> Things that are thrown at weddings; protecting the bride/couple from evil.

2 Students work individually before comparing answers with a partner.

3 Students work individually.

4 Students work individually before checking answers with a partner, and then open-class.

> **ANSWERS**
>
> 1 D   2 I   3 B   4 G   5 A   6 E

Listening: away from home p.24

▶ Paper 4 Part 4 (multiple choice)

1 Read the exam information and suggested procedure aloud to the class.

2 (p.25) Give students time to read through the questions and mark key words in the **Tapescript** on pp.113–114. Before playing the recording, students follow the **Tapescript**.

> **SUGGESTED UNDERLINING**
>
> 1 … he had the chance of a job back in the UK, in London. So we agreed that we'd go there …
> 2 … it was much harder to make friends than I'd imagined it would be. There was also something about the English which I found quite hard … I often felt I didn't know if people really meant what they were saying to me.

3 Students compare answers in pairs before checking open-class.

> **ANSWERS**
>
> 1 B untrue: 'had always been her dream' too strong and too long term for 'I was really excited about it'.
> C not referred to.
> 2 A partially but not completely true: work was only 'part of the problem'.
> B not referred to.

4 Allow time for students to read through the rest of the questions. Play the cassette once straight through as students answer individually. Students then compare answers with a partner. Play the cassette again. Check answers open-class, replaying the cassette and pausing after the relevant section. Get students to say why the other options are wrong.

ALTERNATIVE PROCEDURE: after students have heard the recording twice and checked answers open-class, distribute copies of the **Tapescript** on pp.113–114. Students study the **Tapescript** and say why the other options are wrong.

> **ANSWERS**
>
> 3 C   4 B   5 C   6 B   7 C   8 A   9 B   10 B

EXTRA ACTIVITY: Put the following question up on the board: 'What experiences have you had of the cultural behaviour of people in other countries which has surprised you?'
Begin by telling the students some things that have surprised you. They work in groups of four, appointing a representative to report back to the rest of the class.

FURTHER PRACTICE: *Advanced Gold Exam Maximiser* **pp.20–21.**

Grammar check: modals p.26

1 Students work in pairs before checking answers open-class.

ALTERNATIVE PROCEDURES:
a) Work through each pair of sentences eliciting differences open-class.

b) Students work in pairs using their grammar reference books or the **Grammar reference** in the *First Certificate Gold Coursebook* to decide on answers. Check answers open-class. Accept alternative terminology to that used in the answer key.

ANSWERS

1 First sentence expresses certainty; second sentence expresses possibility.
2 First sentence expresses strong obligation; second sentence expresses weak obligation and recommendation.
3 First sentence expresses present ability; second sentence expresses past ability.
4 First sentence expresses permission; second sentence expresses weak obligation and recommendation.
5 First sentence expresses complete certainty; second sentence expresses weak probability.
6 First sentence expresses lack of strong obligation; second sentence expresses prohibition.
7 First sentence expresses present inability; second sentence expresses prohibition.
8 First sentence expresses strong obligation; second sentence expresses possibility.

2   Students work in pairs before comparing answers open-class.

POSSIBLE ANSWERS

1 … everyone has lost confidence in her.
2 … it's a holiday.
3 … we have to be up very early tomorrow morning.
4 … they're in tiny print.
5 … I can just make out some claws.
6 … it's only a month before the exams start.

3   Look at the example with the whole class. Students work in pairs before comparing answers open-class.

POSSIBLE ANSWERS

2 I could play the clarinet badly, the piano a little better and the recorder quite well.
3 Can I smoke in here?
4 He might be in the library or he could have gone to the coffee bar.
5 You don't have to. I've got my bike with me.
6 That must be Sam. He said he'd ring about now.
7 You may go home early this afternoon.
8 We have to bring our calculators for the maths exam.

4   Demonstrate the first dialogue with a confident student, taking the role of Student 1. Students work in pairs, starting with 1 and working though the other situations. Get confident pairs to act out their dialogues for the whole class at the end. The class monitors and makes suggestions of any corrections and situations where other modal verbs could be used.

POSSIBLE CONTINUATIONS

1
S1: You know, I really want to get fit …
S2: You should join the local gym. It's great. But, anyway, why this sudden desire to get in shape?
S1: Well, don't laugh but I want to take part in next year's marathon.
S2: Really … Are you sure? You have to train gradually over a period of years, you know.
S1: Well, there's a half-marathon in October so I thought I'd see how I got on in that and then if I'm fit enough, register for the full city marathon.
S2: It still sounds like you've got a lot of heavy training ahead of you.

2
S1: Did you play any musical instruments when you were a child?
S2: I could play the clarinet badly, the piano a little better and the recorder quite well.
S1: Wow! Can you still play any of them?
S2: I sometimes play the recorder and I might take up the piano again.
S1: Wouldn't you need to have access to a piano, though?
S2: I suppose so, but I might buy one of those electronic keyboards.

3
S1: Can I smoke in here?
S2: I'd rather you didn't. My mother says we mustn't smoke inside the house.
S1: Shall we go outside, then?

4
S1: Where's Mark?
S2: He might be in the library or he could have gone to the coffee bar.
S1: He can't have gone to the coffee bar. It doesn't open till four.
S2: I guess he must be in the library then.
S1: But the library is closed today.
S2: Well, I don't know where he could have gone.

5
S1: Can we drop you off somewhere?
S2: You don't have to. I've got my bike with me.

S1: We could put the bike in the back of the car if you like.
S2: Oh you don't need to go to all that trouble. It's not very far.
S1: But it might rain.
S2: I won't get too wet. I've got my rain-proof hat and jacket with me.

6
S1: That must be Sam. He said he'd ring about now.
S2: You mustn't tell him what I said about him.
S1: You can trust me. I can keep a secret, you know.

7
S1: You may go home early this afternoon.
S2: Do we have to come early tomorrow?
S1: Yes. You should all be here by 8 a.m.

8
S1: We have to bring our calculators for the maths exam.
S2: Can we bring our maths books too?
S1: Of course not.

FURTHER PRACTICE: Advanced Gold Exam Maximiser p.20.

Writing: information sheet p.26

1   Students work in groups discussing possible areas for inclusion and appointing a representative to report back to the rest of the class. List the areas students have suggested on the board.

SUGGESTED ANSWERS

giving gifts, talking on the telephone, showing emotions, e.g. anger, how close you stand in relation to other people, parts of the body you shouldn't touch or use to gesture with, telling jokes, religious celebrations, clothing, paying for food and drink in bars and restaurants

2   (p.27) Students work individually. Monitor and offer suggestions to anybody who is stuck.

3   Students read and study the information sheet in the **Writing reference** on p.203 of the *Advanced Gold Coursebook*. They work individually planning their sheets.

SUGGESTED ANSWERS

1 (possible titles) 'How to be the "perfect visitor"' OR 'Etiquette tips for travellers'.
2 Five or six: an introduction and conclusion plus sections for each of the three or four areas.
3 Relatively formal and polite as the visitors could be any age and the subject matter is slightly delicate.

4 Inform, advise and warn. It will be necessary to use a lot of modal verbs to soften what is expressed in the sheet … e.g. 'people might be offended' rather than 'people will be offended'. Not too much 'You should/shouldn't/ must/mustn't'. Alternate with 'You can … You needn't/don't have to …'.
5 With a brief explanation of the reason for the custom.

4   Students write the first draft of their information sheet individually.

5   Students exchange drafts and check each other's work.

6   Students work in pairs discussing each other's comments.

7   Rewriting can be done as homework.

FURTHER PRACTICE: Advanced Gold Exam Maximiser p.23.

Exam focus p.28

▶ **Paper 3 English in Use: Part 3** (error correction – extra word)

Read the exam information aloud to the class. Draw students' attention to the suggested procedure and do step 1 with the whole class. Accept all predictions. Students work through the other steps in the procedure under exam conditions.

Write answers up on the board so students can correct their own work.

ANSWERS

1 to   2 so   3 that   4 of   5 ✓   6 did   7 ✓
8 themselves   9 they   10 ✓   11 quite   12 ✓
13 because   14 ✓   15 which   16 the

FURTHER PRACTICE: Advanced Gold Exam Maximiser p.22.

Unit 2 review p.29

ANSWERS

1 1 B   2 A   3 D   4 D   5 A   6 C   7 B   8 A   9 D
10 B   11 C   12 A   13 D   14 A   15 C

2 1 friend's   2 horse   3 bath   4 mint tea
5 film about a lost violin   6 kitchen   7 train timetable
8 bird's nest   9 lamb's wool   10 box of matches
11 child's   12 tax on educational books

3 1 patiently   2 sincerely   3 intuitively   4 drastically
5 neatly   6 abominably   7 helplessly   8 intimately

3 The root of all evil?

Advance preparation

■ Remind students to bring dictionaries to class for the **Vocabulary** exercise on page 36, or arrange to bring a class set yourself.

Listening: a mystery p.30

▶ **Paper 4, Part 3** (sentence completion)

1 Focus attention on the pictures. Students discuss them in pairs, and then open-class.

2 Play the interview once straight through. Ask the class if any of their suggested connections were right.

ANSWERS

(picture 1) People who were looking for the owl communicated with Max Valentine via Minitel, a computer network similar to the Internet. This picture shows a Minitel terminal.
(picture 2) These are some of the treasure hunters who have tried to find the golden owl.
The golden owl (picture 3) has been buried somewhere in France by Max Valentin.

3 Read the exam information aloud to the class. Students work in pairs completing the sentences before comparing answers with the rest of the class.

4 Play the first part of the interview. Students complete the sentences individually before checking answers open-class. If necessary, play the cassette again, pausing on relevant sections.

ANSWERS

1 treasure hunters   2 the (eleven) clues

5 Students read the other gapped sentences through. Play the interview once straight through. Students work individually before comparing answers in pairs. Play the cassette a second time. Check answers open-class, replaying relevant sections of the cassette where necessary.

ALTERNATIVE PROCEDURE: after students have heard the interview a second time, distribute copies of the **Tapescript** on p.115. Students check their answers by consulting the **Tapescript**.

ANSWERS

3 sculpted an owl   4 the best-seller lists   5 digging up
6 twelfth   7 primitive version   8 his health
9 betrayal   10 publish a clue

6 (p.31) Students discuss the questions in groups, appointing a representative to report back to the whole class.

Vocabulary: expressions with *carry* p.31

1 Look at the example with the whole class. Students work individually before comparing answers with a partner, and then open-class.

ANSWERS

b) vii)   c) iv)   d) ix)   e) i)   f) v)   g) iii)   h) viii)   i) vi)

2 Students work individually before checking answers open-class.

ANSWERS

1 carried away   2 carries   3 carry … weight
4 carried … off   5 carry on   6 carried
7 carried out   8 carried … through   9 carried … too far

3 Students discuss the questions in groups, appointing a representative to report back to the whole class.

FURTHER PRACTICE: **Advanced Gold Exam Maximiser p.26.**

Reading pp.32–33

▶ **Paper 1, Part 1 and Part 4** (multiple matching)

1 Students discuss the difficulties in groups before sharing their views open-class.

2 Set a two-minute time limit. Students work individually before comparing answers open-class.

ANSWERS

Tom Hartley: selling used cars
Simon Cunliffe-Lister: £10 million inheritance
Tracey Makin: lottery win
Karl Crompton: lottery win

3 Read the procedural information aloud to the class. Set a ten-minute time limit. Students work individually before checking their answers open-class. Insist on students justifying their answers by referring to the parallel expressions in the text.

ANSWERS

1 D lines 128–129 & 149–150   2 B lines 78–81
3 A lines 36–40   4 A lines 24–25
5 A lines 43–50   6 C lines 98–101
7 C lines 118–121   8 D lines 146–147 & 149–150
9 C lines 90–93   10 A lines 43–47
11 C lines 104–109   12 D lines 135–139

4 Students work individually, writing questions which they then answer in pairs.

ALTERNATIVE PROCEDURE: students work individually and give you written versions of their questions. Compile and edit a list of questions to copy and distribute in a subsequent class. Students answer questions individually. Check answers open-class, asking students to link their answers to parallel expressions in the text.

5 Students discuss the questions in groups, appointing a representative to report back to the whole class.

POSSIBLE JUSTIFICATIONS

Tom Hartley: like: humble and tolerant (lines 32–36);
    dislike: extravagant tastes (lines 23–25 & 49–50)
Simon Cunliffe-Lister: dislike: sexist (lines 80–82)
Tracey Makin: like: not greedy (lines 88–90)
Karl Crompton: dislike: slovenly (line 140); like: honest
    and realistic (lines 150–155)

6 Divide the class into As and Bs. Allow students a few minutes to work individually, planning what they will say. Students work in A–B pairs. Monitor and select a confident pair to perform their role-play for the rest of the class.

ALTERNATIVE PROCEDURE: divide the class into two groups: A and B (N.B. in large (16+) classes you may need four or eight groups). Each group appoints a representative to act out the role-play, but plans with that person what they will say. The role-play is then performed once. Those students not performing take note of any changes they would make.

The representatives then return to their groups and re-plan the interaction in the light of what the other student said. The role-play is acted out again.

BACKGROUND INFORMATION: Students may be surprised that Tom Hartley left school at 11. If they are, you can explain that in the UK, Australia, the USA and many other countries it is possible for children to be educated at home. In the UK, the parent is legally responsible for ensuring that the child receives an education, but the law states that children may be educated according to their parents' wishes. Parents don't need special qualifications to teach their children at home or can, as in the case of Tom Hartley, employ private tutors. Students with access to the internet might like to look at:
http://www.heas.org.uk or http://www.homes-cool.com.

FURTHER PRACTICE: *Advanced Gold Exam Maximiser* **pp.24–25.**

Grammar plus: verb tenses p.34

1 Elicit the names of the tenses open-class.

ANSWERS

Past Perfect Simple; Future Perfect Simple; Present Perfect Continuous; Present Perfect Continuous; Past Perfect Continuous

2 Students work individually before checking open-class.

ANSWERS

I bought him a Ferrari because he had earned it. 1
By the time he is 18 he will have become Britain's youngest
    multi-millionaire. 4
I have been serving an apprenticeship for two years. 2
I have not been watching TV, I have been working. 3
I had been waiting three hours before she arrived. 1

3 Students work in groups before comparing answers with the rest of the class.

ANSWERS

1 first sentence: permanent situation
   second sentence: temporary situation
2 first sentence: 'but I haven't finished'
   second sentence: 'and I've finished'
3 first sentence: 'and I don't mind'
   second sentence: 'and it irritates me'
4 first sentence: 'I am the one who has decided this'
   second sentence: 'the situation is beyond my control'

5 first sentence: they only did it once
   second sentence: they continued doing it for some time
6 first sentence: as a general rule, though not necessarily
   at the moment of speaking
   second sentence: at the moment of speaking.

4   Students work in pairs before checking their answers open-class.

ANSWERS

1 ✓
2 inappropriate: 'splitting up' happens quickly, though the lead up to the actual event may take a long time. Answer: 'I had split up … '
3 inappropriate: walking into the room only takes a few seconds. Answer: 'Our boss had walked … '
4 inappropriate: cutting yourself only takes a second. Answer: 'I cut myself … '
5 ✓
6 ✓
7 inappropriate: 'hear' with this meaning is not normally used in the continuous form/it only takes a minute or so to 'hear the news'. Answer: 'Have you heard … '
8 ✓
9 ✓

5   1 & 2 Students work in pairs before comparing answers open-class.

ANSWERS

1 like/love/care (feelings/emotional states)
   believe/know/understand (knowledge/mental states)
   possess/own/belong (possession)
   agree/deny/promise (communicating)
   smell/taste/hear (receiving sensations/sensory perception)
2
a) not possible: 'think' = believe, i.e. mental state
b) ✓: 'think' = consider, i.e. mental process
c) ✓: 'see' = meet, i.e. action
d) not possible: 'see' = understand, i.e. mental state
e) ✓: 'taste' = try, i.e. action
f) not possible: 'taste' = receive sensation, i.e. sensory perception
g) not possible: 'feel' = believe, i.e. mental state
h) ✓: temporary, ongoing situation: 'feel' = experience condition of the body

6   (p.35) Elicit examples of each of the tenses in the box. Students work individually before checking answers open-class and practising the dialogue in pairs.

ANSWERS

1 have you been doing   2 I'll be sharing   3 belongs
4 were moving   5 're joking   6 failed
7 had completely forgotten   8 'll be
9 will have unpacked   10 've done

7   Start by telling students about yourself. Allow time for them to think of a couple of answers. Students get up and mingle, telling everyone in the class about their achievements and future plans, and trying to find out how many people have achieved the same things and/or have the same future plans.

8   Students work in pairs and then in groups. Get a confident pair who use the Future Continuous well to tell the whole class about their dream holiday.

FURTHER PRACTICE: **Advanced Gold Exam Maximiser pp.28–29.**

Refer students to the **Grammar reference**, *Advanced Gold Coursebook*, p.195.

Speaking: giving opinions p.35

▶ **Paper 5, Part 3** (problem-solving task)

1   Read the exam information aloud to the class. Give examples to illustrate the meaning of 'prompts', e.g. question marks, single words or short lists. Play the cassette. Students work individually, noting what the candidates are asked to do. Check the answers open-class.

ANSWERS

To look at the pictures, to rank the areas of life in order of importance to them, and to give reasons to explain their choices.

2   Students listen and then discuss their answer open-class.

ANSWER

The female student asks the male for his opinion and gives her opinion some of the time, but he doesn't ever ask for her opinion.

She always agrees with him, whereas he almost always disagrees with her.

3   Students listen and note their answers individually before comparing in pairs, and then open-class. Put the expressions on the board.

ANSWERS

Asking for opinions	Giving opinions
So, what would you put first?	I'd have to go for …
What do you reckon is most important to you?	… you see, as far as I'm concerned …
Really? Not family?	'Work' certainly takes up a lot of time, but it's not really that important to me.
And how do you feel about what would go next?	In terms of quality of life, books are very high up on the list.
So that would be your number 2, would it?	There's nothing I like more than …

Agreeing	Disagreeing
Yes, I guess you're right.	No, well you see …
Yes, I think so …	… but, on the other hand, …
Yes, that's the same for me too …	… but you do need money …
	I'm not sure that I'd totally go along with that.

4   Students work in pairs. Choose a confident pair who use the expressions to repeat the task for the rest of the class. The others should tick off any of the expressions they hear the pair use.

FURTHER PRACTICE: Advanced Gold Exam Maximiser p.27.

Vocabulary: compound adjectives p.36

1   Students work individually before checking answers open-class.

ANSWERS

1 c   2 c   3 b   4 a   5 b   6 c   7 c   8 a   9 b   10 a

2   Students work in pairs before checking answers open-class.

ANSWERS

1 **self-'made** a self-made man or woman has become successful and rich by their own efforts, and did not have advantages like money or a high social position when they started
2 **'bullet proof** something that is bullet proof is designed to stop bullets from going through it
3 **absent-'minded** likely to forget things, especially because you are thinking about something else
4 **last-'minute** happening or done as late as possible within a process, event or activity (N.B. noun is not hyphenated)

5 **so-'called** a word used to describe someone or something that has been given a name that you think is wrong
6 **mass-pro'duced** produced in large numbers using machinery, so that each object is the same and can be sold cheaply
7 **tight-'fitting** fitting very closely or tightly
8 **'air-conditioned** kept cool and dry by means of a system of machines to control air temperature
9 **long-'standing** having continued or existed for a long time
10 **level-'headed** calm and sensible in making judgments or decisions
[NOTE: The stress can shift when the items are used in context.]

3   Students work individually before checking answers open-class.

ANSWERS

1 d   2 h   3 f   4 a   5 e   6 g   7 b   8 c

4   Students work in pairs, exchanging sentences with another pair.

ALTERNATIVE PROCEDURE: students work individually and hand in their sentences to you. You compile and edit their sentences and distribute a handout for revision work to be done in a subsequent class or for homework. The students' sentences could also be used as test material.

FURTHER PRACTICE: Advanced Gold Exam Maximiser p.28.

Exam focus p.37

Paper 3 English in Use: Part 6 (gapped text)

Read the exam information and suggested procedure aloud to the class. Set a fifteen-minute time limit for the task. Students work individually under exam conditions. Check answers open-class.

ANSWERS

1 F   2 G   3 C   4 A   5 B   6 E

FURTHER PRACTICE: Advanced Gold Exam Maximiser p.31.

Grammar check: articles p.38

1   Students work individually before checking their answers open-class.

ANSWERS

1 the   2 a   3 the   4 the   5 0   6 the   7 a   8 a
9 0   10 0   11 the   12 0   13 the   14 0   15 0
16 the   17 the   18 the   19 0   20 the   21 a
22 the   23 a   24 a   25 the   26 0   27 the

2   Students work in pairs before comparing answers with the whole class.

ANSWERS

a)   (suggested) We took a paddle steamer along the Mississippi. The Atlantic is a much darker blue than the Mediterranean.
b)   11 and 25
c)   1 and 17
d)   20
e)   4
f)   (suggested) He works as a bank teller and she's a stockbroker.
g)   2, 7, 8 and 21
h)   14, 19 and 26
i)   5, 10, 12 and 15.

FURTHER PRACTICE: **Advanced Gold Exam Maximiser p.26.**

Writing: informal/formal letters p.38

1   Students work individually before checking answers open-class.

ANSWERS

formal: a   b   c   e   f   g   i   l
informal: d   h   j   k   m   n

2   Students work in pairs before checking answers open-class.

SUGGESTED ANSWERS

a)   With reference to your letter of 3rd May, I wish to inform you that we no longer have the item in stock.
b)   I am writing to express my concern about the appalling condition of the pavement in Harcourt Avenue.
c)   I would therefore be very grateful if you would refund my money.

d)   I'm really sorry for not getting in touch sooner, but I've been incredibly busy settling in.
e)   I look forward to hearing from you in the near future.
f)   It was highly frustrating to discover that my room was immediately above the hotel discotheque.
g)   If this matter is not resolved in the very near future, I will be forced to report your company to the Consumer Protection League.
h)   Do write soon and tell me all your news.
i)   I am writing to enquire whether there are any positions for administrative assistants available with your company.
j)   It was lovely to get your letter with the photos of Kim and Simon.
k)   This is just a quick note to let you know how much we enjoyed our dinner with you on Tuesday.
l)   I am sure that you will be aware that many guests in the hotel were disturbed by the noise.
m)   I just wanted to let you know that I won't be able to come to the meeting on Thursday.
n)   Please give my love to your parents ... and to Olivier!

3   Students work in groups before checking their answers with the **Writing reference**, *Advanced Gold Coursebook* pp.201 and 204, and then open-class.

ANSWERS

1   In letters to friends it is usual to put the date on the right-hand side at the top of the page, and sometimes your address or the name of the place you are writing from. For formal letters to companies, if you are not using writing paper with a printed address, your address goes in the top right-hand corner. The address and the name and title of the person you are writing to go on the left, starting a line below your address. The date in full is written a line below the recipient's address on the left.
   N.B. Students do not need to include addresses in CAE Paper 2 writing tasks.
2   Letters to friends can begin 'Dear' + first name or 'Hi' + first name. 'My dear' + first name or 'Dearest' + first name or first name + 'my darling' can also be used with loved ones. Letters to acquaintances and people you do not know very well typically end with phrases such as 'Yours', 'With best wishes', or 'All the best'. 'Love' or 'Lots of/All my love' are used with close friends and loved ones. These are sometimes followed by the symbols for kisses and hugs: XXX OOO. Formal letters to companies begin with 'Dear' + the person's title and surname if you know it. If you do not know the title or the person's sex, it is increasingly acceptable to begin 'Dear' + first name and surname. If you know neither

the name or title you can begin 'Dear Sir/Madam'. Letters to companies normally end with the formula 'I/We look forward to … + ing' or 'Should you require … , please do not hesitate to contact me/us.' In situations where you do not know the person's name and have begun 'Dear Sir/Madam', the final salutation is 'Yours faithfully' + your signature and full name typed or clearly printed. 'Yours sincerely' + your signature and full name typed or clearly printed are used where you know the name of the person you are writing to. (In US English, 'Sincerely yours' and 'Yours truly' are also used.)

3 In informal letters, new paragraphs can begin on the next line with a small indent (1 cm). An acceptable alternative paragraphing style is full out, with a space between paragraphs.
Formal letters typically use block style, where a two-line space is left between paragraphs. Indents are not obligatory but can be used as well.

4 (p.39) Students work individually before comparing answers with a partner, and then open-class.

ANSWERS AND SUGGESTED CHANGES

Just thought I'd drop you a line to tell you about …
   ➜ I am writing to inform you of …
over the moon ➜ astonished
And this wasn't just a one-off either.
   ➜ In fact this was not an isolated incident
The bit about this that really got on my nerves …
   ➜ What I found particularly irritating …
I can't believe it but everything still seems really up in the air at the moment …
   ➜ Incredible as it may seem, the situation remains unclear …
… get their act together and sort this mess out pretty soonish!
   ➜ … find a way to resolve the matter as soon as possible.
NB: The fact that she has written only her first name at the bottom of the letter is also inappropriate in a formal letter. She should sign the letter and then type her full name below the signature.

5 Students work in pairs to complete the informal letter. Monitor, and ask a good pair to read their letter aloud to the rest of the class.

6 The writing task can be done in class or for homework. If done in class, students can exchange their work and suggest further revisions.

FURTHER PRACTICE: Advanced Gold Exam Maximiser p.29.

Grammar check: relative clauses/ pronouns p.40

1 Set a one-minute time limit for the gist reading task. Students work individually before checking their answers open-class.

ANSWERS

1 130 thousand million   2 Hungary

2 Students work individually before checking their answers open-class.

ANSWERS

1 whose   2 when   3 which   4 which   5 who
6 where   7 which

3 Students work in pairs before checking answers open-class.

ANSWERS

1 a) I only have one brother and I am more interested in telling you about the fact that he lives in Glasgow than I am in his being a solicitor.
   b) I have more than one brother. One of my brothers is a solicitor. This brother lives in Glasgow.
2 a) ✗ There should not be a comma after 'hotel'.
   b) ✓
3 a) There were several windows and one of them was left open.
   b) There was only one window and it had been left open.
4 a) All the students were allowed to go home and they got very good marks.
   b) Some students got very good marks. Only these students were allowed to go home.
5 a) ✓
   b) ✗ This should be two separate questions: 'Why don't you tell me? Which evening is best for you?'
6 a) ✗ this gives the impression that there are several Eiffel Towers built in different years.
   b) ✓

4 Students work in pairs writing their questions, and then with a partner, asking and answering them.

ALTERNATIVE PROCEDURE: this can be played as a team game. Divide the class into two teams. Each team works together composing ten quiz questions to put to the other team.

FURTHER PRACTICE: Advanced Gold Exam Maximiser p.30.

Unit 3 review p.41

The unit review can be done in class or set for homework.

ANSWERS

1 1 ~~off~~   2 ✓   3 ~~on~~   4 ✓   5 ✓   6 ~~away~~   7 ✓
    8 ~~over~~ → off   9 ✓

2 1 will be doing
    2 was feeling
    3 She's talking/She's been talking
    4 haven't
    5 have you been doing
    6 is assembled/is being assembled
    7 had gone/was going

3 1 dissatisfaction   2 understand/appreciate
    3 interview/appointment   4 staff   5 delay/situation
    6 rare occurrence/rarity   7 publicity/literature/brochures
    8 limit   9 consultation/notification
    10 arrangement/appointment
    11 individual circumstances   12 apologies   13 caused

UNIT

4 The universal migraine

Advance preparation

▮ Remind students to bring dictionaries to class for Exercises 4 and 6 on page 50. Alternatively, arrange to bring a class set yourself.

▮ Ask students to bring some of their recent written work to class for Exercise 5 on page 50.

Speaking: what is love? p.42

1 1 Students work individually, using their dictionaries to check the meaning of unfamiliar vocabulary in the quotes and deciding which are negative, positive and neutral.

SUGGESTED ANSWERS

Robert Graves quote: negative
Dorothy Parker quote: neutral
Proverb: positive
Oliver Goldsmith quote: negative
William Congreve quote: positive

2 Students discuss the quotes in groups, appointing a representative to report back to the rest of the class.

SUGGESTED ANSWERS

Robert Graves quote: Love is something that everyone experiences. It is a painful experience that initially dazzles us and obscures our perception of reality.

Dorothy Parker quote: If you look desperately for love and are then possessive and dependent on the loved one, you are likely to lose their love; if, on the other hand, you adopt a more relaxed attitude you will have more chance of maintaining the relationship.

Proverb: Even if it seems impossible for you to overcome practical problems, if you really love someone you will find ways round them.

Oliver Goldsmith quote: People establish friendships without any hidden motives and treat one another as equals; people who are in love suffer greatly because the relationship is one of inequality where one partner always loves more and is dependent on the other, who, in turn treats her/him badly.

William Congreve quote: Never having been in love is worse than having been in love and having lost your lover.

EXTRA QUESTIONS FOR DISCUSSION: Which single quote do you think is the best? Why?

BACKGROUND INFORMATION: Dorothy Parker (1893–1967) American writer and critic. Parker wrote reviews for magazines such as *Vogue*, *The New Yorker* and *Esquire*. She also wrote poetry, short stories, plays and film scripts. Parker was a very liberated woman for the times in which she lived and was famous for her witty conversation.
Robert Graves (1895–1985) English poet and writer. He is famous for his autobiography *Goodbye to All That*, which describes his experiences in World War I, and for his two novels about ancient Rome, *I, Claudius* and *Claudius the God*. He also wrote poetry and was professor of poetry at Oxford from 1961–1966. He lived for many years in both Egypt and Mallorca.
Oliver Goldsmith (1730–1774) Poet, playwright and man of letters. He is famous for his play *She Stoops to Conquer* and his novel *The Vicar of Wakefield*, though he also wrote histories of Greece and Rome, as well as works on natural history.
William Congreve (1670–1729) is principally known for his plays, witty satires on seventeenth- and eighteenth-century society. He also wrote librettos for operas.

Grammar check: gerund v. infinitive p.42

1 Set a one-minute time limit for the gist reading task.

ANSWERS

1 No (lines 55–56 and 67–68)   2 Yes (lines 77–78)

2 (p.43) Students work individually before checking their answers open-class.

ANSWERS

1 telling   2 to go   3 to learn   4 to teach/teaching
5 to sing   6 singing   7 to live   8 to have   9 to marry
10 to marry   11 to abide   12 to see/seeing
13 to choose   14 marrying   15 to have   16 to divorce
17 to see/seeing   18 to agree

3   Students work in pairs before checking their answers open-class.

ANSWERS

1 ✓   2 ~~passing~~ → to pass   3 ✓   4 ✓
5 ~~to smoke~~ → smoking   6 ✓   7 ~~to leave~~ → leaving
8 to speaking   9 ~~to run~~ → running   10 ~~to be~~ → being
11 ~~to take~~ → taking   12 ~~to open~~ → opening   13 ✓
14 ~~to go~~ → going

4   Students work individually before comparing answers with a partner and then with the rest of the class.

POSSIBLE ANSWERS

1   As a child I generally wasn't allowed to stay up later than 11 p.m.
2   I once tried riding my bike to university, but I was so exhausted when I got there I never did it again.
3   On Sunday mornings, I generally like to get up quite early and go for a run.
4   I'm not really accustomed to living in the city yet.
5   I generally avoid leaving for work in the rush hour.
6   I must admit that I rather regret selling my mountain bike.
7   In the future, I hope to have more time to spend doing the things that are really important to me.
8   For people who want to give up smoking, I would suggest drinking a glass of water every time they feel like having a cigarette.
9   The earliest childhood memory I have is from when I was about two years old. I remember making a sandcastle on the beach with another little girl.

ALTERNATIVE PROCEDURE: students get up and mingle, taking it in turns to read their sentences with another student until they find someone who has completed a sentence in the same way as they have.

FURTHER PRACTICE: **Advanced Gold Exam Maximiser p.32.**

Vocabulary: similes (*like/as ... as*) p.43

1   Look at the example with the students, drawing attention to the underlined simile. Students discuss the other similes in pairs before checking their answers open-class.

ANSWERS

1   very likely to make someone angry or upset
2   rude to people because you are feeling bad-tempered
3   sleep very well
4   uncomfortable because you are in an unfamiliar place or situation
5   clumsy and tactless

2   Students work in pairs before checking their answers open-class.

ANSWERS

as strong as an ox   as light as a feather
as quick as a flash   as white as a sheet
as cool as a cucumber

3   Look at the example with the class. Students work individually before checking with a partner, and then open-class.

ANSWERS

1 like a fish out of water   2 as cool as a cucumber
3 as quick as a flash   4 as white as a sheet
5 like a log   6 like a bull in a china shop
7 as light as a feather   8 like a red rag to a bull
9 as strong as an ox

4   Put these questions up on the board and ask students to discuss them in groups, appointing a representative to report their discussion to the rest of the class.
• Why do relationships end?
• How do people react when a relationship finishes?

Put these questions up on the board:
• How long ago do you think this relationship ended?
• How has the singer reacted to the ending of the relationship?

Students listen to the song and answer individually before checking answers open-class.

ANSWERS

The relationship ended a long time ago and the singer reacted so badly that she has been unable to get over the break-up.

Ask students what simile they heard.

ANSWER

like the deserts miss the rain

5   Students work individually before comparing answers with a partner and checking by listening to the song.

ANSWERS

1 d   2 f   3 a   4 e   5 c   6 b

BACKGROUND INFORMATION: The duo 'Everything but the girl' ('EBTG' for short) are Tracey Thorn and Ben Watts. They met in Hull, where they were both studying, in 1981. The name of the band came from the name of a shop in Hull which sold furniture to newly-wed couples. Both Ben and Tracey had already been in pop groups in London when they formed EBTG. Ben Watts was very ill for several years with a very rare, near-fatal disease. He wrote an autobiographical account of his illness, *Patient* (1992), which has been widely acclaimed by the critics. Their official website includes extracts from *Patient* as well as audio and video material. It can be found at: http://www.ebtg.com.

EXTRA ACTIVITY: Students work in pairs, taking it in turns to give the first part of a simile and seeing how quickly their partner can finish it off.

Example: Student A: Like a red … Student B: … rag to a bull.

FURTHER PRACTICE: *Advanced Gold Exam Maximiser* p.33.

Reading p.44

▶ **Paper 1, Part 4** (multiple matching)

1   Focus attention on the cartoon and the cliché. Discuss the question open-class. Tell students to look at the other clichés in the reading text and discuss their meaning with a partner before comparing answers open-class. Emphasise that they should NOT read the text at this stage.

SUGGESTED ANSWERS

absence makes the heart grow fonder used to say that being away from someone makes you like them more

out of sight out of mind used to say that you will soon forget someone if you do not see them for a while

familiarity breeds contempt an expression meaning that if you know someone too well, you find out their faults and respect them less

the seven-year itch the idea that after seven years of being together, couples feel less satisfied with their relationship

birds of a feather flock together we are attracted to people like ourselves

opposites attract we are attracted to people who are completely different from us

to play hard to get to pretend that you are not romantically interested in someone so that they will become more interested in you

beauty is in the eye of the beholder used to say that different people have different opinions about what is beautiful

2   (p.45) Read the rubric to the class. Go through the suggested procedure, reading it aloud and pausing for students to action each point. Set the following time limits:
1 5 minutes (three minutes reading and underlining; two minutes comparing with another student)
2 5 minutes (three minutes reading; two minutes comparing with another student)
3 10 minutes
4 5 minutes (two minutes checking answers; three minutes comparing with another student)

Check the answers open-class, insisting on parallel expressions to justify answers.

ANSWERS

1 E (lines 56–58)   2 H (lines 79–82)
3 A/4 B (lines 32–33)   5 D (lines 46–51)
6 B (lines 38–39)   7 F (lines 55–56)
8 A/9 B (lines 32–35)   10 C (lines 42–44)
11 F (lines 58–60)   12 B (lines 35–37)   13 G (lines 68–72)

3   Students work individually before checking answers open-class. Where students share the same L1, accept translation equivalents.

ANSWERS

1 clearly expressed in a few words
2 to give opinions, excuses, reasons, etc. that you have used too often to seem sincere
3 directly and firmly
4 to say that what someone is saying is true
5 strong desire to do or have something
6 using words in a clever and amusing way
7 an opinion that everyone in a group will agree with or accept

4   Students discuss the question in groups, appointing a representative to report their discussion to the rest of the class.

FURTHER PRACTICE: *Advanced Gold Exam Maximiser* pp.34–35.

Speaking: language of speculation p.46

1   Students discuss the photographs in pairs.

2   Play the cassette. Pairs compare their impressions to those of the people on the cassette and report back to the rest of the class.

ANSWERS

One speaker thinks the woman with the long hair and the man with the plaid shirt are boyfriend and girlfriend, whereas the other thinks they could be brother and sister.

The speakers agree that the people in the street are having a relationship because of the way the woman is leaning in towards the man.

The two speakers disagree about the picture of the elderly man and the child. The first speaker is sure that the man is the girl's grandfather or great-grandfather, while the other speaker thinks he could just be a family friend.

3   Students work individually, completing the sentences before checking their answers open-class.

ANSWERS

2 guess is that   3 get the impression that
4 bet   5 reckon it's pretty unlikely that
6 wouldn't be at all surprised if
7 suppose it's just possible

4   Students work in pairs. Get confident students who have used the language of speculation well to describe a photograph for the rest of the class. The class notes which expressions of speculation were used.

FURTHER PRACTICE: **Advanced Gold Exam Maximiser p.37.**

Exam focus pp.46–47

Paper 4 Listening: Part 3 (sentence completion)

Read the exam information aloud to the class. Read the exam procedure aloud, pausing for students to action each point. Check answers, replaying relevant sections of the cassette.

ANSWERS

1 difficult and inaccessible
2 moodiness and self-absorption   3 language
4 today's teenagers   5 revolution   6 short segments
7 pupils   8 mime   9 direct   10 videos

ALTERNATIVE PROCEDURE: distribute copies of the **Tapescript** on pp.116–117. Students correct their own work.

Grammar plus: modals (advanced features) p.48

1   Students work individually before checking answers open-class.

ANSWERS

1 theoretical possibility   2 ability   3 strong obligation
4 prohibition   5 weak obligation   6 deduction
7 lack of obligation   8 permission

2   Students work in pairs before checking answers open-class.

ANSWERS

1   theoretical possibility: *may, might*
2   ability: *can*
3   strong obligation: *must, need to*
4   prohibition: *must not, may not*
5   weak obligation: *should, had better*
6   deduction: *can't, may, might*
7   lack of obligation: *do/does not have to*
8   permission: *may, might*

3   Students work in pairs before checking their answers open-class.

ANSWERS

… it must be true. (line 16 = deduction)
You can use either cliché … (line 32 = theoretical possibility)
… might play its part (lines 38–39 = theoretical possibility)
… there can be problems. (line 50 = theoretical possibility)
… the theory may work (line 65 = theoretical possibility)
… or it could hopelessly backfire. (line 66 = theoretical possibility)
… the majority can agree … (line 77 = ability)
… you can't argue … (line 81 = negative theoretical possibility)
… people cannot agree … (line 82 = ability)

4   Students work individually before checking their answers with a partner, and then open-class.

ANSWERS

1 You must not bring …   2 ✓   3 May I leave …
4 You had better …   5 Can't you play …   6 ✓
7 You can/may stay up …   8 ✓   9 ✓   10 ✓
11 She must have misunderstood …   12 ✓   13 ✓

5   Students work individually before checking their answers open-class.

ANSWERS

1 You shouldn't drink/oughtn't to drink …
2 … be happier.
3 … can get very cold …
4 can't/couldn't have taken …
5 … must register/will register/need to register …
6 … didn't need to/didn't have to/needn't have put up …
7 … may/might not have realised …
8 better not book …
9 you have to/need to switch …
10 … couldn't have let you …
11 … shouldn't/ought not to have called …

6   Students work in pairs before checking their answers open-class.

ANSWERS

1 can/should   2 must   3 could/might   4 must
5 could/can   6 shouldn't (N.B. 'haven't to' acceptable in
   some varieties of English)   7 might   8 might
9 could/can/might   10 should/could
11 have to/need to/ought to   12 should/may
13 shouldn't have/needn't have   14 can/might

7   (p.49) The writing can be done in pairs or individually in class, or for homework.

ALTERNATIVE PROCEDURE: divide the class into two groups. All the students in group A should write a letter to an 'agony aunt/uncle' as a homework activity. The letter can be about going to have dinner at their boyfriend's/girlfriend's home or another 'relationship' problem. They bring their letters to the next class and give them to the students in group B. The students in group B then reply to the letters for homework and bring their replies the next day. Stick the letters and replies up round the room so that everyone can read them. Students vote on who had the most difficult problem and who gave the best advice.

Watch Out!   *didn't need to/needn't have*

Students work individually before checking their answers open-class.

ANSWERS

1 a)   2 b)

Refer students to the **Grammar reference**, p.194 of the *Advanced Gold Coursebook*.

*FURTHER PRACTICE: **Advanced Gold Exam Maximiser** p.36.*

English in Use p.50

▶ Paper 3, Part 3 (error correction, spelling and punctuation)

1   Students read the exam information silently.

2   Set a one-minute time limit for this.

ANSWER

By naming their child after the airline.

3   Students work individually.

4   Students work in pairs before checking their answers open-class.

ANSWERS

1 ~~german~~ ➔ German
2 ~~launtch~~ ➔ launch
3 ~~fliht~~ ➔ flight
4 wedding, the airline (i.e. add comma)
5 ~~beseaged~~ ➔ besieged
6 ✓
7 no)
8 ✓
9 no ; after *married*
10 ~~traditionall~~ ➔ traditional
11 ✓
12 wedding (i.e. lower-case 'w')
13 no apostrophe after *newlyweds*
14 ✓
15 ~~espesially~~ ➔ especially
16 ✓

5   Students work individually.

6   Students work individually before checking their answers in a dictionary, and then open-class.

ANSWERS

2 ✓   3 whether   4 quite   5 ✓   6 inconvenient
7 lose   8 ✓   9 wonderful   10 ✓

Refer students to the **Editing checklist** on p.214 of the *Advanced Gold Coursebook*.

Vocabulary: noun collocations (with *of*) p.51

1   Students work in pairs.

2   Students check their answers to Exercise 1 by listening to the cassette.

ANSWERS

a grain of 'truth   pearls of 'wisdom   a load of 'rubbish
a slip of the 'tongue   a difference of o'pinion
a heart of 'gold   a lapse of concen'tration
a term of en'dearment   the price of 'failure
(without) fear of contra'diction   a question of 'time

3   Students work individually before checking their answers open-class.

ANSWERS

1 (have) a heart of gold   2 a grain of truth
3 the price of failure   4 a difference of opinion
5 a question of time   6 a slip of the tongue
7 a term of endearment   8 without fear of contradiction
9 a lapse of concentration   10 a load of rubbish
11 pearls of wisdom

4   Students work in pairs. Ask confident pairs to describe situations to the whole class.

*FURTHER PRACTICE: **Advanced Gold Exam Maximiser** p.38.*

Listening: messages p.51

1   Students discuss the questions in groups, appointing a representative to report back to the whole class.

2   Students read the questions through before answering individually and comparing answers with a partner. Play the cassette again so that students can check their answers. Check answers open-class, replaying sections of the messages where necessary.

ANSWERS

1 b   2 c   3 a   4 b   5 b (see **Tapescript** on p.117)

3   Students work individually before comparing answers with a partner and checking open-class.

SUGGESTED ANSWERS

1 Debbie phoned. Says she'd like to get in touch with someone she met last night. Wants his number.
2 Message from Health Clinic. Dr Sengupta is ill. Won't be able to see you until next week. If that's too late, phone them on 0171 491 2588.
3 Sara phoned. Arrived safely and had a good flight. Said not to forget to feed Pickles!!!
4 SIMON MCLACHLAN phoned about your mountain bike. Wants to know if he can come round and see it. Phone him on 0181 771 9458.
5 Jenny phoned. Says she got the job and is going on a mad spending spree. Call her at home before 2 p.m. if you want to go along.

Writing: notes/messages p.52

1   Students work in groups before checking their answers open-class.

SUGGESTED ANSWERS

1 Note on windscreen of car. Warning, identifying self. Angry resident to owner of car.
2 Note on coffee machine in company/college. Apologising, warning, informing. Member of catering staff to members of staff and/or students.
3 Note left on kitchen table. Informing, suggesting. Boyfriend/Girlfriend written before leaving for work to girlfriend/boyfriend still asleep after late night at party.

2   Students work in pairs before comparing lists with the rest of the class.

SUGGESTED ANSWERS

Notes are usually particularly informal. As a result special punctuation is used: dashes, exclamation marks, multiple question marks; numbers are used instead of words: *6 p.m.*; abbreviations are used: *asap* (= as soon as possible), *p.m.* (after midday, Latin *post meridiem*) *a.m.* (before midday, Latin *ante meridiem*); symbols replace words: + (= and), xxx (= kisses/love), xxx ooo (= kisses and hugs/love).

3   Students work in pairs before checking answers open-class.

ANSWERS

1 *e.g.* = for example   *etc.* = et cetera
2 *pto* = please turn over (and read what's on the other side)
3 *NB* = please note (Latin *nota bene* = note well)
4 *info.* = information   *i.e.* = that is, what is meant is (Latin *id est* = that is)   *incl.* = including

4   Students work individually before comparing notes with a partner and deciding on a final version. Each pair reads their notes to the rest of the class.

SUGGESTED ANSWERS

1 Locked myself out. Next door having a coffee with Julie. Come and get me. XXX Sandra
2 Brian, Not feeling well so have gone home early. Can you finish report? Leave on my desk. Will read first thing tomorrow a.m. Sarah

Unit 4 review p.53

ANSWERS

1 1 criticism   2 surprisingly   3 dismissive
4 commitment   5 expectation   6 defiantly   7 hopeful
8 relationship

2 1 better   2 must   3 can't   4 couldn't   5 might/could
6 needn't   7 won't/shouldn't/mightn't   8 Do/Don't

3 1 lapses   2 tongue   3 endearment   4 grain
5 failure   6 pearls   7 contradiction   8 opinion

4 SUGGESTED ANSWERS
She felt like a fish out of water when she got to the party and no one she knew was there.
That new mattress is so comfortable I slept like a log.
Our new jackets are very warm, yet light as a feather.
When she confronted him he was as cool as a cucumber.
Tony isn't particularly well built, but he's as strong as an ox.
He went as white as a sheet when he saw the newspaper headline.

UNIT

5 Where will it end?

Advance preparation

▪ (Optional) Bring the review sections of a selection of newspapers and magazines in English to class for Exercise 1 on page 56.

▪ (Optional) Get a copy of the video of the film *Blade Runner* for the class to watch as an extra activity to follow Exercise 2 on page 56.

▪ Remind students to bring dictionaries to class for Exercise 3 on page 59, or arrange to bring a class set yourself.

Listening: cryonics p.54

1   Students discuss the questions in pairs before comparing their reactions with the rest of the class.

2   Students listen and take notes before comparing answers with the rest of the class.

SUGGESTED ANSWER

They are planning to have themselves frozen so that they will be ready for any advances in science that extend the natural life expectancy of a human.

3   Play the cassette again. Students compare answers with a partner. Check answers, replaying relevant sections of the cassette.

ANSWERS

1 the United States   2 be together
3 liquid nitrogen   4 changes his mind
5 serious   6 life insurance   7 Michael Jackson
8 seven/7   9 emigrating

ALTERNATIVE PROCEDURE: distribute copies of the **Tapescript** on p.118. Students correct their own work.

4   Students discuss the questions in groups, appointing a representative to report back to the rest of the class.

Speaking p.54

▶ Paper 5, Part 3 + Part 4

1   Students read the exam information silently.

2 & 3   (pp.54–55) Focus attention on the magazine cover designs and on Exercises 3–5. Students discuss the usage of the phrases with a partner, and then open-class.

SUGGESTED ANSWER

They are all used to pick up on a point made by another speaker so as to clarify and/or develop it. They would be particularly useful in situations where one speaker is less accurate and/or has a more limited range than another. The stronger speaker would use the phrases to check understanding by re-expressing what the less able speaker has said more accurately and with more sophisticated language. The phrases would also be used in situations where both speakers are equally competent so as to check understanding and show interest.

4   Play the recording. Write the phrases on the board, marking the stress and intonation.

'So, what you really 'mean by that 'is … '

'If I under'stand you co'rrectly then … '

'What I under'stand by that is … '

Students listen and repeat.

5   Students listen to the recording again before performing the task in pairs. Go round monitoring, and choose a pair who are using the phrases well to perform for the rest of the class.

6   Students discuss the questions in groups, appointing a representative to report back to the whole class.

7   Students listen before discussing the questions open-class.

8   Play the recording. Students complete the phrases individually before checking open-class. Play the recording again. Students listen and repeat.

ANSWERS

1 to follow on from   2 generally agreeing with that
3 to what you've just

9 Students work in groups of three. Monitor and choose a confident group to perform for the rest of the class. They listen and note examples of the expressions in Exercises 3 and 8.

FURTHER PRACTICE: *Advanced Gold Exam Maximiser* **p.39.**

Writing: review p.56

1 Students discuss the questions in groups, appointing a representative to report their discussion to the rest of the class.

ALTERNATIVE PROCEDURE: bring in the review sections of newspapers and magazines in English. Students examine the material in groups and report their findings to the rest of the class.

2 Read the review information aloud to the students. They then read the review individually before locating each of the elements with a partner and discussing the other questions. Check answers open-class.

SUGGESTED ANSWERS

Paragraph 1: Background information with elements of 2 and 3.
Paragraph 2: A brief account of the plot with elements of 3.
Paragraph 3: Critical comment + personal opinion and recommendation.
It is a good review because it includes all four elements and uses a good range of vocabulary and structure.

EXTRA ACTIVITIES: **1** Students watch the film *Blade Runner* (available on video), or an extract from the film, and decide if they agree with the reviewer or not.
2 Students analyse one of the reviews they looked at in Alternative procedure Exercise 1 for the elements in 2 and present their findings to the rest of the class.
3 Students with access to the Internet might enjoy looking at the network of *Blade Runner* web fan magazines at: http://www.devo.com/bladerunner.

3 (p.57) Ask students to find the examples of the adverb + adjective/participle collocations in the review (lines 3, 11 and 22 respectively). Make it clear that some of the adverbs collocate with more than one adjective/participle. They work individually, matching the adverbs and adjectives/participles

before comparing answers with a partner and checking open-class.

SUGGESTED ANSWERS

highly successful/amusing/entertaining
profoundly moving
utterly ridiculous/tedious
excruciatingly tedious
hugely successful/disappointing/impressive
amazingly successful/entertaining

4 Refer students to the **Writing reference**, pp.206–207 of the *Advanced Gold Coursebook*. They compare with a partner and check open-class.

5 Students can write their reviews in class or for homework.

EXTRA ACTIVITY: Put up a Reviews Notice Board in the classroom. Encourage students to write reviews of films they see (on TV and at the cinema), books they read, and records or concerts.

FURTHER PRACTICE: *Advanced Gold Exam Maximiser* **pp.40–41.**

Listening: song p.57

BACKGROUND INFORMATION: Dr Jekyll and Mr Hyde are characters in the novel of the same name written by the Scottish writer Robert Louis Stevenson and published (by Longman) in 1886. The novel tells the tale of Dr Jekyll, who believes he can separate the good and evil sides of human nature. To this end, he invents a potion that turns him into the evil Mr Hyde. Soon Dr Jekyll finds that the potion is too strong and he can no longer control his diabolical counterpart. The story may have been based on Stevenson's personal experiences. He was from a very respectable family but had a fascination with the marginal elements in Edinburgh society. There are no less than ten film versions of the novel, the most recent of which was made in 1941, and starred Ingrid Bergman, Lana Turner and Spencer Tracey.

1 Students discuss the questions with a partner, and then open-class.

SUGGESTED ANSWERS

See background information above. A Jekyll and Hyde person is one who has two different natures and can change from one to the other. They are sometimes, for example, very sweet and kind and sometimes angry and cruel.

2   Students work in pairs, predicting the missing words.

3   Students listen to the song to check their answers.

ANSWERS

1 dreams   2 found   3 sad   4 alive   5 survive
6 fools   7 care

BACKGROUND INFORMATION: The song is by the Australian
(Melbourne) band, Men at Work. Founded in 1979, Men at
Work had several international hits in the early 1980s.
Many will recognise titles such as 'Down Under' and 'Who
can it be now?'. Although they had not performed or
recorded together for many years, the members of Men at
Work toured South America in 1996 and 1997 and
recorded a live album in Brazil (entitled *Brazil*) in 1998.
Students might like to look at their website at:
http://www.menatwork.com.au.

4   (p.58) Students discuss the questions in pairs before
comparing answers open-class.

SUGGESTED ANSWERS

1   The experiment is not a normal scientific experiment
    and quickly gets out of control.
2   He has gone slightly mad and/or is excited because his
    experiment has 'broken new ground'.
    to break new ground to do something completely
    new that no one has ever done before, or find out new
    information about a subject
3   He carries out the experiment on himself.
4   **to set your sights on something** to be determined to
    achieve something or decide that you definitely want to
    have it
5   **the underdog** a person, country etc. that is weak and
    is always treated badly
6   The greatest experiment; better or worse than all others
    i.e. The experiment of changing himself into Mr Jive
    and/or being able to control human personality.

5   Students read the text on *Advanced Gold Coursebook*
p.222 before comparing answers with a partner and then with
the rest of the class.

ANSWERS

He has created a living creature. He is horrified and
    terrified.

BACKGROUND INFORMATION: Mary Shelley, the wife of the poet
Percy Shelley, wrote the story that formed the basis of the
novel while on holiday with her husband and the poet Lord
Byron in Italy. The story was the result of a party game in
which everyone was to write a ghost story. Mary Shelley's
story is about Doctor Frankenstein, who tries to create a
living thing but ends up creating a monster. There are
many interpretations of the novel, which she wrote when
she was only eighteen. One of these suggests that Shelley
was afraid of giving birth to a deformed child or to a child
she could not love. There are innumerable films loosely
based on the events of the novel, the most famous of
which are the 1930 version with Bela Lugosi and the 1938
re-release of the 1931 version, starring Boris Karloff. The
entire text of the novel and an enormous amount of
information can be found at:
http://www.georgetown.edu/irvinemj/english016/franken/
franken.html.

6   Students discuss the question in groups, appointing a
representative to report their discussion to the rest of the
class.

Grammar check: conditionals p.58

1   Students work individually before checking answers
open-class.

ANSWERS

1 will not pass/are not going to pass
2 would not have started   3 would be going/would go
4 say   5 did/were to do   6 get   7 adds   8 promise
9 had come   10 has

2   Students work in pairs before checking answers open-
class.

ANSWERS

1 Present Simple   2 Present Simple   3 Past Simple
4 Past Perfect

3   Students work individually before getting up and
mingling. They should ask each other questions formed from
the prompts, e.g.:
A: What will you do if you have some free time this evening?
B: I'll phone my friend Veronica and have a chat.
What will you do when you become completely fluent in
English?
What would you do if you won £1,000 on the lottery?
Where would you go if you had the chance to visit anywhere
in the world?
What would you have done if things had been different when
you were younger?

They ask and answer until they find someone with similar answers to their own. The pair with the most similarities read their sentences to the rest of the class.

FURTHER PRACTICE: **Advanced Gold Exam Maximiser p.40.**

Vocabulary: science and medicine p.59

1   Students work individually before checking with a partner, and then open-class.

ANSWERS

1 h   2 l   3 f   4 a   5 i   6 b   7 k   8 e   9 c   10 j
11 d   12 g

2   Students read the words and expressions aloud to a partner.

ANSWERS

1 clone /kləʊn/
2 cell /sel/
3 sexual reproduction /ˌsekʃuəl riːprəˈdʌkʃən/
4 organ /ˈɔːgən/
5 tissue /ˈtɪʃuː/
6 embryo /ˈembriəʊ/
7 genetic engineering /dʒəˌnetɪk endʒəˈnɪərɪŋ/
8 fertilisation /ˌfɜːtəlaɪˈzeɪʃən/
9 technique /tekˈniːk/
10 physicist /ˈfɪzəsəst/
11 ethics /ˈeθɪks/
12 DNA /ˌdiː en ˈeɪ/

3   Students work in pairs before checking answers open-class.

ANSWERS

1 a clone   2 reproduce reproductive
3 embryonic   4 gene/genetics   5 fertilise
6 physics   7 (un)ethical

4   1 Students discuss the questions in groups, appointing a representative to report their discussion to the rest of the class.

2 Play the cassette and allow time for the groups to discuss the comments (see **Tapescript** on p.118).

3 Students discuss the questions in groups, appointing a representative to report their discussion to the rest of the class.

FURTHER PRACTICE: **Advanced Gold Exam Maximiser p.46.**

Reading p.60

▶ **Paper 1, Part 2** (gapped text)

1   Students discuss the question in pairs and then open-class. Explain that the title involves a pun or play on the word 'cell' and that a 'cell mate' is the person with whom you share a prison cell.

2   Set a two-minute time limit for this gist reading task. Students discuss their answers in pairs, and then open-class.

ANSWER

He seems rather impressed by him, though he also considers him to be arrogant and odd.

3   Work through the instructions step by step with the class.

ANSWERS

1   Some reference to the first cloning method somewhere in the main text. Paragraph G fits gap 2. See lines 21–26.
2   They refer to some process and a male person previously mentioned in the text. It will fill gap 1, referring back to 'clone human beings' and Richard Seed.

3 Students work individually before checking answers with a partner, and then open-class. Insist on students explaining the relationship between the underlined words and the base text.

ANSWERS

3   A: He in paragraph A refers back to Seed (and subsequent uses of 'he') in base text line 39; procedure refers back to the technique for transferring embryos in cattle (lines 47–48) in the base text.
4   H: This refers back to 'research' (line 68, base text).
5   B: my refers back to Steve Jones (line 74, base text).
6   F: They refers back to 'clone' (line 80, base text).
7   D: This refers back to 'human cloning raises a hundred questions' (lines 90–91, base text).

4   Students read the article all the way through.

5   Students discuss the questions in groups, appointing a representative to report their discussion to the rest of the class.

FURTHER PRACTICE: **Advanced Gold Exam Maximiser pp.43–44.**

Grammar plus: conditionals (advanced forms) p.62

1   Students work individually before comparing answers with a partner and checking open-class, or by referring to the **Grammar reference** on p192 of the *Advanced Gold Coursebook*.

ANSWERS

1 True   2 True
3 False: They are similar to 'if', i.e. no more or less polite.
4 True   5 True

2   Students work individually before checking their answers open-class.

ANSWERS

1 If I were **to** say that I …
2 **Had** we spent more time with her …
3 If you **will/would** just be patient …
4 … **would** that be a problem?
5 If you happen **to** see Mr Parker …
6 **Were** you to go through with legal action …

3   Students work individually before checking with a partner, and then open-class.

ANSWERS

1   Supposing you got all the necessary grades, would you go to college?
2   If you'll do the shopping, I'll make dinner.
3   Had you listened to my advice, you wouldn't be in this situation.
4   If they were to discover a cure for the common cold, they'd make a fortune.
5   If you happen to see my address book, could you tell me?

4   Students work in pairs. Ask a confident pair who have incorporated the sentence naturally to perform their dialogue for the rest of the class.

5   Allow time for students to work individually, thinking of dilemmas. They then work in groups, discussing their dilemmas. Each group should appoint a representative to report back to the rest of the class on the dilemma which produced the most controversy in their group.

*FURTHER PRACTICE: **Advanced Gold Exam Maximiser** p.44.*

Vocabulary: collocations (body) p.63

1   Students work in pairs before checking answers open-class.

ANSWERS (CLOCKWISE)

Picture 1: l lick your lips
Picture 2: k shake your fist
Picture 3: h twist your ankle
Picture 4: d wrinkle your nose
Picture 5: c shrug your shoulders

2   Students work in pairs before checking answers open-class.

ANSWERS

a) viii)   b) xi)   c) vii)   d) vi)   e) x)   f) i)   g) v)   h) xii)
i) ix)   j) iii)   k) iv)   l) ii)

3   Students work in pairs taking it in turns to mime the actions.

4   Students work in pairs, miming and asking for explanations.

*FURTHER PRACTICE: **Advanced Gold Exam Maximiser** p.45.*

Grammar check: future p.64

1   Students work individually before checking answers with a partner, and then open-class.

ANSWERS

1 are you doing   2 will probably go   3 'll have saved
4 'll begin   5 do you start/are you going to start

2   Students work in pairs before checking answers open-class.

SUGGESTED ANSWERS

2   We use the Present Simple to talk about events which are part of a timetable or something similar. Example: *Our train leaves at 11:47 a.m.*
3   We use *will* when we make predictions. Example: *It'll be hot in Tenerife, so take plenty of light clothing.*
     We often use *will* when we tell people about a decision as we make it. Example: (phone ringing) *I'll get it!*
     We also use *will* to make threats and promises. Example: *I'll never smoke another cigarette as long as I live.*

4 We use *going to* to talk about plans, especially in informal contexts. Example: *I'm going to invite Pedro and Clara over for dinner next Thursday.*
We also use *going to* to make predictions on the basis of present evidence. Example: *You're going to drop that vase if you're not careful.*

5 We use the Future Continuous to talk about events in progress in the future. Example: *This time next month I'll be sitting in a lecture theatre listening to some of the best teachers our country has to offer.*
We also use the Future Continuous to say what we think is probably happening somewhere else. Example: *Tina will be walking down the aisle round about now.*

6 We use the Future Perfect to say what will have been done, completed or achieved by a certain time in the future. Example: *Why don't you come and stay in September? The builders will have finished the renovations by then.*

Exam focus p.64

▶ **Paper 3 English in Use: Part 3** (error correction – spelling and punctuation)

Read the exam information aloud to the class. Students read the suggested procedure silently. Set a ten-minute time limit for completion of the task. Check answers open-class.

ANSWERS

1 ~~pear~~ ➔ pair
2 ~~moveing~~ ➔ moving
3 ~~diferent~~ ➔ different
4 ~~'I'm thirsty,~~ ➔ 'I'm thirsty',
5 ✓
6 ~~tecnology~~ ➔ technology
7 ✓
8 ~~its~~ ➔ it's
9 ✓
10 ~~nerves, in~~ ➔ nerves in
11 ✓
12 ~~patiente~~ ➔ patient
13 ~~impulses'~~ ➔ impulses
14 ~~dr~~ ➔ Dr
15 ~~trainning~~ ➔ training
16 ✓

FURTHER PRACTICE: Advanced Gold Exam Maximiser p.46.

Units 1–5 progress check pp.65–67

The Progress check can be treated as an open-book exam in which students do the exercises, looking back to relevant sections of the units as necessary. It can be done in class or for homework. Alternatively, students can revise the vocabulary, grammar and English in use sections of the previous five units before tackling the Progress check, once again either in class or for homework.

Check answers open-class or provide students with copies of this key so that they can correct their own work.

1 See Unit 2 for training and Unit 3 for Exam focus.

ANSWERS

1 D   2 H   3 E   4 I   5 B   6 G

2 See Unit 1 Vocabulary: Word formation (suffixes).

ANSWERS

a 2 indecision   b 10 resentful   c 7 hospitality
d 3 heroism   e 1 kindness   f 9 intelligent
g 6 childish   h 11 privatise   i 5 development
j 8 spacious   k 4 loyal

3 See Unit 1 Grammar plus: verb patterns 1.

ANSWERS

1 They've **raised** the life expectancy of people living … OR The life expectancy of people living in the developed world has risen …
2 I'm sure our team can **beat** the other team … OR I'm sure our team can win if they …
3 I feel rather unwell.
4 … but I forgot. OR … but I forgot to.
5 He **bought** me a ticket … OR He paid **for my** ticket …
6 ✓
7 … I'm still **waiting**.
8 Before you close **the door**…
9 … I love **it**!
10 ✓

4 See Unit 2 Vocabulary: adverbs of manner.

ANSWERS

1 intuitively   2 patiently   3 bitterly   4 sincerely
5 imperceptibly

5 See Unit 1 for training and Unit 2 for Exam focus.

ANSWERS

1 the   2 ✓   3 them   4 ✓   5 ✓   6 being
7 into   8 he   9 up   10 it   11 ✓   12 so
13 ✓   14 some   15 does   16 ✓

6   See Grammar check and Grammar plus sections for the first five units.

ANSWERS

1 carried   2 unless   3 wearing   4 more   5 number
6 will   7 having   8 of   9 you   10 one
11 may/might/could   12 can   13 have/need
14 should/must   15 them

7   See Unit 2 Grammar plus: noun phrases.

ANSWERS

1 lambs' wool   2 the artists' entrance
3 a boat show   4 a three-year degree
5 a cheese sauce   6 a living-room ceiling
7 a children's choir   8 a rabbit's tail
9 Poland's national monuments   10 a cupboard door

8   See Unit 2 Grammar plus: noun phrases.

POSSIBLE ANSWERS

1 a bowl of cherries   2 a carton of fruit juice
3 a herd of wild elephants   4 a set of keys
5 a bunch of flowers   6 a clove of garlic
7 a packet of washing powder   8 a litter of kittens

9   See Unit 2 Vocabulary: words with similar meaning.

ANSWERS

1 B   2 A   3 B   4 D   5 A

10   See Unit 4 for training and Unit 5 for Exam focus.

ANSWERS

1 each-other → each other,
2 ✓
3 coresponded → corresponded
4 tradicional → traditional
5 ✓
6 ✓
7 ocur → occur
8 spiting → spitting
9 ✓
10 twins → twins'
11 tendancies → tendencies
12 doctor's → doctors
13 wait → weight
14 herd → heard
15 People → 'People
16 ✓

11   See Unit 4 Vocabulary: similes.

ANSWERS

1 like a **bull** in a china shop.
2 as white as **a sheet**
3 to sleep like a **log**
4 ✓
5 as cool as a **cucumber**
6 like a red **rag** to a bull
7 like a bear with a sore **head**
8 as quick as a **flash**
9 ✓
10 as light as a **feather**

U N I T
6 The sporting life

Advance preparation

▌ Ask students to collect information about their favourite sports stars for the **Speaking** activity on page 70.

▌ Remind students to bring dictionaries to class for Exercise 2 on page 72, or arrange to bring a class set yourself.

Listening p.68

▶ Paper 4, Part 2 (note taking)

1 Ask students what the people seem to be doing in the photographs. Students discuss the questions in groups, appointing a representative to report their discussion to the rest of the class.

2 Play the extract. Students take notes before comparing answers with a partner, and then open-class.

ANSWERS

There will be new sports, especially for wealthier people. Sports stars will earn even more and they will have the same status as film and music stars. Existing records will be maintained but they will measure times in thousandths of a second.

3 Students read the notes and make predictions individually before comparing with a partner. Play the extract. Students answer and then compare answers with a partner. Play the cassette again. Students answer individually before checking open-class. Replay sections of the cassette as necessary.

ALTERNATIVE PROCEDURE: distribute copies of the **Tapescript** on p.119. Students correct their own work.

ANSWERS

1 long history   2 urban areas   3 basketball
4 baseball   5 Bouncy Boxing   6 football
7 fewer performances   8 10.2 seconds   9 9 seconds

4 Students work in groups, taking it in turns to ask and answer.

ALTERNATIVE PROCEDURE: play this as a team game. Divide the class into two teams. Allow a few minutes for the teams to think of a list of sports. The teams then take it in turns to ask and answer questions. The team who guesses the most sports with the smallest number of questions wins.

Grammar plus: future (advanced features) p.69

1 Students work individually before referring to the **Grammar reference** on p 193 of the *Advanced Gold Coursebook*. Check answers open-class.

ANSWERS

3 to say something will be completed at a particular time in the ~~near~~ future
6 to indicate that an event in the future has been officially scheduled

2 Students work individually before checking their answers with a partner, and then open-class.

ANSWERS

1 ... I'm not about to **start** now!
2 I hope we **will** be sitting ...
3 ... is **due to** ...
4 ✓
5 They won't have ~~been~~ realised ...
6 We were on the point of **leaving** ...
7 ✓
8 ✓

3 Students get up and mingle, telling everyone what they are on the point of doing. They should find someone else who has the same plans.

4 Students work with a partner, taking it in turns to ask and answer.

45

POSSIBLE ANSWERS

1 What will you be doing this weekend?
2 Where will you be going for your summer holiday this year?
3 How will you be getting home today?
4 When will you be seeing X next?
5 How long will you be continuing to learn English?

5 Students work in pairs.

DIFFERENCES

Open buffet – 7.15 p.m./7.50 p.m.
8.20 p.m. – Live band 'DeLuxe'/Live band 'Delirious'
Disco – 9 p.m./9.30 p.m.
10 p.m. – Results of charity raffle/'Coolest couple' award
11.30 p.m. – Karaoke competition/Fireworks

6 Students can write their answers in random order on a piece of paper. Their partner should then try to guess when they hope to do each of the things they have written down.

EXAMPLE

Student A: So, you hope you will have finished university in one year's time.
Student B: No. Actually, I hope I will have finished in three months' time. We've got exams then.

FURTHER PRACTICE: *Advanced Gold Exam Maximiser p.47.*

Speaking p.70

1 Students use the information they have compiled on their favourite sports stars.

2 Students work in groups, taking it in turns to read out their facts and guess the identity of the sports star.

ALTERNATIVE PROCEDURE: this can be played as a team game. Divide the class into two teams. Allow time for each team to choose five sports stars to test the other team with. The teams take it in turns to read out facts and guess. The team who guesses the most identities having heard the smallest number of facts wins.

Exam focus p.70

▶ Paper 1 Reading: Part 1 (multiple matching)

Read the exam information and Suggested procedure aloud to the class. Set a twenty-minute time limit. Warn the class when only five minutes remain. Students work individually, before checking their answers open-class.

ANSWERS

1 C (lines 61–62, 66–67 and 78–79)
2 B (lines 35–37)
3 B (lines 56–57)
4 A (lines 10–13)
5 D (lines 89–91)
6 B (lines 57–58)
7 D (lines 103–108)
8 B (lines 36, 37, 38 and 58)
9 B (lines 45–48)
10 D (lines 94–95)
11 C (lines 62–64 and 65–68)
12 B (lines 50–51)
13 C (lines 71–77)
14 A (lines 6–8)

FURTHER PRACTICE: *Advanced Gold Exam Maximiser pp.48–49.*

Vocabulary: competitive sports p.72

1 Point out that the words and phrases come from the reading text. Students work in pairs before checking answers open-class.

ANSWERS

1 f 2 b 3 e 4 h 5 k 6 a 7 i 8 d 9 j 10 c
11 g

2 Students work in pairs, checking pronunciation in their dictionaries.

3 Students work in groups before comparing answers with the rest of the class.

ALTERNATIVE PROCEDURE: students research answers to the questions and report back in a subsequent class.

SUGGESTED ANSWERS

1 gold and silver
2 javelin long jump high jump triple jump hammer
3 100 metres long jump shot put high jump
  400 metres 110 metres hurdles discus pole vault
  javelin 1500 metres
4 When Manchester United football team played Bayern Munich in 1999, the German team were leading and seemed assured of a 1–0 victory until the last few minutes when the English team scored two goals in quick succession.

5 a) Monica Seles. She was stabbed by a spectator and had to retire from championship tennis for a period of two years. She has also had a number of injuries that have prevented her playing for long periods of time. Her father died, further preventing her from playing at her usual standard.
b) Vance Armstrong, winner of the Tour de France in 1999 and 2000. Armstrong recovered from cancer to return to cycling.
6 To withstand the rigours of training and competing, athletes need to have a tremendous desire to win. Achieving success is the compensation for all the *suffering that has gone into their preparation for an important sporting event.

Speaking p.72

▶ Paper 5, Part 3 (problem-solving task)

1 Students work in pairs.

2 (p.73) Play the cassette. Students listen and then compare notes with a partner. Check answers open-class.

ANSWERS

Making an additional point: on top of that
What's more   Not only that
Indicating lack of complete agreement:
Having said that though   We do need to remember that
That's all very well but

3 Students discuss the questions in groups, appointing a representative to report their discussion to the rest of the class (see Tapescript on p.119).

Listening: no football for girls p.73

1 Students discuss the questions in groups, appointing a representative to report their discussion to the rest of the class.

ALTERNATIVE PROCEDURE: debate. Divide the class into two groups. One group should prepare arguments in favour of separation and the other against. Each group should choose a representative to present their case. At the end of the debate the class votes.

2 Focus attention on Questions 1 and 2. Play the extract. Students work individually before comparing answers with a partner.

ANSWERS

1 cricket   golf   skiing   horseriding
[NB: Netball is mentioned on the recording, but this is not the same as basketball. The difference between the two sports is that repeated bouncing of the ball is not permitted in netball.]
2 They are glad that she enjoys sport so much and have supported her efforts to continue to play football, though her mother is less keen on her playing rugby because she fears she will get hurt.

3 Focus attention on the words and phrases. Students should try to recall their significance before listening to the extract again. Check answers open-class, replaying the cassette as necessary.

ANSWERS

1 finishing position in London mini-marathon
2 height
3 age at which she started to play sport
4 position she played in football team
5 injury her mother fears she'll get in rugby
6 number of triathlons she won last year
7 day she is involved in drama
8 one of the jobs she might like to do when she grows up
(See Tapescript on pp.119–120.)

4 Students discuss the questions in groups, appointing a representative to report their discussion to the rest of the class.

Vocabulary: language of gender p.74

1 Students work in pairs before checking answers open-class.

ANSWERS

flight attendant   headteacher   police officer
spokesperson   firefighter   salesperson

2 Students work in groups, checking understanding of meaning and then discussing acceptability and potential replacements. They should choose a representative to report their discussion to the rest of the class.

SUGGESTED ANSWERS

1 meaning: the average man or the average person
alternatives: the man or woman in the street OR the average person

2   meaning: a man you can trust, who will do what he has promised to do
alternative: man or woman, according to the gender of the person being spoken about

3   meaning: to behave and think independently without worrying about what other people think
alternatives: be your own person OR be true to yourself

4   meaning: if a group of people do something as one man, they do it together
alternative: as one person

5   meaning; to work at, use, or operate a system, piece of equipment, etc.
alternatives: staffed OR open

6   meaning: all humans considered as a group
alternatives: humanity OR the human race OR humankind

7   meaning: used to say that people will not help each other
alternative: It's everyone for themselves

8   meaning: a man who understands and expresses the views and opinions of ordinary people
alternative: man or woman, according to the gender of the person being spoken about

3   Students discuss the questions in groups, appointing a representative to report their discussion to the rest of the class.

FURTHER PRACTICE: *Advanced Gold Exam Maximiser p.52.*

Grammar check: modifiers/intensifiers p.74

1   Students work individually before checking answers with a partner, and then open-class.

ANSWERS

1 really   2 both   3 extremely   4 really   5 both
6 both   7 both   8 both   9 extremely

2   (p.75) Students work individually before checking answers open-class.

ANSWERS

Gradable: very   rather   extremely   fairly   terribly   really   quite   pretty
Non-gradable: absolutely   really   completely   quite   totally

FURTHER PRACTICE: *Advanced Gold Exam Maximiser p.50.*

3   Students work in pairs. Monitor, and ask confident students who are using the modifiers and intensifiers successfully to tell the whole class.

Watch Out! *quite*
Focus attention on the two sentences and read them aloud to the class. Students work in pairs before discussing their answers open-class.

ANSWERS

1 rather   2 completely

English in Use p.75

▶ **Paper 3, Part 4** (word formation)

1   Set a one-minute time limit for the gist reading task. Students work individually before checking answers open-class.

ANSWER

3

2   Students work individually on Questions 1 and 2 before checking their answers with a partner, and then open-class.

ANSWERS

1 adjective   2 noun   3 noun   4 adjective   5 noun
6 noun   7 verb (negative form)   8 adverb

3   Students work individually before comparing answers in groups and checking their dictionaries.

ANSWERS

1 watered   2 excitement   3 celebration   4 disastrous
5 representatives   6 awareness   7 disregard(s)
8 appallingly

4   Students follow the same step-by-step procedure, comparing answers in groups and checking in a dictionary before checking open-class.

ANSWERS

1 agility   2 basically   3 traditional   4 equivalents
5 lightness   6 permissible   7 effectiveness
8 protection

FURTHER PRACTICE: *Advanced Gold Exam Maximiser p.51.*

Writing: formal letter/informal note p.76

▶ **Paper 2, Part 1** (compulsory)

_1_   Students work individually before checking answers in pairs, and then open-class.

ANSWERS

Valid advice: points 2 and 5

_2_   1 Students work with a partner before discussing their answers open-class.

SUGGESTED KEY WORDS

holiday   did not live up to   original advertisement   write Director   complain   Read original advertisement
notes you wrote   part of letter from a friend you wrote to write letter   200 words   to Director   telling how feel
note 50 words   friend   telling what decided do

2 Students work individually before discussing their answers with a partner, and then open-class.

SUGGESTED DIFFERENCES

a) The letter begins with the formal phrase 'I am writing on behalf of … ', whereas the note begin 'Here's … '.
   The letter is divided into paragraphs, each of which covers a separate point. The note is a single paragraph.
   The letter does not use contractions, whereas the note does.
   The letter uses formal linkers such as 'Furthermore', whereas the note has informal linkers such as 'Anyway'.
   The letter demands a response with a formal phrase, 'If we do not receive … ', whereas the note uses a question tag, 'don't you?', to elicit a response.
   The letter ends with the conventional phrase 'I look forward to hearing from you … ', whereas the note ends with the informal 'let me know …,'.
   The final salutation in the letter is 'Yours sincerely', whereas in the note it is 'All the best'.
b) All of these apply in principle to the letter and note in the task on pp.76 and 77.

3 Discuss the questions open-class.

ANSWER

The purpose of the letter is to complain about the mismatch between the advertisement and reality.
The purpose of the note is to tell Tina you have decided to write a letter of complaint.

_3 & 4_   The writing can be done in class or for homework.

SUGGESTED ANSWERS

3

   I am writing as a result of my recent two-week stay in Brighton on a LangSports Co. 'sports break'. Unfortunately, the holiday was extremely disappointing for a number of reasons.
   To begin with, it was not in fact two weeks, as your brochure stated, but twelve days, since the course didn't start till the day after we arrived and finished the day we left. A second problem was that the quality of the course itself did not live up to my expectations. Your brochure implied that students would come from a variety of countries, but almost all of them were German. A more serious problem was that the teaching staff were not appropriately qualified. Many of them were in fact students themselves. This criticism applies equally to the sports instructors, some of whom were no better at the sports than we were. A third area in which the holiday proved a disappointment was in relation to the social programme. I was surprised to discover that there was a charge for several of the evening activities. Furthermore, there were no activities for the first weekend, which meant we all sat at home with our host families. Although my family were perfectly pleasant, I was seriously inconvenienced by the fact that their house was so far from the college.
   As a result of this experience, I think it only fair if you refund a proportion of the substantial fee I paid.
   I look forward to hearing from you in due course.
   Yours faithfully,
   Fabiana Judice

4
Hi Tina,
Thanks for your letter. This is just a quick note to tell you that I've written to the holiday company asking for a refund. I was interested to read about your brother's experience. Could you send me the details? If I get my money back I might be able to go to the UK with the same organisation as your brother.
Love,
Fabrice

*FURTHER PRACTICE: **Advanced Gold Exam Maximiser pp.52–53.***

English in Use p.78

▶ Paper 3, Part 5 (register transfer)

1 Read the exam information aloud to the class.

2 Students read individually before summarising with a partner. Get someone with a good summary to tell the whole class.

SUGGESTED SUMMARY OF MAIN POINTS

Rob has taken an active part in sports and has improved his strength, stamina and ability. He was a significant member of the school football and swimming teams and was captain of the football team for three matches. Nevertheless, he doesn't always attend practice sessions, and he arrives late and in the wrong clothes. He also loses his temper when playing matches. If he doesn't improve these things, he'll be dropped from the teams.

3 Students work in pairs, taking it in turns to re-express these points in informal language. Choose a good confident pair to perform for the rest of the class.

4 Read through the Suggested procedure. Students work individually before checking their answers with a partner, and then open-class.

ANSWERS

1 keen/involved   2 progress   3 a lot   4 win   5 made
6 few   7 play/work together   8 going/turning up
9 regularly/on time   10 wearing   11 lost   12 disqualified
13 let

FURTHER PRACTICE: **Advanced Gold Exam Maximiser p.54.**

Unit 6 review p.79

ANSWERS

1 1 pulled   2 comeback   3 set   4 resume   5 setbacks
6 bronze   7 decathlon   8 glory   9 put
10 competitors

2 1 ... you won't **have** seen ...
2 ... about **to** buy ...
3 Will you **be** taking ...
4 ... due **to** kick off?
5 ... people **will** be running ...
6 ... on **the** point ...
7 ... are **to** assemble ...

3 1 attendant   2 officers   3 person (man)   4 fighter
5 person   6 teacher

4 (SUGGESTED ANSWERS)
1 they cut his pocket money by half
2 she can be a little bit impatient at times
3 they have not fulfilled their promises with regard to education
4 he had injured his ankle and was in terrible pain
5 but he offered to correct as much extra written work as we were prepared to give him

5 1 Every   2 as   3 Apart   4 to   5 the   6 which
7 lasted/continued   8 when   9 of   10 him
11 would   12 by   13 to   14 made   15 at

UNIT

7 The ties that bind us

Advance preparation

▌ Ask students to bring some examples of their recent written work to class for Exercise 5 on p.85.

▌ Remind students to bring dictionaries to class for **Vocabulary** Exercise 1 on p.86, or arrange to bring a class set yourself.

▌ (Optional) Bring some examples of leaflets (in English or in the students' L1) to class for the work on leaflets on p.88.

Speaking: family dynamics p.80

1 Play the cassette while students read the quotations.
1 & 2 Students work in groups, appointing a representative to report their discussion to the rest of the class.

SUGGESTED ANSWERS

Ugo Betti: We behave with members of our own family in ways in which we would not even consider behaving with other people.

Florida Scott-Maxwell: Mothers never stop being mothers.

John Lennon: The younger generation always finds fault with the older generation.

André Malraux: Without a family you have no one to rely on in times of hardship.

John Cleese/Robin Skinner: It is not good if only one parent is the authority figure and doesn't share this responsibility with other family members.

Anthony Powell: We expect this to be the other way round, i.e. 'Children are sometimes a bit of a disappointment to their parents … '.
Children often adore their parents when they are young but come to see them as ordinary people, with all the usual weaknesses, as they grow older.

Ethel Watts Mumford: We often find our relatives unsatisfactory in various ways.

2 Students work in groups.

ANSWERS

Our 'children will 'hate us 'too.

With'out a 'family, 'man, a'lone in the 'world, 'trembles with the 'cold.

In the 'healthiest 'families, the 'power is 'shared by a'greement. In the 'others, 'one 'parent or the 'other is 'usually more 'powerful.

'Parents are 'sometimes a 'bit of a disa'ppointment to their 'children. They 'don't ful'fil the 'promise of their 'early 'years.

The 'family is the 'place where the 'most ri'diculous and the 'least re'spectable things in the 'world 'go on.

No 'matter 'how 'old a 'mother 'is, she 'watches her 'middle-'aged 'children for 'signs of im'provement.

'God gives us our 'relatives: 'thank 'God we can 'choose our 'friends.

FURTHER PRACTICE: Advanced Gold Exam Maximiser p.55.

3 The representatives from each group go to another group to read the quotations that their group chose.

Students might enjoy looking at the following websites, where there are collections of quotations about a number of themes, including families:
http://www.startingpage.com/html/quotations.html AND
http://www.geocities.com˜spanoudi/quote.html/.

EXTRA ACTIVITY: Students work in pairs. They should take it in turns to play the role of interlocutor reading these instructions to their partner:
    'Here are some photos showing family relationships. I'd like you to talk about two or three of the photographs, saying what kind of family relationship they show and how the people in the photographs might be feeling.'
  The students should take it in turns to describe the photographs on p.80. The other student listens and tries to work out which photographs are being described.

Exam focus p.81

▶ Paper 4 Listening: Part 2 (note taking)

Read the exam information aloud to the class. Read the Suggested procedure, pausing for students to action each of the points up to point 4. Play the monologue. Allow time for students to check their work before checking answers open-class.

ANSWERS

1 eyes   2 8/eight   3 actor   4 shy   5 extremely poor
6 £40 million   7 his siblings   8 humanity

Play the cassette again, pausing as necessary.

ALTERNATIVE PROCEDURE: give students copies of the **Tapescript** on p.121, so that they can correct their own work before listening to the cassette again.

Reading p.82

▶ **Paper 1, Part 3** (multiple choice)

1   Students discuss the questions in groups, appointing a representative to report their discussion to the rest of the class.

2   Set a two-minute time limit for this.

ANSWER

No. It simply discusses how your position in the family can affect your personality.

3   (p.83) Students read the article again before checking their answers with a partner, and finally open-class.

ANSWERS

1 C (lines 14–16)   2 A (lines 25–29)
3 C (lines 39–44)   4 B (lines 51–52)
5 D (lines 65–69)   6 B (lines 86–88)

4   Students discuss the questions in groups, appointing a representative to report their discussion to the rest of the class.

FURTHER PRACTICE: **Advanced Gold Exam Maximiser pp.56–57.**

Grammar plus: substitution/ellipsis p.84

1   1 & 2 Students work with a partner before checking their answers open-class.

ANSWERS

1 you   child   the
2 a) your place in the family

b) your place in the family can have a major influence on the rest of your life
c) a noticeable reduction in the amount of attention they give you
d) try to please adults, to become even more like them – conservative and responsible – in an effort to win back what you've lost.

2   Read the information on Substitution aloud to the class. Students work individually before checking their answers open-class.

ANSWERS

1 do   2 there   3 so   4 one   5 not   6 It

3   Read the information on Ellipsis aloud to the class. Students work individually before checking their answers open-class.

ANSWERS

1 they feel   2 take some holiday   3 to eat
4 he is leaving on Friday   5 towels   6 trainers
7 come and visited me
8 phone me when you get to the hotel   9 get so angry

4   Students work in pairs before checking their answers open-class.

ANSWERS

1 I certainly hope **so**.
2 No, I'm afraid I can't afford **to**.
3 Our old **one** is still perfectly OK.
4 ~~So~~ **Neither** will we.
5 OK, I'll drop by ~~so~~ after work.
6 ... but they ~~hadn't~~ **haven't**.
7 I ~~do~~ **will**.
8 Oh I think it's Joan's ~~one~~.
9 I expect ~~it~~ so.
10 ... than we used **to** (have).

Refer students to the **Grammar reference** on pp.196–197 of the *Advanced Gold Coursebook*.

FURTHER PRACTICE: **Advanced Gold Exam Maximiser pp.58–59.**

5   (p.85) Students work in pairs before comparing their answer with the rest of the class.

SUGGESTED ANSWER

It is well-known that relationships between children and their parents fundamentally affect adult behaviour. But now their importance is being challenged as new research shows that a child's relationship with its siblings may have a more important effect. Psychologist Francine Klagsbrun says 'Our relationship with our siblings is unmatchable. We have them whether we like them or not. As parents die, friends drift away, marriages dissolve, that relationship continues and the memories of a life shared with them remain with us long after childhood has ended.'

6   Students work individually before sharing their written work with a partner.

Vocabulary: word + prepositions (1) p.85

1   Students work individually before checking their answers against the text on pp.82–83 of the *Advanced Gold Coursebook*.

ANSWERS

1 for   2 with   3 on   4 by   5 by   6 to   7 of   8 in
9 to   10 for

2   Students work in pairs before checking their answers open-class.

ANSWERS

in: result   specialise   confide
for: pay   apologise   apply
with: plead   coincide
from: benefit   refrain   suffer
on: congratulate   concentrate   insist
to: refer   confess   react

3   Students work individually before working with a partner. They should read their sentences and explain the background to them.

POSSIBLE ANSWERS

I asked my doctor to **refer** me **to** a specialist.
Tony was the first to **congratulate** me **on** passing my driving test.
I didn't have enough money to **pay for** all the things I had put in the supermarket trolley.
I think he should **apologise for** being so rude to you.
She **pleaded with** her parents to let her keep the kitten.
Santa Cruz has **benefited from** European Union funding.

My exams will **coincide with** Chris's visit.
We were asked to **refrain from** smoking indoors.
Some physical illnesses can **result in** quite violent mood changes.
I decided to **concentrate on** finishing tidying up the study and to leave the rest of the housework until the next day.
More and more children around the world **suffer from** asthma.
I **specialised in** Medieval History when I was at university.
Marie always **insists on** paying when we have coffee together.
She **confided in** us that she had been feeling quite depressed.
She **confessed to** having always had a tremendous crush on Brad Pitt.
I didn't know how to **react to** the news that she had decided to get married.
I'm thinking of **applying for** a position as a volunteer worker in Sierra Leone.

FURTHER PRACTICE: *Advanced Gold Exam Maximiser* p.55.

Speaking: talking about families p.85

1   Students listen to the cassette and complete the family tree before comparing notes with a partner. Play the cassette again, pausing as necessary for students to check their answers.

ANSWERS (see family tree on page 58)

Tony's father (first box) married his mother (second box).
They only had two children: Tony and his brother Matthew (third box).
Tony's father had two sisters: Margaret and Jessica.
Tony says he doesn't see them very often, but thinks he should make more of an effort.
Matthew is married to Sofía, who is Spanish.
They met when Matthew went to Spain on holiday, but live in England now.
They have three daughters, called Isabella, Cristina and Natalia.
Tony says that there is some tension between Sofía and his mother.
In general, he says that his family is rather small, and wonders what it would be like to have a bigger family.

2   Students work in pairs. Ask a confident student to talk to the whole class.

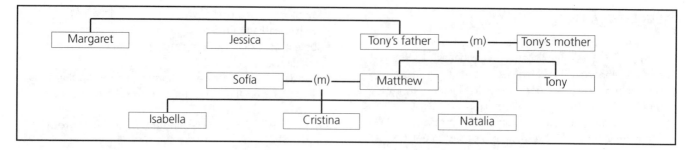

Grammar check: hypothetical meaning p.86

1   Students work individually before checking answers with a partner, and then open-class.

ANSWERS

1 I wish my dad ~~couldn't~~ **wouldn't** always be so cross with me. OR ... **weren't** always ~~be~~ so cross with me.
2 ✓
3 If only I ~~would~~ **could** spend more time with my family!
4 I'd rather we ~~don't~~ **didn't** spend the whole evening with your parents.
5 ✓
6 ✓
7 ✓
8 ✓
9 ✓
10 It's time the children ~~go~~ **went** to bed.
11 ✓
12 Suppose somebody ~~will see~~ **sees** us taking the money.

2   Students work individually before checking answers with a partner, and then open-class.

ANSWERS

b) 1   c) 11   d) 7   e) 3   f) 10   g) 4   h) 12

FURTHER PRACTICE: **Advanced Gold Exam Maximiser p.55.**

3   Students work individually before reading their sentences to a partner.

POSSIBLE ANSWERS

1 I wish I was better at tennis.
2 I wish I hadn't given up playing the piano when I was so young.
3 I wish Olivier wouldn't play that awful techno music all the time.
4 I wish I could give up smoking.
5 It's definitely time I started to work on my essay.

Vocabulary: commonly confused words p.86

1   Divide the class into four groups made up of 2, 4, 6, 8, etc. students. Allot a group of words (A, B, C or D) to each of the four groups. Divide the groups into pairs. Students work in pairs finding the differences in meaning.

2   Form groups with one student from each of the four original groups. They exchange information on the words. Check answers open-class.

ANSWERS

A
childish/childlike: one is derogatory, the other is appreciative
childish /ˈtʃaɪldɪʃ/ *adj* **1** related to or typical of a child: *a high childish laugh* **2** behaving in a silly way that makes you seem much younger than you really are: *Stop messing around, it's so childish.* – compare CHILDLIKE.
childlike /ˈtʃaɪldlaɪk/ *adj* having qualities that are typical of a child, especially qualities such as INNOCENCE and trust: *an expression of childlike innocence* – compare CHILDISH
effect/affect: one is usually a verb, the other is usually a noun
effect[1] /ɪˈfekt/ *n* **1** [C; U] the way in which an event, action, or person changes someone or something: [+ **of**] *the harmful effects of smoking* | **have an effect on** *Inflation is having a disastrous effect on the economy* | **have/achieve the desired effect** **9** [C usually singular] an idea or feeling that an artist, speaker, book etc tries to make you think or feel: *Turner's paintings give an effect of light.*
effect[2] *v* [T] *formal* to make something happen: *efforts to effect a reconciliation between the warring factions*
affect /əˈfekt/ *v* [T] **1** to do something that produces an effect or change in someone or something: *How will the tax affect people on low incomes?* | *a disease that affects the central nervous system* | *emergency relief for the areas affected by the hurricane* **2** [usually passive] to make someone feel strong emotions: *We were all deeply affected by the news of her death.*

lose/loose: pronunciation of final 's'; one is a verb, the other is an adjective

lose /luːz/ v 1 [T] to stop having something that is important to you or that you need: *I can't afford to lose my job, I have a family to support.* | *I lost a lot of money on that deal.* | *We're going to lose five teachers when the schools are merged.*

loose /luːs/ adj 1 not firmly fixed in place: *One of my buttons is loose.* | *a loose floorboard*

specially/especially: These two words can often be used with the same meaning; the difference is that *especially* can pre-modify an adjective.

specially /ˈspeʃəli/ adv 1 for one particular purpose, and only for that purpose: *I had this dress made specially for the wedding.* 2 *especially spoken* much more than usual, or much more than other people or things; ESPECIALLY: *We specially wanted to visit Disneyland.* – see ESPECIALLY (USAGE)

especially /ɪˈspeʃəli/ also specially *spoken adv* 1 [sentence adverb] used to emphasize that something is more important or happens more with one particular thing than with others: *Crime is growing at a rapid rate, especially in urban areas.* 2 [+ adj/adv] to a particularly high degree or much more than usual: *I was feeling especially tired that evening.* | *"Do you feel like going out for a drink?" "Not especially, no."* 3 [+ for] for a particular person, purpose etc: *I bought these chocolates especially for you.*

B

stationery/stationary: one is a noun, the other is an adjective

stationery /ˈsteɪʃənəri/ n [U] 1 materials that you use for writing, such as paper, pens, pencils etc 2 paper for writing letters on, usually with matching envelopes: *a letter on hotel stationery*

stationary /ˈsteɪʃənəri/ adj standing still instead of moving: *How did you manage to drive into a stationary vehicle?*

principle/principal: one is only a noun, the other can be an adjective or a noun

principle /ˈprɪnsɪpəl/ n 1 a) [C, U] a moral rule or set of ideas which makes you behave in a particular way: *She resigned on a matter of principle.* b) strong ideas about what is morally right or wrong, that you try to follow in everything you do: *He has no principles; he'll do anything as long as it's profitable.* 2 [C] a rule which explains the way something such as a machine works, or which explains a natural force in the universe: *the principle of the internal combustion engine* | *Archimedes' principle* 3 [C] a belief that is accepted as a reason for action: *the principle of free markets*

principal[1] /ˈprɪnsɪpəl/ adj [only before noun] most important; main: *My principal source of income is*

teaching.* | *The principal character in the book is called Scarlett.*

principal[2] n 3 [C] *especially BrE* someone who is in charge of a university, college, or school

lonely/alone: one can only be an adjective, the other can be both an adjective and an adverb

lonely /ˈləʊnli/ adj 1 unhappy because you are alone and feel that you do not have anyone to talk to: *Don't you get lonely being on your own all day?* 2 *especially literary* a place that is lonely is a long way from where people live and very few people go there: *a lonely beach* – see ALONE (USAGE)

alone[1] /əˈləʊn/ adj 1 [not before noun] without any other people: *She lives alone.* 2 without any friends or people who know you: *It was scary being all alone in a big city.*

alone[2] adv 1 if you do something difficult alone you do it on your own: *Brian was left to put up the tent alone.*

memory/souvenir: different meaning

memory /ˈmeməri/ n 1 [C; U] the ability to remember things, places, experiences etc: *Grandpa was getting old and his memory wasn't so good.* 2 [C usually plural] something that you remember from the past about a person, place, or experience: *memories of the war* 3 a) [C] the part of a computer in which information can be stored b) [U] the amount of space that can be used for storing information on a computer: *32 megabytes of memory*

souvenir /ˌsuːvəˈnɪə/ n [C] an object that you keep to remind yourself of a special occasion or a place you have visited: [+ of] *I bought a model of the Eiffel Tower as a souvenir of Paris.* | *a souvenir shop* | *a souvenir programme from the Gala Concert*

C

lie/lay: one is intransitive, the other is transitive

lie[1] /laɪ/ v 1 a) [I always + adv/prep] to be in a position in which your body is flat on the floor, on a bed etc: *He was lying on the bed smoking a cigarette.* | *Don't lie in the sun for too long.* b) also lie down [I always + adv/prep] to put yourself in a position in which your body is flat on the floor or on a bed: [+ on/in/there etc] *Lie on the floor and stretch your legs upwards.* c) [I always + adv/prep] to be in a flat position on a surface: *The papers were lying neatly on his desk, waiting to be signed.*

lay[2] v /leɪ/ 1 [T always + adv/prep] to put someone or something down carefully into a flat position: *Laying my coat carefully on the bed, I crept towards the door.* | *The bodies were laid under the trees to await burial.* | *Sharon laid her hand on my arm.*

raise/rise: meaning; one is transitive, the other is intransitive

raise /reɪz/ *v* [T] **1 a)** to move or lift something to a higher position, place, or level: *Can you raise your arm above your head? | They're thinking of raising the ceiling in the kitchen. | The teacher raised his finger to his lips for silence.* **b)** to move or lift something into an upright position: *The bridge can be raised in the middle to allow ships through.* **c)** to move your eyes or face so that you are looking upwards: *She raised her eyes from the newspaper when he came in.* **d)** also **raise up** to lift the upper part of your body from a lying position: *She raised herself up on her arms and looked around sleepily.* **2** to increase an amount, number, or level: *We have no plans to raise taxes at present. | The reaction is started by raising the temperature to 140°C.*

rise¹ /raɪz/ *v* [I] **1** to increase in number, amount or value: *House prices are likely to rise towards the end of this year.* **2** to go upwards: *The polar ice caps will melt and the sea level will rise. | Smoke rose from the chimney. | The road rises steeply from the village.* **6** to appear in the sky: *The sun rose and the sea turned gold.*

practice/practise: one is a noun, the other is a verb (in AmE it is the other way round)

practice /præktɪs/ *n* **1 a)** [U] regular activity that you do in order to improve a skill: *It takes hours of practice to learn to play the guitar. | With a little more practice you should be able to pass your test.* **b)** [C] a period of time you spend training to improve your skill in doing something: *choir practice | We have two rugby practices a week.*

practise /præktɪs/ *v* **1** [I, T] to do an activity regularly in order to improve you skill or to prepare for a test: *John's practising the violin. | Today we're going to practise parking.*

ensure/insure: meaning (in AmE the meanings are reversed)

ensure *especially BrE* /ɪnˈʃʊə/ *v* [T] to make it certain that something will happen: *All the necessary steps had been taken to ensure their safety. | His wife ensured that he took all his pills every day.*

insure /ɪnˈʃʊə/ *v* **1** [I, T] to buy insurance to protect yourself against something bad happening to you, your family, your possessions etc: *Have you insured the contents of your home?*

D

channel/canal: meaning

channel /tʃænl/ *n* [C] **1** a television station and all the programmes broadcast by it: *We watched the news on Channel 4 | This is boring – I'm going to switch to another channel.* **4** a passage that water or other liquids flow along: *an irrigation channel* **5 a)** a passage of water connecting two seas: **the Channel** (= the English Channel) **b)** the deepest part of a river, harbour, or sea passage, especially one that is deep enough to allow ships to sail in

canal /kəˈnæl/ *n* [C] a passage dug out of the ground, either to connect two areas of water so boats can travel between them, or to bring or remove water from somewhere: *the Panama Canal*

worthless/priceless: meaning

worthless /wɜːθləs/ *adj* **1** having no value, importance, or use: *a completely worthless exercise*

priceless /praɪsləs/ *adj* **1** so valuable that it is difficult to give a financial value: *priceless antiques*

imply/infer: meaning

imply /ɪmˈplaɪ/ *v* [T] **1** to suggest that something is true without saying this directly: *She managed to imply she'd contributed the money without actually saying so. | an implied threat –* see INFER (USAGE)

infer /ɪnˈfɜː/ *v* [T] to form an opinion that something is probably true because of other information that you already know: *facts that can be inferred from archaeological data | It would be wrong to infer that people who are overweight are just greedy.* USAGE NOTE: In formal English the speaker or writer **implies** something and the listener or reader **infers** it.

hard/hardly: one can be both an adjective and an adverb, the other is only an adverb; meaning

hard¹ /hɑːd/ *adj* **1** firm and stiff, and difficult to press down, break, or cut: *Diamond is the hardest substance known to man. | The plums are much too hard to be eaten now. | The chairs in the waiting room felt hard and uncomfortable.* **2** difficult to do or understand: *This year's exam was much harder than last year's.*

hard² *adv* **1** using a lot of effort, energy, or attention: *She had been working hard all morning. | I tried as hard as I could to remember his name.* **2** with a lot of force: *Tyson hit him so hard that he fell back on the ropes. | The boys pressed their noses hard against the window. | It's raining hard.*

hardly /hɑːdli/ *adv* **1** almost not: *I hadn't seen him for years but he had hardly changed at all. | The children were so excited they could hardly speak. | I can hardly believe it.*

3 (p.87) Students work individually before checking answers open-class.

ANSWERS

1 worthless   2 stationery   3 lay   4 implying
5 hardly   6 effect   7 ensure   8 lose   9 principles
10 especially

FURTHER PRACTICE: Advanced Gold Exam Maximiser **p.61.**

Listening: song p.87

1   Students work in groups, appointing a representative to report their discussion to the rest of the class.

2   Students work individually before comparing answers with a partner.

3   Play the song for students to check their answers.

ANSWERS

1 eyes   2 bed   3 breath   4 eye   5 angels   6 before
7 future   8 colour   9 languages   10 perceived
11 experience   12 days

BACKGROUND INFORMATION: The song is by the Canadian (Toronto) band Barenaked Ladies, or BNL for short, all of whom are male. It is taken from their 1998 album *Stunt*. The band have toured in North America and Britain, playing at the Glastonbury Festival in 1993. More information about the band, as well as audio and video clips, can be found at: http://bnl.org.

4   Students work in pairs.

Writing: leaflet p.88

1   Discuss the questions open-class.

ALTERNATIVE PROCEDURE: distribute the leaflets you have brought to class. Students work in groups, analysing the purpose of each leaflet.

ANSWER

A leaflet is a small piece of printed paper giving information or advertising.

2   Students work individually before checking their answer in pairs, and then open-class.

ANSWER

To tell people about the London Eye and persuade them to visit it.

3   Students discuss the questions in groups, appointing a representative to report back to the rest of the class.

SUGGESTED ANSWERS

1   The leaflet is very effective. The title is clever and eye-catching; the headings provoke the reader's curiosity. The

style is informal and friendly without being patronising; the information given is interesting and the information in the box is particularly clear and well-handled. The tone sets a balance between informing and persuading.

4   Students work individually before discussing their impressions with a partner, and then open-class.

ANSWER

Not very good.

5   (p.89) Students work in pairs before checking their answers open-class.

ANSWERS

Noticeable lifting: This is a leaflet for the increasing numbers of tourists coming to this country. It is produced by the National Tourist Office … an important attraction in this country.
Errors that sometimes obscure communication:
builded   expositions   tells many informations
they won't get boring   have visited it still
the luck of a lifetime   easyest   the trains are often
not too much expensive   to the Dome place
I am recommending   how the Dome was building
Content not clearly organised: No headings.

6   Students work individually before comparing their answer open-class.

ANSWER

Yes. The student has taken all the advice, though s/he has not needed to correct many of the errors in the original because s/he has changed the language so much.

7   Students work individually before comparing answers with a partner.

8   Read the suggested procedure aloud to the class, pausing for students to action each of the points. They work in pairs for 1, 2, 3, 4 and 5. For 6, the actual writing, and 7, the editing, work can be done in class or for homework.

9   Students work in groups reading each other's leaflets.

FURTHER PRACTICE: Advanced Gold Exam Maximiser p.61.

English in Use p.90

▶ Paper 3, Part1 (multiple-choice cloze)

_1_   Students work in groups, appointing a representative to report back to the rest of the class.

_2_   Students work individually before discussing the question open-class.

_3_   Students work individually.

_4_   Students work individually before checking their answers open-class.

ANSWERS

1 C   2 A   3 B   4 D   5 A   6 D   7 B   8 A   9 C
10 D   11 A   12 B   13 C   14 C   15 A

_5_   Students work in groups, appointing a representative to report back to the rest of the class.

EXTRA ACTIVITY: Ask students what point they think the cartoon is trying to make.

FURTHER PRACTICE: _Advanced Gold Exam Maximiser_ p.60.

Unit 7 review p. 91

_1_ 1 I went **there** just last weekend.
2 No, I don't think **so/they will.**
3 Of course I **won't.**
4 **Neither have I.**
5 Which **one?**
6 I think they **will (do).**

_2_ 1 Take as much time as you need ~~to take~~.
2 I'm sorry Sir. We don't have any silk sheets left. Just cotton ~~sheets~~.
3 I don't know whose that car is; this ~~car~~ is mine.
4 I'm surprised ~~that~~ he forgot to ring you. I'm sure ~~that~~ he intended to ~~ring you~~.
5 I thought she would have got me a present but she hasn't ~~got me one~~.
6 She is excited by the new job but ~~she is~~ also a little apprehensive ~~about it~~.

_3_ 1 E   2 G   3 A   4 B   5 I   6 C

UNIT

8 As luck would have it

Advance preparation

▮ Remind students to bring dictionaries, thesauruses or *Activators* to class for Exercises 3 and 5 on page 95 and Exercise 1 on page 97. Alternatively, arrange to bring a class set yourself.

Speaking: merely superstition? p.92

Students work in groups, appointing a representative to report their discussion to the rest of the class.

Reading p.92

▶ Paper 1, Part 3 (multiple choice)

▮ **1** Set a two-minute time limit for this.

ANSWER

3

▮ **2** (p.93) Set a ten-minute time limit. Students work individually before checking their answers with a partner, then open-class.

ANSWERS

1 C (lines 14–20)
2 D (lines 25–26 and 35–41)
3 A (lines 44–48 and 90–91)
4 B (lines 96–97 and 99–101)
5 C (lines 103 and 108–110)

▮ **3** Students work in pairs.

▮ **4** Students work in pairs before checking their answers open-class.

ANSWERS

1 What number did she think she had found on the notice board?
2 Where was Paula Dixon flying to when she fell ill?
3 Why did Doctors Wallace and Wong win world acclaim?

4 Why is it not so surprising for two strangers at a party to have a friend in common?
5 How many people do most of us regard as 'close'?
6 What are the chances of getting a double six in twenty-five throws of two dice?
7 When did Mendeleev publish his Periodic Table?
8 What other discovery benefited from a coincidence?

▮ **5** Students work in pairs before reporting back to the rest of the class.

FURTHER PRACTICE: **Advanced Gold Exam Maximiser p.62.**

Grammar plus: verb patterns (2) p.94

▮ **1** Students work in pairs before checking their answers open-class.

ANSWERS

line 4: 'decided to call'
lines 8–9: 'began to explain'
line 10: 'stopped her saying'
lines 11–12: 'happened to be'
line 37: 'seem to fall into'
line 95: 'seemed to follow'
line 105: 'finished doing'
lines 40–41: 'needed to help'
Followed by infinitive: decide   happen   seem
Followed by -ing form: finish
Followed by both: stop   begin   need-

▮ **2** Students work individually before checking their answers with a partner, then open-class.

ANSWERS

1 She doesn't remember **learning** to ride the bicycle.
2 I couldn't imagine **living** in a big city.
3 ✓
4 ✓
5 ✓
6 ✓
7 I'm sorry but they made me ~~to~~ **tell** them where I had hidden the money.

8 ✓

9 They encouraged me ~~starting~~ **to start** playing the piano from a very early age.

10 ✓

11 We didn't expect you ~~being~~ **to be** home so soon.

12 ✓

13 They begged **me/you/her/him/us/them** to lend them the money they needed.

14 ✓

15 ✓

3 Students work in pairs before checking their answers open-class.

ANSWERS

avoid, etc. 4   beg, etc. 6   allow, etc. 3
forget, etc. 1   make, etc. 5   begin, etc. 2

4 Students work individually before checking answers open-class.

ANSWERS

1 forward to the future   2 before the main verb

5 Students work individually before checking answers open-class.

ANSWERS

1 persuaded me to ask   2 regret leaving
3 let me help   4 expected me/us to work
5 avoid having   6 try seeing
7 intended to be   8 urged her, etc. to reconsider
9 deserve to be treated   10 I have neglected to keep
11 I'm going to threaten to tell
12 dared me to do
13 have attempted/attempt to lift   14 stop to check
15 miss talking

6 (p.95) Students work in pairs.

Refer students to the **Grammar reference** on pp.197–198 of the *Advanced Gold Coursebook*.

FURTHER PRACTICE: Advanced Gold Exam Maximiser p.64.

Vocabulary: synonyms p.95

1 Students work individually before comparing answers with a partner.

2 Play the cassette. Allow time for students to compare answers with a partner, and then check open-class.

ANSWERS

	A chance	B many	C normally	D unlikely	E increase
boost					✓
far-fetched				✓	
typically			✓		
countless		✓			
maximise					✓
coincidence	✓				
inconceivable				✓	
generally			✓		
luck	✓				
numerous		✓			

(See **Tapescript** on p.122.)

3 1 Divide the class into five groups. Allot a group of words (A, B, C, D or E) to each of the five groups. 2 Form new groups with at least one representative of each of the original groups. Students exchange information.

ANSWERS

chance how possible or likely it is that something will happen, especially something that you want; the way some things happen without being planned or caused by people

many a large number of people or things

normally usually, or under normal conditions; in a normal ordinary way

unlikely not likely to happen; not likely to be true

increase to become larger in amount, number or degree; to make something larger in amount, number, or degree

boost to increase something such as production, sales etc because they are not as high as you want them to be: *The advertising campaign is intended to boost sales.*

maximize to increase something such as profit or income as much as possible: *The company's main function is to maximise profit.*

far-fetched extremely unlikely to be true or to happen: *His explanation sounds pretty far-fetched to me.*

inconceivable too strange or unusual to be thought real or possible: *A few years ago a car fuelled by solar energy would have been inconceivable.*

typically in a way that a person or group is generally believed to behave: *It's a typically British bureaucratic response.*

generally usually or most of the time: *Jonathan says he generally gets in to work by 8.00.*

countless too many to be counted: *It has saved my life, and the lives of countless others.*

numerous *formal* many: *Numerous attempts have been made to hide the truth.*

coincidence a surprising and unexpected situation in which two things that are connected happen at the same time, in the same place, or to the same people: *What a coincidence! I didn't know you were going to be in Geneva too!*

luck something good that happens by chance: *Did you have any luck with the job application?*

4   Students work individually before checking answers open-class.

ANSWERS

1 maximise   2 countless   3 typically   4 inconceivable
5 boost   6 luck   7 generally   8 Numerous
9 far-fetched   10 coincidence

5   Students work in pairs before comparing answers in groups.

POSSIBLE ANSWERS

meeting
conference: lots of people; business
convention: large meeting; politics, once a year
summit: government leaders
gathering: crowd
encounter: unexpected; unpleasant
remember
ring a bell: remind one of something
be on the tip of your tongue: not quite able to be
    remembered
interesting
absorbing: taking all your attention; very interesting
riveting: holding your attention completely; very interesting
    and exciting
gripping: holding your attention completely: very
    interesting and exciting
problem
stumbling block: something that prevents action, advance
    or development
hitch: a difficulty which delays something for a while
hurdle: a difficulty that must be dealt with
quickly
swiftly: at great speed, esp. without effort
rapidly: at great speed; fast
in a/like a/as quick as a flash: very quickly; suddenly or soon

6   Students work individually, recording the words.

FURTHER PRACTICE: Advanced Gold Exam Maximiser p.65.

Listening: five bizarre tales p.96

▶ Paper 4, Part 4

1   Tell students to read the instructions and look at the prompts for task one. Play the extracts.

2 Tell students to read the instructions and the prompts for task two. Play the cassette. Students compare answers to both tasks in pairs before checking open-class. Replay the cassette, pausing where necessary.

ANSWERS

1 F   2 D   3 G   4 B   5 A   6 E   7 G   8 D   9 A   10 C

3   Play the cassette. Students complete the sentences individually before checking their answers with a partner, and then open-class.

ANSWERS

1 'd have thought it
2 imagine my surprise
3 to my amazement
4 you believe it
5 you'll never guess what happened next!

4   Play the extracts again. Students listen and repeat (see **Tapescript** on p.122).

5   Students work individually.

6 Students get up and mingle, telling their story to as many other students as possible. Ask a couple of students with particularly good intonation and effective stories to tell theirs to the whole class.

FURTHER PRACTICE: Advanced Gold Exam Maximiser p.65.

Grammar check: reported speech p.96

1   Students work in pairs before checking their answers open-class.

ANSWERS

2 He said he would never forget the day he had had a premonition that he should phone his dad.
3 She said she had often wanted to find out what had happened to her cousins.

4 He asked me if I was married to a Cancerian.
5 She said she couldn't believe her eyes when she realised who it was.
6 He said that he didn't know why, but that he had to go to that address the following morning.

2 (p.97) Students work in pairs before checking their answers open-class.

ANSWERS

1 for   2 on   3 with   4 of   5 from   6 for   7 of   8 on

3 Students work in pairs before checking their answers open-class.

ANSWERS

2 She warned him not to hang/against hanging around with those boys.
3 She suggested going/(that) we went/(that) we should go/(that) we go out to that new Italian restaurant.
4 She apologised for borrowing/having borrowed my car without telling me.
5 He promised to help me with my essay the following day.
6 He denied stealing/having stolen any money from the till.
7 She accused him of taking her CD.
8 He admitted that he had been seeing a lot of Debbie.
9 She agreed to go and help him with the shopping.

*FURTHER PRACTICE: **Advanced Gold Exam Maximiser** p.66.*

4 Students work individually before reporting their conversations and dialogues to a partner.

Vocabulary: word formation (prefixes) p.97

1 Students work in pairs, before comparing their words with those of the rest of the class.

POSSIBLE ANSWERS

unfortunately unhappy   dishonest disconnect
immobilise impossible   illegal illegible
irrational irresistible

2 Students work in pairs, taking it in turns to contradict each other. Check answers open-class.

ANSWERS

1 Actually, I think it's completely relevant.
2 Actually, I think it's always disobedient.
3 Actually I found his story quite unbelievable.
4 Actually I think this argument is completely illogical.
5 Actually I think he's very immature for his age.

3 Students work in pairs before checking their answers open-class.

ANSWERS

1 j   2 f   3 c   4 a   5 g   6 i   7 e   8 b   9 d   10 h

4 Students work individually before comparing answers with a partner and checking open-class.

ANSWERS

semicircle   postgraduate   monosyllable   auto-pilot
rebuild   anticlockwise   overestimate   mispronounce
pseudo-intellectual   ex-husband

*FURTHER PRACTICE: **Advanced Gold Exam Maximiser** p.66.*

Speaking p.98

▶ Paper 5, Part 2 (comparing and contrasting)

1 Students work in pairs before checking their answers open-class.

ANSWERS

Part 1 is a three-way conversation between the candidates and the interlocutor using general interactional and social language. It largely involves conveying personal information.

In **Part 2** each candidate speaks for about a minute about a set of photographs. When they have finished speaking, the other candidate responds to a question briefly.

In **Part 3** the two candidates speak to each other. They try to solve a problem of some kind using the visual prompts the interlocutor gives them.

In **Part 4** the interlocutor asks the candidates questions related to the theme of Part 3.

In **Part 2** the interlocutor usually asks each candidate to compare and contrast the photographs and to comment on them from a particular perspective. Sometimes the second candidate is asked which photographs the first candidate talked about. Sometimes the second candidate is asked to comment on the photographs from another perspective.

2   Students work in pairs before getting up and mingling. How many students had the same kind of 'good news'?

3   Students work in pairs before checking answers open-class.

> **ANSWERS**
>
> Sentence 2 would be the most appropriate of the three, because it describes what the man is doing and then relates that to the second photograph.
> Sentence 1 only focuses on the man's physical appearance, and Sentence 3 only provides a description of the landscape.

4   Students work in pairs.

English in Use p.99

▶ Paper 3, Part 5 (register transfer)

1   Students read the instructions and complete the task individually before comparing answers with a partner and then checking open-class.

> **ANSWERS**
>
> 1 vacancies   2 suggestion   3 degree   4 column
> 5 considering   6 journalism   7 provide   8 experience
> 9 flexible   10 willing/prepared   11 contacted
> 12 let   13 information

Writing: competition entry p.100

1   Read the exam information aloud to the class.

2   Students work in pairs.

3   (p.101) Students work individually before comparing their answers with a partner and then checking open-class.

BACKGROUND INFORMATION: 'Eastenders' is a long-running BBC soap opera about people living in the fictional East London borough of Walford. It was first broadcast in 1985, and is now shown all over the English-speaking world. Students might like to look at the official website at: http://www.bbc.co.uk/eastenders/.

> **ANSWERS**
>
> The answer includes plenty of varied and interesting vocabulary. Examples:
> Para 1: *watching avidly*

Para 2: *glued to the set ... absolutely exhausted ... pleaded in exasperation*
Para 3: *pouring with rain ... splashed through the puddles ... an enormous box of popcorn ... stumbled through the darkness ... gratefully discovered ...*
Para 4: *hallucinating ... the hairs on the back of my neck stood up ... sitting right behind me ... it dawned on me ...*
The writing is organised as follows:
Para 1: Background information/setting the scene
Para 2: Specific background to the main event in the story, i.e. the trip to the cinema including the main participants (Michelle, the writer, her/his friend Jo)
Para 3: The complicating action (difficulty of getting to the cinema, getting tickets and finding a seat)
Para 4: The climax (Michelle in the cinema) and resolution (realising that she didn't really have anything wrong with her leg and could logically be there).
The linking words/phrases used are:
As it happens ... After it had finished ... Nevertheless, ... Finally, ... After a few minutes though ... At first ... and then ....
The entry is clever and amusing. It would have a good chance of winning the competition. It is written in a relatively informal style, which is entirely appropriate.

4   Students work individually. Read the suggested procedure aloud to the class, pausing for students to action each of the points. Point 4 can be done in class or for homework.

5   Students work in pairs.

6   This can be done in class or for homework.

FURTHER PRACTICE: **Advanced Gold Exam Maximiser p.68.**

Exam focus p.102

▶ Paper 3 English in Use: Part 1 (multiple-choice cloze)

Read the exam information aloud to the class. Read the suggested procedure, pausing for students to action each of the points. Students work individually before checking answers open-class.

> **ANSWERS**
>
> 1 D   2 A   3 C   4 B   5 A   6 C   7 C   8 A   9 D
> 10 A   11 C   12 A   13 D   14 C   15 A

FURTHER PRACTICE: **Advanced Gold Exam Maximiser p.67.**

Unit 8 review p.103

ANSWERS

1
1 Simon persuaded me to apply for that job at the post office.
2 My teacher wouldn't let me leave the class before the bell went.
3 I really regret not revising/having revised more for my exams.
4 You deserved to win the competition. Your poem was by far the best.
5 When do you intend/are you intending leaving/to leave?
6 Do you think he'll manage to move all that rubble by himself.
7 He made me promise never to see them again.
8 I don't mind if I can't smoke in the office.
9 They avoid eating meat if at all possible.
10 I can't believe that he admitted (to) stealing that car.

2
1 boost   2 inconceivable   3 Generally   4 numerous   5 coincidence

3
1 I'm sorry I've overcooked this meat.
2 John's ex-wife rang me at home last night.
3 Sarah is sometimes disloyal to her friends.
4 They kept raising issues which were irrelevant.
5 He lives by himself and is very anti-social.
6 We overestimated how long the work would take.
7 We misunderstood her.
8 Concealing this information is illegal.

4
1 retired   2 coincidentally   3 discovery   4 amazement   5 marriages   6 presidency   7 assassination   8 alive

UNIT

9 Where there's a will …

Advance preparation

▣ Remind students to bring dictionaries to class for Exercise 8 on page 106 and Exercise 2 on page 110, or arrange to bring a class set yourself.

Reading p.104

▶ Paper 1, Part 2 (gapped text)

1 Students work in pairs before discussing their answers with the rest of the class.

ALTERNATIVE PROCEDURE: discuss the photos open-class.

BACKGROUND INFORMATION: The first photograph is of American actor **Jodie Foster**. Jodie Foster began her career acting in advertisements and later as a child star in *Bugsy Malone* and *Taxi Driver*. She has gone on to act in many films and to direct several herself. Foster also holds a degree from Yale. More information on Jodie Foster can be found at: http://www.celebritypro.com/jodie_foster.htm.

The second photograph is of the scientist **Marie Curie**. Born Marya Sklodowska in Warsaw, Poland, Marie Curie moved to Paris where, despite terrible poverty and hunger, she became the first woman to graduate in physics from the Sorbonne. She is famous for her discovery of radioactivity, for which she was awarded the Nobel Prize for physics, the first woman to win such an award. More information on Marie Curie can be found at: http://ampolinstitute.org/sklodowska.html

Richard Branson is an extremely successful British businessman. Apart from Virgin Cola, depicted in the photograph, Branson owns Virgin airlines and a railway network. Branson began his career publishing a student magazine while still at school. He then went on to found his company Virgin, which began as a record shop, and later became a recording company.

ANSWER

Foster, Curie and Branson all share a powerful will to succeed, often against very high odds.
They had an achievement publicly recognised.

2 Set a two-minute time limit for this. Make it clear that students need only read the base text at this stage.

ANSWERS

1 (lines 13–17)   2 (line 5)   3 (lines 27–37)
4 (lines 40–45 and 53–56)   5 is not mentioned

3 (p.105) Students work individually. Enforce the fifteen-minute time limit.

4 Students check answers in pairs, and then open-class.

ANSWERS

1 F: Para F: *there's a big difference …*
   Base text: *these differences*
2 C: Base text: *the motivation comes from some adverse life events in early childhood …*
   Para C: *this*
3 G: Base text: *two main types of motivation …*
   Para G: *These two styles*
4 E: Base text: *It could be a socialisation thing …*
   Para E: *So that's the theory*
5 B: Base text: *what you need to do to be successful is to focus on the outcome of what you want and how that will affect your life …*
   Para B: *Apart from adjusting your mental attitude …*
6 A: Para A: *Other ways …*
   Base text *Use anything that works, no matter how strange.*

5 Students work individually before checking answers with a partner, and then open-class.

SUGGESTED ANSWERS

1 Because they experienced adverse circumstances as children.
2 'Task motivation' (the motivation to play well and improve) and 'achievement motivation' (motivation to win).
3 He means that people learn a motivational style through their parents' reactions to their performance.

4 The ideas are: i) improving your diet; ii) doing more exercise; iii) taking extra training; iv) burning energising oils; v) analysing your motives to work out whether or not you really want to do the thing; vi) reading self-help books.

6   Students work in groups, appointing a representative to report their discussion to the rest of the class.

7   (p.106) Students work individually before checking their answers open-class.

ANSWERS

2 motivate   3 psychological   4 rely   5 unsuccessful
6 powerless   7 failed   8 developments   9 improvement
10 determined   11 energetic   12 Theoretically

Watch Out!   *few*

Students work individually before checking their answers open-class.

ANSWERS

Negative: 1b 2a   Positive: 1a 2b

8   Students work in pairs before checking their answers open-class.

POSSIBLE ANSWERS

3 psychology *n*, psychologist *n*
4 unreliable *adj*, reliance *n*, reliably *adv*, reliability *n*
5 (un)successfully *adv*, success *n*, succeed *v*, unsuccessful *adj*
6 powerful(ly) *adj/(adv)*
7 failing *n*, failure *n*, failed *adj*
8 underdeveloped *adj*, developing *adj*
9 improved *adj/past participle*
10 determination *n*
11 energetically *adv*, energy *n*
12 theorise *v*, theorist/theoretician *n*

9   Students write their resolutions on pieces of paper without their names. Collect the resolutions and put them in a hat. Each student draws out two resolutions and writes her/his advice. Display the resolutions and advice on the classroom notice board for everyone to read.

Vocabulary: expressions with *make/get/ keep/gain/resolve* p.107

1   Students work in pairs before checking their answers open-class.

ANSWERS

1

make	get	keep
a difference	*into trouble*	*a resolution*
someone feel something	even with someone	your word
an impression	a promotion	on at someone

2

gain	resolve
control	*a problem*
an advantage	to leave
experience	your doubts

2   Students work individually before checking their answers open-class.

ANSWERS

1 You **made a** very good **impression** on my mother. She thinks you're great!
2 She **gained** a lot of useful **experience** through working for her uncle and now she'd like to start up her own business.
3 They **resolved** the **problem** of where to send their son to school by letting him choose.
4 His teacher told him he would **get into** serious **trouble** if he continued to hang around with that group of boys.
5 She **made me feel** terribly guilty when she said how upset she was that I hadn't been in touch.
6 She was so unhappy in her job that she **resolved to leave** by the end of the year.
7 I think we can **gain a** definite **advantage** over the competition if we launch our new model in January.
8 You can never believe Jim when he promises to do something. He just seems unable to **keep his word**.
9 I can't believe that Fiona humiliated me like that. I'll **get even** with her if it's the last thing I do.
10 I wish my boss wouldn't **keep on at** me all the time to finish the report. It doesn't have to be done until the end of the month.
11 He's managed to **keep his resolution** to stop smoking for six weeks now.
12 My sister has just **got a promotion**. Now, she's head of her department.
13 If he **gains control** of any more newspapers, he will have a virtual monopoly of the media.
14 Passing her exams has **made an** amazing **difference** to her levels of self-confidence!

3   Students discuss the questions in groups, appointing a representative to report their discussion to the rest of the class.

*FURTHER PRACTICE: **Advanced Gold Exam Maximiser** p.69.*

Grammar plus: emphasis p.108

1   Play the conversation and check the answer open-class.

ANSWER

She told him that she was having a 'Roman toga' party. He had a costume specially made, but when he arrived he discovered that he was the only one in fancy dress.

2   Play the cassette. Students answer individually before checking their answers open-class.

ANSWER

1 what I really like about her
2 what Amanda did was to tell
3 what happened was that he arrived
(See **Tapescript** on p.123.)

3   Students study the questions individually before checking their answers open-class.

ANSWERS

1 It places greater emphasis on the information in the last part of the sentence.
2 whole sentence = c)   the verb = b)   the thing = a)
3 whole sentence = 3   the verb = 2   the thing = 1

4   Students work individually before checking their answers with a partner, and then open-class.

ANSWERS

1 What she did was to learn all the irregular verbs off by heart.
2 What annoys me most is people who are always late.
3 What happened was that he failed all his exams at school and that made him determined to be successful in business.
4 What she did was to go on a management course at the end of last year.
5 What I'd really like is to have a new computer.
6 What happened was that she decided finally to ask her boss for promotion, but the company went bust and she lost her job.
7 What I did was to start going swimming first thing in the morning.
8 What happened was that she went and told her boss about how she felt.

5   Students listen to the cassette, marking the stress, and then compare answers with a partner. Check answers open-class, getting individuals to read the sentences.

ANSWERS

1 What **did** was to learn **all** the ir**reg**ular verbs off by **heart**.
2 What **annoys** me **most** is **people** who are **always late**.
3 What **happened** was that he **failed all** his **exams** at **school** and that made him de**term**ined to be su**ccessful** in **business**.
4 What she did was to **go** on a **man**agement **course** at the **end** of **last year**.
5 What I'd **really** like is to have a **new** com**pu**ter.
6 What **happened** was that she de**cided finally** to **ask** her **boss** for promotion, but the **company** went **bust** and she **lost** her **job**.
7 What I **did** was to **start going swimming first** thing in the **morning**.
8 What **happened** was that she **went** and **told** her **boss** about **how** she **felt**.

6   Students work individually before forming groups of four and taking it in turns to speak for a minute each. Each group should choose someone to make their speech to the whole class (see **Tapescript** on p.123).

SUGGESTED ANSWERS

What I particularly need to do to improve my English is to **read more novels and short stories in English** because **that would help me to improve both my reading and vocabulary.**

I had a slightly strange experience a little while ago. What happened was **that I was just thinking of an old friend of mine when he phoned all the way from Australia.**

What I value most about my best friend is **her tremendous patience and kindness** because it's not always easy to be kind and patient, after all!

What really annoys me is people **who get pets for their children** because the children are often too young to look after them properly.

My friend Diana really surprised me the other day. What she did was to **order a wonderful book for me via the Internet.**

7   (p.109) Remind students about the layout and stylistic features of formal letters (see **Writing reference**, p.201 of the *Advanced Gold Coursebook*). Also make it clear that they should try to use the emphasis structures in their letters. Students work individually before exchanging drafts with a partner. They should then suggest any revisions or corrections. The final version can be written in class or for homework.

*FURTHER PRACTICE: **Advanced Gold Exam Maximiser pp.70–71.***

Speaking p.109

▶ **Paper 5, Part 2** (comparing and contrasting)

1   Students briefly discuss the photographs in pairs.

ALTERNATIVE PROCEDURE: conduct an open-class discussion of the photographs and the questions.

2   Read the exam information aloud to the class. Students study the box with the phrases and the example. Play the cassette. Students note the words and phrases and compare with a partner. Check answers open-class.

ANSWERS

appearance	contrast	qualifier
seems	–	a good deal
gives the		
impression		

(See **Tapescript** on p.123.)

3   Students work in pairs. Monitor and ask confident students who are using the words and phrases to talk about their photographs again for the whole class. The other students listen and say which photographs have been described.

FURTHER PRACTICE: Advanced Gold Exam Maximiser p.00.

Vocabulary: leisure activities p.110

1   1 Tell students that they can use dictionaries if they need to. They work individually before checking answers with a partner, and then open-class.

ANSWERS

an oar   an easel   a script   a crash helmet   lyrics

2 Elicit answers open-class.

ANSWERS

scuba diving   photography   singing   riding reading/writing.
a wetsuit a piece of clothing, usually made of rubber, that underwater swimmers wear to keep warm
an oar a long pole with a wide flat blade at one end, used for rowing a boat
a snorkel a tube that allows a swimmer to breathe air under water
flippers large flat rubber shoes worn to help you swim faster

a mask something that covers all or part of your face, to protect or hide it
a tripod a support with three legs, used for a camera, telescope etc.
a lens the part of a camera through which the light travels before it hits the film
an album a book in which you put photographs, stamps etc.
an easel a wooden frame that you put a painting on while you paint it
a darkroom a dark room where film is taken out of a camera and made into a photograph
a choir a group of people who sing together, especially in a church or school
a rehearsal a period or a particular occasion when all the people in a play, concert etc. practise it before a public performance
a conductor someone who stands in front of a group of musicians or singers and directs their playing or singing
to sight-read to play or sing written music when you look at it for the first time, without practising it first
a script the written form of a speech, play, film etc.
a bridle a set of leather bands put around a horse's head and used to control its movements
a whip a long thin piece of rope or leather with a handle used for making animals move or punishing people
a crash helmet a very strong hat that covers your whole head, worn by racing car drivers, motorcyclists etc.
reins long narrow bands of leather that are fastened around a horse's head in order to control it
a saddle a seat made of leather that is put on a horse's back so that someone can ride it
a chapter one of the parts into which a book is divided
lyrics the words of a song, especially a modern popular song
a blurb a short description giving information about a book, new product etc.
an author someone who writes books
a paperback a book with a stiff paper cover

3 Students work in pairs, testing each other.

2   Students work individually, researching their chosen leisure activity and preparing to speak about it. They then work in groups, giving their short speeches. Each group should choose a representative to tell the class what leisure activities were presented.

FURTHER PRACTICE: Advanced Gold Exam Maximiser p.72.

English in Use p.110

▶ Paper 3, Part 3 (error correction, spelling and punctuation)

1   Students discuss the questions in groups, appointing a representative to report their discussion back to the rest of the class.

2   Set a two-minute time limit for this. Students work individually before checking their answers open-class.

ANSWERS

Children should be able to succeed (or fail) independently of wealthy parents.
It is better to leave money to charity than to one's children.
Money doesn't make you happy, but success can.

3   Students discuss the question in groups, appointing a representative to report their discussion to the rest of the class.

4   Students work individually.

5   Students check their answers with a partner, and then open-class.

ANSWERS

entrepreneurs. Including ➜ entrepreneurs, including
there ➜ their
welth ➜ wealth
british ➜ British
thought ➜ though
like minded ➜ like-minded
dye ➜ die
succesful ➜ successful
milionaire ➜ millionaire
legacies the ➜ legacies. The
beleive ➜ believe
There ➜ 'There
goverment ➜ government
peoples ➜ people's
either' Sykes ➜ either.' Sykes
a link, between ➜ a link between
definitaly ➜ definitely

*FURTHER PRACTICE: **Advanced Gold Exam Maximiser** p.74.*

Grammar check: tenses p.111

1   Students work individually before checking their answers with a partner, and then open-class.

ANSWERS

1 are   2 have lived/lived   3 broke   4 was walking
5 had taken/took   6 survived   7 had travelled   8 died
9 walked/had walked   10 reached   11 had lost
12 had gone   13 had drifted   14 are probably thinking
15 are   16 have conducted

2   Students work in pairs before checking their answers open-class.

ANSWERS

1 T   2 T   3 F   4 T   5 F   6 T   7 T   8 T

*FURTHER PRACTICE: **Advanced Gold Exam Maximiser** p.73.*

3   Students work in pairs. Monitor, and get a confident narrator to tell her/his story to the whole class.

Writing: report (1) p.112

1   Students read the report individually.

2   Students discuss the question in groups, appointing a representative to report their discussion to the rest of the class.

3   (p.113) Students work individually before comparing impressions with a partner, and then open-class.

ANSWER

Linking words and phrases are a problem as links between sentences and paragraphs are not explicitly marked.

4   Students work individually before comparing answers with a partner, and then open-class.

SUGGESTED ANSWERS

Paragraph 1: Introduction/Purpose and method
Paragraph 2: Reasons for lack of success/Contributing factors
Paragraph 3: Ideas for improvement/Suggestions for change
Paragraph 4: Conclusion/Recommendations and concluding remarks

5   Students work in pairs before checking their answers open-class.

ANSWERS

1 T   2 T   3 F   4 F   5 T

6   Students work individually before checking answers open-class.

ANSWERS

1 consequently   2 both   3 first and foremost
4 both   5 moreover

7   Students work individually before checking answers open-class.

ANSWERS

addition	consequence	significance
As well as this	So	The main priority is …
in addition to this	consequently	most importantly
		above all
furthermore	clearly	first and foremost
moreover	therefore	
	as a result of this	

8   Students work individually before comparing versions with a partner, and then open-class.

POSSIBLE VERSION

MOTIVATING STUDENTS TO ACHIEVE A HIGH LEVEL OF ENGLISH.

INTRODUCTION This report is intended to explain why so many students finish secondary school with a low level of English. A number of students and teachers were interviewed and their suggestions for changes to the teaching methods are summarised.

REASONS FOR LACK OF SUCCESS There seem to be a variety of reasons why our school students fail to reach a good level of spoken English. The main problem seems to be the fact that teachers appear to place so much significance on grammar. **As a result of this,** students appear to know a lot about grammar but can't actually speak with much confidence. **In addition to this,** what students complain about most is that lessons are boring with too many grammar exercises and gapfills.

IDEAS FOR IMPROVEMENT **Having said this,** what steps can be taken to improve the situation? **Above all,** what teachers need to do is to place more emphasis on developing the listening and speaking ability of students. **Furthermore,** they need to introduce greater variety into their teaching and use more games, role-plays, drama and so on. **As well as this,** they should use as much authentic material as possible: newspaper articles, songs, extracts from films etc. (This will also help to increase student motivation.)

CONCLUSION **Clearly** there are serious problems with the way that English is taught in our schools at the moment, leading to low motivation on the part of students. We believe that, **most importantly,** it is the way English teachers are trained that needs to be changed, with more emphasis on preparing students to use English in practical situations rather than approaching it as another academic subject.

9   Students work individually, deciding which of the topics they will write on. Form groups made up of students who have chosen the same topic. Go through the suggested procedure step by step, pausing for the groups to action each of the points. Point 4 can be done in class or as homework. Point 5 can be done with a partner.

Refer students to the report in the **Writing reference,** pp.208–209 of the *Advanced Gold Coursebook.*

FURTHER PRACTICE: **Advanced Gold Exam Maximiser p.75.**

Exam focus p.114

▶ **Paper 4 Listening: Part 4** (multiple matching)

Read the exam information aloud to the class. Read the 'Before you listen' section of the Suggested procedure and pause for students to action the two points. Read the 'As you listen the first time' section. Play the cassette. Students answer individually. Read the 'As you listen the second time' section. Play the cassette.

Check answers open-class, replaying sections of the cassette as necessary.

ALTERNATIVE PROCEDURE: give students copies of the **Tapescript** on p.123. They correct their own work.

ANSWERS

1 D   2 A   3 F   4 G   5 H   6 H   7 E   8 D   9 F   10 A
(See **Tapescript** on p.123.)

FURTHER PRACTICE: **Advanced Gold Exam Maximiser p.70.**

Unit 9 review p.115

ANSWERS

1 1 gets an important promotion 2 ✓ 3 ✓
   4 get into trouble 5 ✓ 6 ✓ 7 get some experience
   8 ✓ 9 keep his word 10 makes me feel

2 1 is 2 happened 3 did 4 that/how/when
   5 how 6 was

3 1 a darkroom 2 a tripod 3 an album 4 an oar
   5 a snorkel 6 a choir 7 a conductor 8 a saddle
   9 a whip 10 the lyrics

4 1 as 2 was 3 by 4 who 5 Although/Though
   6 has 7 with 8 been 9 other 10 what 11 told
   12 for 13 the 14 of 15 on

10 The trials of technology

Advance preparation

▉ (Optional) Prepare revision questions for Extra Activity: Criss-Cross Quiz on page 79. Use material from Units 1–9. Devote a square to vocabulary, pronunciation and grammar from each unit. You will need from ten to fifteen questions per square.

▉ Remind students to bring dictionaries to class for Exercise 1 on p.126, or arrange to bring a class set yourself.

Exam focus p.116

▶ Paper 1 Reading: Part 2 (gapped text)

Read the exam information aloud to the class. Students read the Suggested procedure silently and action each point. Enforce an eighteen-minute time limit, warning students when ten minutes and fifteen minutes have passed. Check answers open-class. Insist on justifications for answers.

ANSWERS

1 D (para D 'a new breed of agent ready to fight back against the infiltrator'; base text line 16)
2 H (base text lines 20–21; para H 'Sitting among the debris')
3 B (base text lines 28–29; para B 'It was futile.')
4 F (base text lines 35–36; para F 'But how?')
5 A (base text lines 42–43; para A 'The agents had informants who cruised the Internet ... ';
   para A 'Datastream Cowboy hung out at Cyberspace, an Internet service provider based in Seattle.'; base text line 45)
6 E (base text line 55; para E 'Having identified his location ...')
7 C (para C '... they saw a teenager hunched in his chair ...'; base text line 63)

Vocabulary: computers p.118

1 Students work with a partner before checking their answers open-class. In classes where students share the same L1, accept translation equivalents plus explanations.

ANSWERS

a **network** a set of computers that are connected to each other and can be used to send information or messages
to **download a file** to move information or programs from one part of a computer system to another
a **(computer) screen** the flat glass part of a computer
to **delete a file** to remove a file from a computer's memory
to **crash a system** if a computer crashes or you crash the computer, it suddenly stops working
a **computer terminal** a piece of computer equipment consisting of at least a keyboard and a screen, that you use for putting in or taking out information from a large computer
a **computer hacker** someone who secretly uses or changes the information on other people's computer systems
to **be online** to be directly connected to or controlled by a computer or telecommunications system
an **Internet service provider** a company that provides individuals or other companies with access to the Internet
a **keyboard** the set of keys on a machine such as a computer

2 Students discuss the questions in groups, appointing a representative to report their discussion to the rest of the class.

POSSIBLE USES OF THE INTERNET

The Internet can be used for displaying and accessing a wide variety of information. It can be used for professional or leisure purposes. There are lots of websites that are related to education and research. There are also enormous numbers of sites devoted to games and chat.

SOUND: There is a huge amount of music on the Internet. Groups, individual musicians and record companies have websites where it is possible to listen to songs and see video clips. The Napster and MC3 sites also allow you to download music on to your hard drive. Some musicians, e.g. David Bowie, have released albums 'online'. Many radio stations have websites and it is possible to listen to broadcasts. Some university linguistics departments have recorded material on their sites. The majority of websites have some sound (background music or snippets of speech).

IMAGE: It is possible to see an enormous variety of images on the Internet. There are sites that specialise in images, some of which allow you to send an image to a friend in an e-mail message, to use it as a screensaver or to buy it as a poster. One of these, Webshots, also allows you to publish your photographs on the Internet. Almost all websites include images, though it is also sometimes possible to view a 'text-only' version of a site. This takes less time to come up on the screen.

TEXT: You can read the vast majority of the world's newspapers online and also access enormous quantities of text of all kinds. The novelist Stephen King published a novel which was only available on the Internet. Many books are now available in electronic form as 'e-books'.

FURTHER PRACTICE: **Advanced Gold Exam Maximiser p.77.**

Grammar plus: *it* as preparatory subject/object p.118

1   Students work in pairs before checking their answers open-class.

ANSWERS

1 c   2 b   3 a

2   Students work individually before checking their answers with a partner, and then open-class.

ANSWERS

1 It is unbelievable how easy it is to hack into government computers.
2 It was futile to try and find out where he was based.
3 It seems likely that an outside person knows the password to our system.
4 It is absolutely vital for us to find out who it was.
5 It doesn't really matter when you give me back that book.
6 It was announced yesterday that the Prime Minister will resign.

3   Focus attention on the box and go through the examples open-class. Students work individually on the exercise before checking their answers open-class.

ANSWERS

1 His headache made **it** difficult for him to work.
2 They thought **it** strange that he hadn't called.
3 I found **it** surprising to be asked to be on the committee.
4 He made **it** impossible for me to continue working there.
5 She considered **it** a mistake to sign the contract.

4   (p.119) Students work in pairs before checking their answers open-class.

ANSWERS

1 I cannot bear ~~it~~ to see people being cruel to animals.
(i.e. there should be no 'it' after bear)
2 ✓   3 ✓   4 ✓   5 ✓
6 I knew ~~it~~ that they didn't really want to come with me.
(i.e. there should be no 'it' after knew)
7 ✓   8 ✓   9 ✓

5   Students work in pairs. When they have been right through the exercise, get each pair to perform one or two of their mini-interviews for the rest of the class.

POSSIBLE ANSWERS

A: It's surprising how many businesses still close for the whole month of August.
B: Why do you find it surprising?
A: Because they must lose so much money.

A: It's exciting when the local football team is playing in the first division.
B: Why do you find it so exciting?
A: Because there's always a chance that they'll win the cup.

A: It's definitely worth getting an Internet connection.
B: Why do you think so?
A: Well, you can get almost every imaginable kind of information in almost no time at all.

A: It's often said that people are their own worst enemies.
B: Do you agree?
A: Yes, I do. I think we often create problems for ourselves.

A: I find it quite difficult to correct my own mistakes in the writing I do.
B: Why do you think that is?
A: I suppose because I'm so used to making some of the mistakes that I don't even recognise them as such.

A: I find it very interesting to look at advertisements for the same product in different countries.

B: Oh really? Why does it interest you so much?

A: Well, sometimes differences in the campaigns highlight important cultural differences that we wouldn't be aware of otherwise.

A: I find it embarrassing to be always having to ask if I can stay with people when I go to London.

B: Why do you find it embarrassing?

A: Well, I always feel it would be very awkward for them to say 'no'.

Refer students to the **Grammar reference** on pp.194–195 of the *Advanced Gold Coursebook*.

FURTHER PRACTICE: *Advanced Gold Exam Maximiser* **p.77.**

Listening: computers p.119

▶ **Paper 4, Part 1** (sentence completion)

1 Discuss the questions open-class.

ANSWER

Bill Gates, the Chairman of Microsoft.

BACKGROUND INFORMATION: Bill Gates is one of the wealthiest people on earth. His company Microsoft dominated the computer software industry throughout the 1990s and still has few true rivals. Microsoft manufacture the well-known Windows operating systems. Students might enjoy looking at one of the websites devoted to jokes about Bill Gates and Microsoft. One of the better ones can be found at: http://www.cyberint.com.au/billy/index.html. The official Microsoft site is at: http://www.microsoft.com.

2 Discuss the question open-class.

ANSWER

The game is played by two players or two teams: one uses noughts (**0**) and the other uses crosses (**X**). Each player or team tries to fill a line of squares with either noughts or crosses. The players or teams take it in turns to put a nought or cross in a square. The first team or player to complete a line of noughts or crosses (including diagonals) wins.

EXTRA ACTIVITY: Play Criss-Cross Quiz. Divide the class into two teams. One team has the right to put noughts in the squares if they correctly answer a vocabulary, grammar or pronunciation question, the other team has the right to put

a cross in a square if they answer correctly. If a team either cannot answer or gets the answer wrong, the other team has the right to challenge them and to try to answer the question. If they answer correctly they put their mark in the square. Once a team has a complete line of noughts or crosses (including diagonals) they have won. Play as many rounds of the game as necessary to cover the language you want to revise from the first nine units of the *Advanced Gold Coursebook*.

BACKGROUND INFORMATION: Students might enjoy playing noughts and crosses online. They may do so at the following website: http://www.netrover.com/~kingskid/tic.html.

3 Focus attention on the topics. Play the talk. Check answers open-class.

ANSWER

The last two points are not mentioned.

4 Students try to complete any of the gaps they can before listening. Play the cassette. Students work individually, completing the answers before comparing answers with a partner, and then open-class.

ANSWERS

1 slow   2 a Mothers' Club   3 a printing device
4 a lunch period   5 control it   6 feedback   7 really fast
8 won most   9 more
(See **Tapescript** on p.124.)

FURTHER PRACTICE: *Advanced Gold Exam Maximiser* **p.79.**

Speaking: language of approximation p.120

1 Students work in pairs.

2 Students work individually, noting the phrases. Play the cassette. Check answers open-class (see **Tapescript** on p.124).

ANSWERS

… I'm not exactly sure but it seems to have a sort of metal bar attached to …
I could be wrong but could that be … ?
I can also just about make out a yellowy box like thing … and there's also a white box **of some kind, like a** big dice …

3   Students work in pairs. Get a confident student who uses the language of approximation well to describe the pictures for the rest of the class.

4   Students work in pairs. Get a confident student who uses the language of comparison and contrast well to perform for the rest of the class.

FURTHER PRACTICE: Advanced Gold Exam Maximiser p.78.

English in Use p.121

▶ Paper 3, Part 2 (open cloze)

1   Students discuss the questions in pairs before comparing their answers with the rest of the class.

2   Set a two-minute time limit for this. Students discuss their answer open-class.

> **ANSWERS**
>
> 1
> 1   40 hours +
> 2   It allows you to escape into a fantasy world in which no one knows who you are.

3   Students work individually.

4   Students work in pairs before checking their answers open-class.

> **ANSWERS**
>
> 1 has (auxiliary verb)
> 2 who (relative pronoun)
> 3 if (conjunction)
> 4 to (part of infinitive)
> 5 the (article)
> 6 how (conjunction)
> 7 to (part of infinitive)
> 8 Anybody/Anyone (pronoun)
> 9 are/include (verb)
> 10 being (present participle of the auxiliary verb)
> 11 from (preposition)
> 12 of (preposition)
> 13 Nobody/No one (pronoun)
> 14 can (modal verb)
> 15 that/which/and (relative pronoun/conjunction)

5   Discuss the question open-class.

> **ANSWER**
>
> Nouns

EXTRA ACTIVITY: Students work in pairs to design a three- or four-step suggested procedure for dealing with open cloze. They can draw on the advice on pp.120–121 of the *Advanced Gold Coursebook* and/or come up with their own ideas. Each pair presents their procedure to the rest of the class.

FURTHER PRACTICE: Advanced Gold Exam Maximiser p.80.

Listening: cyber dating p.121

1   Play the conversation. Students discuss the question in pairs before comparing summaries with the rest of the class.

> **ANSWER**
>
> Cathy and Andrew are both very disapproving and can hardly believe what Ben tells them. Andrew also seems irritated by the whole idea of the Internet. Ben becomes rather defensive when Andrew and Cathy discover that he plans to meet up with someone he's met on the Internet. Cathy's scepticism then changes to concern.

2   Check understanding of the words. Play the cassette again. Students compare answers in pairs before checking open-class (see **Tapescript** on pp.124–125).

> **ANSWERS**
>
> Only 7 and 8 are not expressed.
> **disbelief:** … her husband of fifteen years is leaving her to … wait for it … go and live with a woman in Australia who he met on the Internet eight weeks ago.
> How can people do something like that … they must be completely nuts.
> **irritation:** I think all this Internet stuff is awful. It's really sad that people have to resort to meeting each other by computer. Why can't they just go out and get a life for goodness' sake.
> **scepticism:** So, you actually have first-hand experience of this, do you Ben?
> Yeah, right …
> **concern:** Listen, you've got to be careful about that kind of thing.
> **defensiveness:** That's really unfair. You know, Andrew, you can be incredibly narrow-minded sometimes! What's wrong with chatting to people on the Internet? You'd be really surprised. You get to meet people from all over the world.

dismissiveness: What rubbish! It's very easy to work out if someone is genuine or not.

3 Students discuss the question in groups, appointing a representative to report their discussion to the rest of the class.

Grammar check: making comparisons p.122

1 Students work individually before checking their answers with a partner, and then open-class.

ANSWERS

Ann and Bill

Bill: ... she says it's **far** ~~much~~ **faster** OR ~~far~~ **much faster** and has **a** lot more memory than the old one.

Ann: ... download things from the Internet **more** ~~quicklier~~ **quickly**.

Ann: Seriously ... I think the most interesting and possibly the ~~less~~ **least** positive thing ...

Clare and David

David: Well, I must say it's probably **the** most difficult thing ...

David: We're thinking of moving to a slightly ~~biger~~ **bigger** flat ... it's not as near the tube **as** our present one and there are far ~~few~~ **fewer** good shops nearby. It's also on the ~~noisyest~~ **noisiest** main road.

EXTRA ACTIVITY: Students act out the conversations, adding beginnings and endings. For example:

Ann: Hi Bill. How was your weekend?

Bill: Not bad apart from the fact that I spent a lot of time being dragged round computer shops.

Ann: So, is Alison going to get her new computer then. etc.

...

Bill: But surely that has all sorts of advantages as well. I mean people don't have to spend hours commuting and loads of money on special 'work clothes' and so on.

Ann: I suppose that's true, but I think it's essential to make sure that people who work from home still have plenty of face-to-face contact with the people they work with.

Bill: Talking of face-to-face contact, I've got a meeting that started five minutes ago. Must rush. See you later.

Ann: Yes, see you later. Say 'hello' to Alison for me, won't you?

Bill: Will do. Bye.

2 Students work in pairs before sharing comparisons with the rest of the class.

POSSIBLE ANSWERS

Cats are not as loyal as dogs. Dogs involve a greater time commitment than cats. Cats are cleaner than dogs. It's easier to train a dog than a cat. Dogs don't live as long as cats.

It's easier to learn to ride a bicycle than it is to drive a car. It's also a lot cheaper because you don't have to pay for lessons or hold a licence. You're much more vulnerable on a bicycle than you are in a car. Bicycles are much less damaging to the environment than cars are. There are fewer bicycles on the road than cars.

Violins are much more expensive than guitars. It's more difficult to learn to make a pleasant sound with a violin than it is with a guitar. You've got a better chance of getting into an orchestra if you play the violin, but you've got less chance of getting into a rock band.

A TV screen is much smaller than a cinema screen. You are less likely to be irritated by other people around you when watching TV. It's cheaper to watch TV than it is to go to the cinema (except in Britain where you have to have a TV licence).

Apples are much better for you. They're not nearly as fattening and they're not as bad for your teeth, but they're nowhere near as delicious as a piece of chocolate cake.

3 Students work in pairs before sharing comparisons with the rest of the class.

FURTHER PRACTICE: *Advanced Gold Exam Maximiser p.81.*

Speaking: Just a minute p.122

1 Students work individually before checking their answers open-class.

ANSWERS

A 3   B 2   D 4

2 Students work individually.

3 (p.123) Students work in groups. They decide who will take the role of 'chair' and read the rules.

BACKGROUND INFORMATION: This game is based on the BBC radio comedy programme of the same name.

4   As they listen, students note down:
1 what the people spoke about;
2 any instances of challenges and why the challenge was made;
3 whether or not it was successful.
Play the cassette.

ANSWERS

1 the use of computers for learning English
2 hesitation
3 yes
(See **Tapescript** on p.125.)

5   Students play the game in groups. Get a good group to perform for the rest of the class.

English in Use p.123

▶ **Paper 3, Part 6** (gapped text)

Read the exam information aloud to the class. Students work individually before checking their answers with a partner, and then open-class.

ANSWERS

1 E   2 H   3 D   4 F   5 A   6 B

*FURTHER PRACTICE: **Advanced Gold Exam Maximiser p.82.***

Exam focus pp.124–125

▶ **Paper 2 Writing: Part 1**

Either devote a whole one-hour class to this or ask students to work at home under exam conditions, giving themselves an hour only to complete the task.

*FURTHER PRACTICE: **Advanced Gold Exam Maximiser pp.82–83.***

Vocabulary: words from other languages p.126

1   Students work in pairs before checking their answers open-class.

ANSWERS

1
1 origami   2 cosmonaut   3 mammoth   4 cobra
5 karate   6 duvet   7 mosquito   8 marmalade
9 chauffeur   10 algebra

Words without illustrations
psychology   kindergarten   piano   siesta   drama
confetti   hamburger   mattress
2
Greek: psychology   Spanish: siesta   Japanese: origami
Italian: piano   French: chauffeur   German: kindergarten
Portuguese: marmalade   Arabic: algebra
Russian: cosmonaut
3
drama plays considered as a form of literature; an exciting and unusual situation or set of events
psychology the study of the mind and how it works
mosquito a small flying insect that sucks the blood of people and animals
siesta a short sleep in the afternoon, especially in warm countries
karate a style of fighting from the Far East, in which you kick and hit with your hands
origami the Japanese art of folding paper to make attractive objects
confetti small pieces of coloured paper that you throw over a man and a woman who have just been married, especially when they come out of church
piano a large musical instrument that you play by sitting in front of it and pressing the keys
duvet a large cloth bag filled with feathers or similar material that you use to cover yourself in bed
chauffeur someone whose job is to drive a car for someone else
hamburger very small pieces of beef pressed together, cooked, and eaten between two round pieces of bread
kindergarten a school for children aged two to five
cobra a poisonous African or Asian snake that can spread the skin of its neck to make itself look bigger
marmalade a jam made from fruits such as oranges, lemons or grapefruit, usually eaten at breakfast
mattress the soft part of a bed that you lie on
algebra a type of mathematics that uses letters and other signs to represent numbers and values
mammoth a large hairy elephant that lived on Earth thousands of years ago; extremely large
cosmonaut an astronaut from the former Soviet Union

4 Students work in pairs and then check their answers open-class, listening to the cassette.

5 Play the cassette. Students listen and repeat.

2   Students discuss the questions in groups, appointing a representative to report their discussion to the rest of the class.

*FURTHER PRACTICE: **Advanced Gold Exam Maximiser p.81.***

Units 6–10 progress check p.127

The Progress check can be treated as an open-book exam in which students do the exercises, looking back to relevant sections of the units as necessary. It can be done in class or for homework. Alternatively, students can revise the **Vocabulary**, **Grammar** and **English in Use** sections of the previous five units before tackling the Progress check, once again either in class or for homework.

Check answers open-class, or provide students with copies of this key so that they can correct their own work.

1   See Unit 7 for training and Unit 8 for Exam focus.

ANSWERS

Paper 3 English in Use: Part 1 (multiple-choice cloze)
1 B   2 C   3 A   4 B   5 B   6 D   7 C   8 D   9 A
10 C   11 B   12 C   13 D   14 A   15 A

2   See Unit 6 Grammar plus: future (advanced features).

ANSWERS

1 point of   2 are to   3 have heard
4 have risen/increased   5 be using   6 be leaving
7 are … to

3   See Unit 7 Vocabulary: commonly confused words.

ANSWERS

1 childlike   2 loses   3 alone   4 hard   5 channel
6 worthless   7 especially

4   See Unit 6. English in Use.

ANSWERS

Paper 3 English in Use: Part 4 (word formation)
1 intensifies   2 ensure   3 strength   4 injury/injuries
5 comfortably   6 toughness   7 interruption   8 childish
9 rivalry   10 painful   11 unresolved   12 competition
13 admiration   14 recognition   15 assertive

5   See Unit 10 Grammar plus: *it* as preparatory subject/object.

ANSWERS

1 It is difficult to know what to do.
2 It is essential that I get in touch with David/for me to get in touch with David.
3 It was Jane that/who lent me the mobile phone.
4 It's on Tuesday that Bill's leaving/Bill leaves for Australia.

5 It is terrible how few people use public transport.
6 It seems she didn't know the meeting had been cancelled.
7 His parents made it clear that they did not like his new girlfriend.
8 It is important to obtain a student visa.
9 I find it hard to understand why I did not get the job.

6   See Unit 8 Vocabulary: word formation (prefixes).

ANSWERS

a 4   b 6   c 10   d 2   e 7   f 9   g 5   h 3   i 1   j 8

7   See Unit 9 Grammar plus: emphasis.

ANSWERS

1 What happened was he left his passport at home.
2 What I'd like to do is stay at home and watch a video.
3 What I like most about Clara is her sense of humour.
4 What she did was to hitchhike to the airport.
5 What really gets on my nerves is the way he's always gossiping.
6 What I need to do is to find out about using my mobile phone outside Spain.

8   (p.129) See Unit 6 and Unit 8.

ANSWERS

Paper 3 English in Use: Part 5 (register transfer)
1 be staffed   2 to encourage   3 to do
4 allowed/permitted to   5 (can) demonstrate
6 attend/have attended   7 prevent damage   8 additional
9 been established   10 as follows   11 are prohibited
12 to have   13 result in

9   See Unit 9 Vocabulary: expressions with *make/get/keep/ gain/resolve*.

ANSWERS

1 made   2 problem   3 feel   4 gained   5 resolve
6 makes   7 keeps   8 got   9 gained   10 trouble
11 experience   12 to get

UNIT
11 Getting away from it all

Advance preparation

▌ Remind students to bring dictionaries to class for Exercise 2 on page 139, or arrange to bring a class set yourself.

Speaking: agreeing to disagree p.130

BACKGROUND INFORMATION: The first postcard shows the Changing of the Guard outside Buckingham Palace in London. The second postcard shows four images of Britain: top left, Anne Hathaway's cottage – Shakespeare's birthplace; top right, Edinburgh Castle; bottom left, the Giant's Causeway in Northern Ireland; bottom right, a Welsh male-voice choir. The third postcard shows a Scottish person in highland dress playing the bagpipes. The fourth postcard shows a Welsh village scene with a typical pub. The fifth postcard shows a woman dressed up for the Nottinghill Carnival, which is celebrated in London every August Bank Holiday weekend (see *Advanced Gold Exam Maximiser* Unit 2 Reading p.17). The sixth postcard shows 'The Angel of the North', a famous modern sculpture just outside Newcastle by Antony Gormley.

▌ **1** Students discuss the postcards in groups, appointing a representative to report their discussion to the rest of the class.

▌ **2** Students work individually. Play the cassette. Check answers open-class.

ANSWERS

The Angel of the North, because it's different and not a cliché;

The four mini-pictures from around Britain, because people may be more likely to buy postcards of familiar well-known scenes, and because it gives an overview of different parts of Britain with places that would interest tourists;

The Nottinghill Carnival, because it shows a different side of the UK, with a sense of diversity and vibrancy. They also comment that it might appeal to Brazilian tourists.

▌ **3** Students work individually. Play the cassette. Check answers open-class.

ANSWERS

That's probably very true … but I do wonder if …
That's certainly an interesting point but I still feel …
Well, I can see what you mean but, having said that, I do think …
(See **Tapescript** on p.126.)

▌ **4** Students discuss the postcards in groups, appointing a representative to report their discussion to the rest of the class.

▌ **5** Divide the class into groups of four or five students. Allow time for students to read the instructions. When they have done this they perform the role-play. Monitor, and ask a good group who are using the language of polite disagreement well to repeat their role-play for the whole class.

Listening p.131

▶ **Paper 4, Part 2** (sentence completion)

▌ **1** Read the exam information aloud to the class.

▌ **2** Students discuss the questions in groups, appointing a representative to report their discussion to the rest of the class.

▌ **3** Read the Suggested procedure aloud to the class. Allow 30–45 seconds for students to read the questions. Play the cassette. Students work individually before comparing answers with a partner. Play the cassette again. Check answers open-class, replaying and pausing the cassette as necessary.

ANSWERS

1 first aid kit   2 a medical emergency   3 in a hurry
4 at the back   5 meals   6 in-flight entertainment
7 peace and quiet   8 leg room

ALTERNATIVE PROCEDURE: after students have heard the cassette twice, distribute copies of the **Tapescript** on p.126. Students correct their own work.

*FURTHER PRACTICE: **Advanced Gold Exam Maximiser** p.84.*

Exam focus p.132

▶ Paper 1 Reading: Part 4 (multiple matching)

Read the exam information aloud to the class. Students read the Suggested procedure silently. Students work individually. Enforce the eighteen-minute time limit, warning students when only five minutes remain. Check answers open-class. Insist on justifications for answers.

ANSWERS

1 A (lines 7–9)   2 D (lines 72–73)   3 H (lines 155–156)
4 A (line 3)   5 G (line 131)   6 H (line 159)
7 A (lines 5–6)   8 C (lines 42–44)   9 H (line 172)
10 F (lines 113–114)   11 A (lines 10–11)
12 B (lines 28–29)   13 D (lines 62–63)   14 E (line 86)
15 C (lines 49–54)   16 B (lines 25–27 and 37–41)

*FURTHER PRACTICE: **Advanced Gold Exam Maximiser** pp.86–87.*

Grammar plus: relative clauses (advanced features) p.134

1   Students work individually before comparing answers with a partner, and then open-class.

ANSWERS

Sentences of the type in a) are known as 'defining' (or 'identifying' or 'restrictive') relative clauses, because the clause defines (identifies or restricts) the noun. They answer the question 'What kind of person, thing, etc. do you mean?'

'Non-defining' ('non-identifying' or 'non-restrictive') relative clauses do not define (identify or restrict). They provide extra information about a previously defined (identified or restricted) noun.

Sentence **a** means that only the 21-day tour went to all the places the speaker/writer wanted to visit. Sentence **b** means that the tour the speaker/writer took (and has previously identified) went to all the places and it happened to be 21 days long.

2   Students work in pairs before checking their answers open-class.

ANSWERS

C   (lines 44–49) 'The service has figured in people's imagination since 1883, <u>when prominent people like princes, spies and film stars started travelling in this sumptuous train across Europe</u>.' (non-defining)

D   (lines 62–64) 'Spacious trains and seats <u>that revolve to face the direction of travel</u> are a few of the features of the Bergen line, a service <u>which operates in Norway</u>.' (both defining)

E   (lines 83–86) 'Travel from one great city to another across the Rockies and the vast, empty Great Plains <u>where buffalo once roamed</u>.' (defining)

(lines 91–95) 'There are also several "historic railroads", such as the Durango & Silverton Narrow Gauge Railroad in Colorado, <u>which takes passengers across parts of the Rockies and the western US</u>.' (non-defining)

H   (lines 151–156) 'A growing number of specialist companies are hosting luxurious private tours, particularly in the palace province of Rajasthan, <u>where you can travel in the sumptuous style of an Indian prince</u>.' (non-defining)

3   Students work individually before checking their answers open-class.

ANSWERS

	defining relative clause	non-defining relative clause
that can be used in place of *who* or *which*.	true	not true
the relative pronoun can be left out	true	not true
commas are generally used before (and after) the relative clause	not true	true

4   Students work individually before checking their answers with a partner, and then open-class.

ANSWERS

1   It's the kind of scenery that you only see once in a lifetime. (no comma).
2   The cost of the trip was much lower than we had imagined, ~~what~~ which came as a pleasant surprise.
3   We met a young man who was terribly helpful when we got lost. (no commas)
4   The company ~~which~~ whose train this is don't seem to want to spend money on improving the state of the interior.

5 The guy **that/who** led the tour was very experienced and very helpful.
6 This is the hotel ~~which~~ **where** we used to stay. OR … which we used to stay **in**.
7 We were unable to discover **who** the documents had been sent **to**./**to whom** the documents had been sent.
8 I took some great photos which everybody wanted copies of ~~them~~ when we got back.

5 Students work individually before checking their answers open-class.

ANSWERS

1 The train, which was at least 35 minutes late, came to a halt again. OR The train, which came to a halt again, was at least 35 minutes late.
2 They didn't understand why he was so angry, which was very upsetting.
3 She was a teacher in my school for whom we all had immense respect. OR … who we all had immense respect for.
4 By Friday, which was the last day of the tour, we had seen an amazing variety of wildlife.
5 This is the gentleman whose son I was telling you about.
6 A young woman who gave me this packet asked me to hand it in to the police. OR A young woman gave me this packet, which she asked me to hand in to the police.
7 Stephanie asked me if I was resigning, to which I only had one thing to say.
8 That's the restaurant where Jim finally proposed to me.

Watch Out!   *what*

Students work in pairs before checking their answers open-class.

ANSWERS

Sentence 1 is correct.
Sentence 2 should read 'We listened carefully to everything that the travel agent was saying.'

Refer students to the **Grammar reference** on pp.195–196 of the *Advanced Gold Coursebook*.

FURTHER PRACTICE: **Advanced Gold Exam Maximiser p.88.**

Listening: on the slow train p.134

1 Students work in groups, appointing a representative to report their discussion to the rest of the class.

2 (p.135) Ask if anyone knows which train appears in the illustration. It is the Nile Express. Students work individually. Play the cassette once. Students compare answers in pairs before checking open-class.

ANSWER

the cost of the travel

3 Students work individually. Play the cassette again. Students compare answers in pairs before checking open-class.

ANSWERS

2 the number of vehicles
3 the gift the governor gave him
4 the time the train left
5 the number of passengers on the train
6 the distance (in km) to Khartoum
7 what could be seen through the rotten panelling
8 what he listened to Van Morrison on
9 what broke and caused a delay
(See **Tapescript** on pp.126–127.)

4 Students work in groups, appointing a representative to report their discussion to the rest of the class.

Vocabulary: expressive description p.135

1 Play the cassette a third time, pausing for students to write down the actual expressions. Check answers open-class.

ANSWERS

2 most warmly   3 wails   4 huge, unwieldy
5 a mass of running figures   6 lends a ghostly glow to
7 spent cigarettes flashing from windows like fireflies

2 Students discuss the expressions in groups before comparing their impressions with the rest of the class.

SUGGESTED ANSWERS

Each of the expressions in the recording is much more vivid than the simple language of 1–7.
1 'milling' gives a sense of rapid, circular movement.
2 'most warmly' conveys the emotion felt.
3 'wails' attributes human or animal qualities to the inanimate train and also suggests sadness or pain.
4 'huge, unwieldy' conveys a sense of both bulk and awkwardness.
5 'a mass of running figures' suggests that the people are not individuals but are inseparable from one another.

6 'lends a ghostly glow' conveys the idea of soft light and of the loneliness and mystery of the desert.

7 'spent cigarettes flashing from windows like fireflies' invites a comparison between something inanimate and prosaic and a thing of natural beauty.

3 1 Students work with a partner. 2 Students work individually. 3 Students work in groups, appointing a representative to read out the expressive words/phrases to the rest of the class.

FURTHER PRACTICE: **Advanced Gold Exam Maximiser p.85.**

Writing: brochure p.136

1 Students work individually before comparing answers with a partner, and then open-class.

SUGGESTED ANSWERS

Durham University

INFORM: Headings organise the information into clearly identifiable categories, each including a digestible amount of information. The use of figures (percentages) helps to convey favourable information about the university in a very succinct form. Travel information is conveyed in terms of distances and duration of journeys.

ATTRACT: The use of the quote from Bill Bryson's *Notes from a Small Island* (see below) uses elements of humour ('Take my car.') and would provoke the reader's curiosity. The section headings involve word plays of various kinds ('High fliers', 'We're accommodating', 'From IT to Italy', 'Take care', 'Easy reach') which would, once again, provoke the reader's curiosity. The use of the first and second person (we–you) throughout establishes a relationship of trust between reader and writer. The use of the future ('you will') transports the reader into an assumed future as a student at Durham University.

Disneyland

INFORM: Titles of attractions in bold serve the same purpose as section headings, allowing readers to focus on the specific information they seek. The box at the bottom of the page with information on special offers (expressed in point form and as noun phrases rather than complete sentences) allows the reader to see what is available at a glance.

ATTRACT: The brochure makes use of a lot of expressive language (including unconventional uses of verbs viz. *thrill* and *amaze* as active verbs and onomatopoeic verbs viz. *whoosh* and *zoom*) to convey the idea of excitement, rapid motion and of 'making your dream come true' – the theme of the brochure. Examples include: 'a marvel-a-minute', 'you'll thrill, amaze and smile your way into whirlwind of impressions', 'Then, in Adventureland, zoom and whoosh your way on a new adventure …', '… before thrilling your way into a spiralling 360-degree loop.', '… a magical symphony of colours and lights', '… you'll see stars in your eyes with the shimmering, glimmering Tinker Bell's Fantasy in the Sky Fireworks Show'. Repetition of the idea of the dream come true in the first paragraph ('A year inspired by the most magical dream of all: yours', 'dream with your eyes wide open'), at the beginning ('This year make your dream come true at Disneyland, Paris') and end of the text ('… it's a year inspired by the most magical of dreams: Yours') serve to personalise and tap into the reader's desire for fantasy and escape. The use of imperatives ('Be prepared for spectacular Disney parades …' , 'So come, dream with your eyes open …', 'Discover the wonderful world of Disney festivities …', 'Start with a magical tour …', 'zoom and whoosh …') and the future ('Here you'll discover …', 'you will be thrilled …', 'you'll see') and the Simple Present ('… you are in the middle of a legendary tale') give a sense of immediacy and involvement, as if the reader had actually been conveyed to Disneyland, Paris by the brochure.

BACKGROUND INFORMATION: **Bill Bryson** is an American travel writer who lived in Britain for almost twenty years. He has written humorous accounts of his travels, including *Notes from a Small Island* (about Britain) and most recently *Down Under* (about Australia). Students may like to look at the following website where extracts from his books can be read:

http://www.randomhouse.com/features/billbryson/home.html.

Durham University has a website with the information contained in the brochure in addition to more detailed information about university services and departments. The site can be found at: http://www.dur.ac.uk.

Students may like to compare this site to those of other universities. UK university websites all end with 'ac.uk', US universities with .edu, and Australian universities edu.au. Most web browsers have long lists of university and college websites.

Disneyland, Paris, also has a website at: http://2000.disneylandparis.com.

2 Students work in pairs or groups of three.

3 Students work individually before comparing answers with the student(s) they worked with in Exercise 2.

4 Students work individually. This stage can be done as homework.

5   Students work in groups.

EXTRA ACTIVITY: Students may like to make poster presentations of their brochures to display in the classroom.

FURTHER PRACTICE: Advanced Gold Exam Maximiser p.90.

Grammar check: linking words p.137

1   Students work individually before checking their answers with a partner, and then open-class.

ANSWERS

1 Firstly/To begin with/In the first place   2 However
3 because of   4 on the one hand   5 on the other hand
6 Despite/In spite of

2 & 3   Students work individually before checking their answers open-class.

ANSWERS

listing ideas	showing consequences	making contrasts
firstly	therefore	however
first of all	as a result	although
in the first place	because	even though
to begin with	because of	though
first and foremost	so	in spite of
secondly	consequently	despite
thirdly	in consequence	but
finally	thus	on the one hand
lastly		on the other hand
last but not least		

4   Students work individually. This can be done as homework.

FURTHER PRACTICE: Advanced Gold Exam Maximiser p.85.

Reading p.138

1   Students work in groups, appointing a representative to report their discussion to the rest of the class.

POSSIBLE ANSWERS

to break a record
to do something no one else has ever done before
to raise money for charity

2   Divide the class into Groups A and B. Students work individually.

3   Students work with a partner before checking their answers to Exercise 2 open-class.

ANSWERS

1

awkward Text A (line 21) 'her own thorny personality'; Text B (lines 24–25) 'Campbell is, to put it mildly, a difficult person.'

determined Text A (line 33) 'Campbell says she got her blind determination from her father …'; (line 53) '… I am determined to do it.'

In both texts there are also references to the distances she walked each day and the suffering she withstood, all of which suggests that she was 'determined'.

self-centred Text A (line 27) 'Unless you're talking about her, she goes into a shell.'; Text B (lines 25–26) 'Restless, self-absorbed, and …'; (lines 68–70) '… seems to have alienated many supporters with her self-involvement and … '.

self-righteous Text B (lines 26–30) '… and prone to moralistic pronouncements, she covers her body with the logos of corporate sponsors while castigating the multinational corporations for destroying the earth.'; (line 70) '… her lecturing manner'.

2

Text A: Because her father was a Royal Marine, the family moved very frequently and Campbell went to fifteen different schools. Her father, who was also very determined, used to take his two daughters on very tough camping trips and reward them for not complaining even if conditions were very harsh. She recently went on holiday with her sister.

Text B: She had a difficult childhood and the family moved very frequently. Her mother found her difficult and Ffyona's relationship with her father was problematic. She ran away from home several times before starting her walk at the age of 16.

3

Text A: She wanted to find out what to do with her life. (line 5) She needed to give herself a tremendous challenge in order to learn about herself. (lines 40–42)

Text B: She had the idea of walking from one end of Britain to the other when she was 16. The dream gradually became an obsession. (lines 44–49)

4

Text A: She argued with them. (lines 23–25)
Text B: She is ambivalent about them. (lines 26–30) She says they put pressure on her. (lines 81–82)

5

Text A: No confession, as such
Text B: That she lied. She let herself be driven for part of her walk across the United States. She was not walking as quickly as she had hoped because she was pregnant.

6

Text A: To get married and have children.
Text B: She doesn't want to say.

Vocabulary: adverbials expressing attitude p.139

1   Students work in pairs.

2   Students work in pairs before checking their answers open-class.

ANSWERS

actually used when you are telling or asking someone what the real and exact truth of a situation is, as opposed to what people may imagine (often used in conversation)
basically used when giving the most important reason or fact about something, or a simple explanation of something
obviously used to mean that a fact can easily be noticed or understood
apparently based on what you have heard is true, although you are not completely sure about it
personally used to emphasize that you are only giving your own opinion about something

3   Students work individually before checking their answers open-class.

ANSWERS

1 obviously   2 basically   3 Actually   4 Frankly
5 apparently   6 Personally   7 Obviously   8 basically

Exam focus p.140

▶ Paper 3 English in Use: Part 5 (register transfer)

Read the exam information aloud to the class. Students read the Suggested procedure silently. Students work individually. Set a fifteen-minute time limit. Check answers open-class.

ANSWERS

1 as minor/small/limited/insignificant   2 read
3 animals   4 careful   5 rubbish/litter   6 camp
7 international   8 used   9 country/area/region
10 supporting/helping   11 keen   12 thought
13 ideas

FURTHER PRACTICE: *Advanced Gold Exam Maximiser* p.89.

Unit 11 review p.141

ANSWERS

1 POSSIBLE ANSWERS
1   I had never been white water rafting before … and now I know why! There were 8 of us crammed into a flimsy rubber boat clutching our paddles as if our lives depended on them. The leader sat in the back, presumably so that he didn't have to look into our terrified eyes. I was scared stiff. I had been extremely reluctant about doing this but had foolishly allowed my friend to persuade me. The river was a churning mass of murky brown water, creamy foam, branches and other debris that was unidentifiable because it was moving so fast. There had been torrential rain only the week before.

The leader gave a few curt instructions and we set off. Almost immediately we were being tossed about violently by the furious torrent. It was almost impossible to hear the instructions the leader was bellowing above the demented roar of the water. Our attention was fully occupied by desperate efforts to avoid the innumerable menacingly jagged rocks that surrounded us on every side. Suddenly we came to this sickening drop. Gallons of water rushed into the boat. Then I felt myself being hurled backwards into the river …

2   Somehow I managed to cling to the leader's paddle. He was screaming something at me, but I had no idea what. The boat was lurching uncontrollably as I tried desperately to heave myself back into it. All I could think was that any second I would hit my head on one of the rocks and that would be it. But no. Just as suddenly as we had come to the drop, we found ourselves in a large expanse of relatively calm water. I finally managed to clamber back into the boat, a quivering mass of sodden terror.

2 1 which   2 ✓   3 ✓   4 him   5 who   6 where
7 was   8 the   9 ✓   10 that   11 who   12 ✓
13 own   14 what   15 ✓   16 was

3 1 ✓   2 ~~basically~~ apparently   3 ~~personally~~ obviously
4 ✓   5 ✓

UNIT 12 Mind over matter

Reading p.142

▶ **Paper 1, Part 2** (gapped text)

1 Students discuss the questions in pairs before sharing their opinions with the rest of the class.

BACKGROUND INFORMATION: The two paintings are by the Surrealist artists **René Magritte** (1898–1967) and **Salvador Dalì** (1904–1989). Magritte, who was Belgian, spent several years in Paris, where he came into contact with the other Surrealists, though he spent most of his life in Brussels. He is famous for his dreamlike paintings, often involving a man in a bowler hat. Another of his paintings was used as the cover for the book *The Man Who Mistook His Wife for a Hat*, by Oliver Sacks, from which the extract is taken. The Catalan artist Salvador Dalì was a member of the Surrealist movement in Paris, but was expelled because of a disagreement over politics. He nevertheless continued to paint his nightmarish images, which have been reproduced in poster form and have, as a result, become familiar.

2 Students work individually before comparing answers with the rest of the class.

3 Students work individually before checking their answers open-class. Enforce the seventeen-minute time limit, warning students when five minutes remain. Insist on justifications for answers.

ANSWERS

1 F: 'these odd mistakes' (para F); 'certain strange problems' (line 3); plus examples in rest of paragraph; '... when <u>diabetes</u> developed' (Para F); 'Well aware that it could affect his eyes ...' (line 12)

2 H: '... came to me.' (line 17); 'It was obvious within a few seconds of meeting him ... ' (Para H); 'I couldn't think why he had been referred to our clinic.' (Para H); 'And yet there was something a bit odd.' (line 18)

3 A: 'his eyes' (line 21); 'These, instead of looking at me ...' (Para A)

4 G: '... they make a sort of symphony, do they not?' (Para G); 'What a lovely man I thought' (line 27)

5 E: '... the first bizarre experience occurred.' (lines 34–35); 'I had taken off his left shoe ... left him to put on the shoe himself.' (Para E); 'To my surprise, a minute later, he had not done this'; 'Can I help?' (line 36)

6 C: 'Did he mis-see?' (line 45); 'My eyes ...' (Para C)

7 B 'I opened out a copy of the *National Geographic Magazine*, and asked him to describe some pictures in it.' (lines 51–53); 'I showed him the cover, ...' (Para B); '... had driven him to imagine the river and terrace.' (Para B); 'I must have looked aghast, but he seemed to think he had done rather well.' (lines 54–55)

4 Students discuss the questions in groups, appointing a representative to report their discussion to the rest of the class.

BACKGROUND INFORMATION: Oliver Sacks, the author of the reading text, is a British neurologist who has written seven books on the relationship between the body and the mind. He went to live in the United States in the 1960s and has worked in hospitals in both San Francisco and New York. His book *Awakenings* (1973), about a group of long-term encephalitis patients, inspired a play by Harold Pinter and was also made it into a film in 1990. It is available on video. Students might also enjoy looking at Oliver Sacks' website at: http://www.oliversacks.com. It contains extracts from the books and interviews.

FURTHER PRACTICE: *Advanced Gold Exam Maximiser* pp.92–93.

Vocabulary: expressions with *take* p.144

1 Students work individually before checking their answers open-class.

ANSWERS

1 i 2 e 3 d 4 h 5 a 6 k 7 c 8 f 9 l 10 b 11 g 12 j

2 Students work in pairs before discussing their answers open-class.

ANSWERS

2 understand
3 start to like
4 start to employ
5 not allow something to annoy you
6 accept (people) as they are
7 treat someone unfairly
8 accept that someone will always be there
9 being amazed
10 decide to do something
11 make someone feel very tired
12 do something about

3 Students work individually before checking answers open-class.

ANSWERS

1 upon   2 up   3 out   4 to   5 granted   6 breath
7 advantage   8 stride   9 on   10 be   11 way   12 in

4 Students work in pairs. Ask each pair to perform one of their stories for the rest of the class.

Listening: song p.145

1 Students listen before discussing the questions in pairs. Check answers open-class.

ANSWER

someone with a serious case of amnesia

2 Students work in pairs.

3 Play the cassette again. Check answers open-class.

ANSWERS

1 papers   2 way   3 gone   4 stomach   5 bed
6 decoder   7 make   8 fear   9 staring   10 nothing

4 Students discuss the questions in pairs, and then open-class.

BACKGROUND INFORMATION: The song is by Peter Gabriel and is from his (1980) album 'Melt'. Peter Gabriel was the founder of the group Genesis, but is now probably better known as a solo artist and the creator of the Womad festivals. Students might enjoy looking at one of the many websites devoted to Gabriel and his work. http://www.primenet.com~carmina/pg/ has explanations of the lyrics of his songs.

Grammar plus: emphasis with inversion p.145

1 Students study the sentences individually before discussing the question open-class.

ANSWER

The a) sentences give more emphasis to the adverbials (*Not only …* and *Seldom*), and thus have a more dramatic impact on the reader.

2 Students study the sentences individually before discussing the question open-class.

ANSWER

There is an auxiliary verb (*did* and *have*) before the subject (*Dr P.* and *I*) in each of the sentences.

3 Students work in pairs before checking their answers open-class.

SUGGESTED ANSWERS

1 witness, providing an account of an armed hold-up to police or reporters
2 politician, making a speech during an election campaign
3 accountant, talking to junior members of accounts department staff
4 university lecturer, giving an inaugural lecture to students, parents and staff at the beginning of the academic year

4 Students work in pairs before checking their answers open-class. Play the recording and get students to repeat chorally and individually.

ANSWERS

1 No **sooner** had I **turned** the **corner**, than I **saw** these **three men** in balaclavas.
2 **Rarely** has this **country** been in **such need** of **strong** leadership.
3 Under **no circumstances** can we be **late** with the figures for **next year**.
4 **At no time** in recent **his**tory have we **seen such rapid** technological **change**.

5 (p.146) Students work individually before checking their answers open-class.

ANSWERS

1 Not only did he miss the meeting, but he failed to finish the report on time.
2 Rarely have I met such an interesting individual.
3 At no time did I ever believe that Ms Stevens took/had taken the money.
4 Hardly had I left the room when I heard someone calling my name.
5 Only after signing/she had signed the agreement did she realise what a terrible mistake she had made.
6 No sooner had the judge entered the courtroom than the defendant started shouting.
7 Scarcely had we got on the plane when the flight attendants asked us to go back to the departure lounge.
8 Under no circumstances were we allowed to enter the building without an identity pass.

6 Play the cassette. Students answer individually before comparing notes with a partner. Check answers open-class.

ANSWERS

1 In a pub; two friends
2 In a hall; a politician speaking to an audience

7 Play the cassette. Students answer individually before comparing notes with a partner. Check answers open-class.

ANSWERS

There is a lot of inversion for emphasis in the second extract, a political speech.

8 Play the cassette. Students answer individually before comparing notes with a partner. Check answers open-class.

ANSWERS

... no sooner had they got into power than they began dismantling the framework of our national health service.
... at no time in living memory have we had such poor provision for our elderly.
Under no circumstances can we allow this government to be re-elected.
Never have I heard such a lame excuse.
(See **Tapescript** on p.128.)

9 Students work in pairs. Choose a good pair to deliver their speech to the whole class.

Watch Out!

Students work in pairs before checking their answers open-class.

ANSWERS

1 No sooner ... **than** ...
2 Hardly ... **when** ...

Refer students to the **Grammar reference** on p.193 of the *Advanced Gold Coursebook*.

FURTHER PRACTICE: **Advanced Gold Exam Maximiser p.96.**

Exam focus p.146

▶ Paper 5 Speaking: Parts 1–4

Students read the exam information silently. Read the Suggested procedure aloud to the class. Play the cassette. Students work in pairs. Monitor, and choose a different pair to perform each part for the rest of the class.

FURTHER PRACTICE: **Advanced Gold Exam Maximiser pp.94–95.**

Grammar check: questions p.148

1 Students work individually before comparing answers with a partner and checking open-class.

ANSWER

No. She feels that she has been tricked into getting on the plane.

2 Students work in pairs before checking their answers open-class.

SUGGESTED ANSWERS

2 How had her fear of flying affected her?
3 What had she decided to do to solve the problem?
4 What did the cabin crew have to do?
5 Where were they taken in the coaches?
6 Why did she think 'they' had won?

3 Students work individually before checking their answers open-class.

ANSWERS

1 ✓
2 Who ~~did give~~ **gave** you permission to leave school early?
3 ✓
4 ~~About~~ **What** is that book you're reading **about**?
5 ✓
6 ✓
7 Will you please tell me where you ~~did go~~ **went** last night?

4 Students write their questions individually. Go round and check that they have the right number of words and are well-formed. Students then get up and mingle, asking as many people as possible their questions. How many people wrote the same questions?

POSSIBLE ANSWERS

1 How long have you lived here?
2 What are you doing next Friday evening?
3 Who is your best friend going out with?
4 Where did you learn to speak such good English?

FURTHER PRACTICE: **Advanced Gold Exam Maximiser p.98.**

Listening p.149

▶ **Paper 4, Part 2** (note taking)

1 Focus attention on the photograph. Ask students what they think is happening. Play the cassette. Students work individually before comparing answers with a partner. Check answers open-class.

ANSWERS

1 1980s   2 headphones   3 armchair   4 ping-pong balls
5 image library   6 3   7 pick out   8 10   9 128
10 39 million

2 Play the cassette again. Students work individually, and then with a partner.

ANSWERS

1 A subject is isolated in a small room with halves of ping-pong balls covering her/his eyes. Once the person is in a relaxed state, an image generated by computer is 'beamed' to the subject by another person outside the room. The computer then shows the subject four images including the one that was 'beamed' and the subject has to say which one it is.

2 The success rate is twice as high as was expected and the chance of this happening by chance are one in 39 million. This is a much greater level of significance than in most scientific experiments.
(See **Tapescript** on p.128.)

BACKGROUND INFORMATION: The writer Arthur Koestler, who was a firm believer in euthanasia, committed joint suicide with his wife in 1983. They left a bequest for the establishment of a parapsychology unit at a British university and Edinburgh was eventually chosen. Koestler is most famous for his novel *Darkness at Noon* (1940) and for his writing on science, particularly for his book *The Roots of Coincidence* (1972). The Koestler Parapsychology Unit has a website which includes an on-line variation of the ganzfeld test. It can be accessed at: http://moebius.psy.ed.ac.uk/

FURTHER PRACTICE: **Advanced Gold Exam Maximiser p.97.**

Vocabulary: sound and light p.149

1 Students work in pairs before checking their answers open-class.

ANSWERS

1 hiss   crash   hum   screech   bang   roar   thud
2 flash   flicker   sparkle   beam   twinkle   glow

2 Students work in pairs before checking their answers open-class.

ANSWERS

1 roar   2 crash   3 hum   4 screech   5 bang
6 hiss   7 thud

3 Students work in pairs before checking their answers open-class.

ANSWERS

Illustration 1: flicker   Illustration 2: beam
Illustration 3: twinkle   Illustration 4: sparkle
Illustration 5: glow   Illustration 6: flash

4 Students work in pairs before checking their answers open-class.

POSSIBLE ANSWERS

hiss: people reacting to the villain in a pantomime or silent film
flash: someone shipwrecked on a desert island trying to attract attention with a mirror

flicker: the visible evidence of an emotion (embarrassment, anger, recognition, etc.) in someone's eyes

crash: a building being demolished

hum: the sound of the audience talking quietly among themselves before a performance begins

screech: the sound of someone's fingernails on a blackboard

sparkle: bubbles in a glass of champagne

bang: a tyre exploding

roar: a swollen river rushing towards the sea

beam: a lighthouse in the fog

thud: someone falling to the floor in a faint

twinkle: the visible evidence of amusement or happiness in someone's eyes

glow: a fluorescent frisbee in the dark

5   (p.150) Students work individually before checking answers open-class.

ANSWERS

1 beam   2 flash   3 flickered   4 roared   5 glowed
6 crash   7 screech   8 humming   9 thud   10 sparkled
11 bang   12 hissing   13 twinkled

6   Students work in pairs. Get each pair to tell one of their stories for the whole class.

FURTHER PRACTICE: **Advanced Gold Exam Maximiser p.97.**

Writing: article p.150

1   Read the exam information aloud to the class.

2   Students read and then discuss titles with a partner.

POSSIBLE ANSWERS

What the mind can do: the biggest unsolved mystery
Can we read one another's minds?
Does 'mind over matter' matter to scientists?
Extraordinary claims and some extraordinary evidence
Improbable truths

3   (p.151) Students discuss the question in pairs before checking their answers open-class.

ANSWERS

1 No, but students have presumably added one in Exercise 2
2 Yes. It establishes an atmosphere of mystery and raises questions (Where is this 'small dark room at Edinburgh University'? What is the 'haze of pink light'? Who is 'sending you a psychic message'? What is going on?)
3 Yes. (lines 23–24)
4 Yes. (Opening paragraph)
5 Yes. 'What' … for emphasis: 'For the past 10 years what they have been attempting to do is … ' (lines 11–12)
Inversion for emphasis: '… under no circumstances do orthodox scientists appear …' (line 22)
6 Yes. (Statistics in para 3)
7 Yes: 'haze of pink light', 'gentle hissing' (Para 1); 'devised a range of rigorous tests', 'startling results' (Para 3); 'fluke, error, even fraud – is more plausible …' (Para 4); '… neatly summed up' (Para 5)
8 Yes. (Statistics in para 3)
9 Yes. (Para 4 lines 27–29; Para 5 lines 32–34)
10 Yes.

4   Students work individually, choosing topics.

5   Pair students according to the topics they have chosen. They read and work through the Suggested procedure. The writing of the final version of the article can be done as homework.

Speaking: memory p.152

1   Students work individually, writing down the names of the objects they remember and then comparing their results in pairs.

2   Students read individually and discuss the question open-class.

3   Students work individually and then in pairs, describing the connections they made. Students then get up and mingle, asking and telling as many others as possible about their connections.

4   Students work individually, preparing their mini-speeches. They then work in groups delivering them. Each group should choose someone to give their speech to the whole class.

English in Use p.152

▶ Paper 3, Part 4 (word formation)

1   Students discuss the question in groups, appointing a representative to report back to the whole class.

SUGGESTED ANSWER

Hypnotism is sometimes used in the treatment of psychological problems such as phobias. It is also used to help people give up smoking and to break other patterns of behaviour that are seen as detrimental, and has even been employed as a substitute for chemical anaesthetics in dentistry, surgery and childbirth.

2   Set a two-minute time limit for this. Check the answer open-class.

ANSWER

He seems positive about it.

3   Students work individually before checking their answers open-class.

ANSWERS

1 subconscious (adj)   2 complaints (noun)
3 anxiety (noun)   4 stress (noun)
5 impressive (adj)   6 injection (noun)
7 understandable (adj)   8 intention (noun)

OTHER POSSIBLE WORD FORMS

consciousness, consciously   complainant   anxiously
stressed   impression, impressionable, impressionism,
impressionist, impressionistic   understood, understandably,
understanding   intended, intent, intently, intentness,
intentional

FURTHER PRACTICE: *Advanced Gold Exam Maximiser p.91.*

Unit 12 review p.153

ANSWERS

1 1 B   2 D   3 B   4 A   5 D   6 B   7 A   8 A   9 D
10 C   11 A   12 C   13 B   14 C   15 D

2 1 Not only did Simon break a bone in his foot but he also dislocated his shoulder.
2 No sooner had he walked through the front door than the phone rang.
3 Only after I had shouted/after shouting at Jerry for not waking me up did I remember it was the weekend.
4 Never before have I been so attracted to someone.
5 Hardly had we moved into our new house when the central heating stopped working.
3 1 If we don't **take on** more people …
2 It really **took my breath away** to hear that she had been fired. …
3 We really **took to** Gail from the beginning. …
4 Looking after my mother after her stroke has really **taken it out of** me.
5 You should **take this matter up** with the council.

UNIT
13 An interesting business

Advance preparation

▍ Remind students to bring dictionaries, *Activators*, thesauruses and lexicons to class for Exercise 6 on page 158. Alternatively, arrange to bring a class set yourself.

▍ They will also need dictionaries for Exercise 3 on page 161.

▍ (Optional) Ask students to bring photographs of the people they have described in Exercise 6 on page 158.

Listening: market place economics p.154

▶ Paper 4, Part 1 (sentence completion)

1 Students discuss the questions in groups, appointing a representative to report their discussion to the rest of the class.

2 Students listen to the cassette before discussing their answers to the questions with a partner, and then open-class.

ANSWERS

He is trying to solve the problem of extreme poverty by lending money to very poor people so that they don't have to borrow at high rates of interest from money lenders.

3 Allow a few moments for the students to read through the sentences. Play the cassette again. Students compare answers with a partner before listening for a third time. Check answers open-class, replaying sections of the cassette where necessary.

ALTERNATIVE PROCEDURE: distribute copies of the **Tapescript** on page 129. Students correct their own work.

ANSWERS

1 an empty feeling   2 a stool   3 13/thirteen
4 repay her loan   5 profit   6 42/forty-two
7 poor they are   8 $35 million

BACKGROUND INFORMATION Students might like to look at the Grameen Bank (the bank founded by Muhammad Yunus) website at: www.grameen-info.org. It has a newsletter with articles by Muhammad Yunus as well as a photo gallery and information on microcredit with links to other sites.

4 Students discuss the questions in groups, appointing a representative to report their discussion to the rest of the class.

POSSIBLE ANSWERS TO 2

Arguments 'for':
it would allow these countries to recover economically instead of being crippled by foreign debt;
the amount of money (usually just a proportion of the interest on the debt) the debtor countries can afford to repay is not significant for the rich countries that lent the money in the first place;
the 'debts' are not truly debts but money 'owed' by the debtor counties, which were often exploited by the richer countries during the colonial period;
the United States owes the United Nations a lot of money but very little pressure is brought to bear on it to repay the debt. Why should poor countries be put under so much pressure to pay?
Arguments 'against':
it would encourage the continuing dependency of the debtor countries on the wealthier nations because they will never learn 'to stand on their own two feet' if they don't take responsibility for their debts;
the money lent has often been misspent or squandered by corrupt rulers. If they know they won't have to pay it back they are even more likely to embezzle in the future.
maintaining the debt allows the World Monetary Fund to put pressure on debtor nations to reform their economies.

Grammar check: passives p.154

1 Students work in pairs. Get a good student to give her/his summary to the whole class.

POSSIBLE SUMMARY

Because there are so many very similar products on the market nowadays, companies rely more and more on a brand image to attract and keep customers. They often use logos which capture the essence of the identity the company wants to project. The use of images to suggest an identity is not new. Medieval knights, for example, used symbols on their shields and battle regalia to distinguish themselves from one another.

2   Students work individually before checking their answers in pairs, and then open-class.

ANSWERS

Paragraph 1:
are being marketing
will instantly be recognised OR will be instantly recognised
Paragraph 2:
which is generally shortened
that is identifies
Paragraph 3:
have been used
were then passing passed on

3   (p.155) Students study the box silently.

4   Students work individually before checking their answers in pairs, and then open-class.

ANSWERS

Sentence 1 = use 2
Sentence 2 = use 1
Sentence 3 = use 3

5   Students work individually before checking their answers open-class.

ANSWERS

1 She is being given an award for bravery.
   (Present Continuous passive)
2 He was asked lots of questions (by journalists).
   (Past Simple passive)
3 She was being shown the new museum of modern art at 9 a.m. this morning.
   (Past Continuous passive)
4 I have been asked by Mr Jacobs to tell you a little about how the company began.
   (Present Perfect passive)
5 I hear he is going to be made chairman of the board.
   ('going to' Future passive)

6 The plane must have been delayed by bad weather.
   (Modal Perfect passive)

FURTHER PRACTICE: *Advanced Gold Exam Maximiser* **p.99.**

Speaking: expressing uncertainty p.155

1   Drill the phrases chorally and individually. Students work in pairs discussing the logos before reporting to the rest of the class.

2   Students work in pairs discussing the logos before reporting to the rest of the class.

Reading p.156

▶ **Paper 1, Part 3** (multiple choice)

1   Focus attention on the photograph. Elicit answers open-class. The title 'The Wind-Up Merchant' is a pun. Trevor Bayliss makes wind-up radios, but a wind-up merchant is also a colloquial expression meaning 'a person who teases other people or who pulls their legs'.

2   Set a two-minute time limit for this. Check answers open-class.

ANSWERS

The blond man in the second photograph is the co-founder of the company 'BayGen', which makes wind-up radios. He was inspired to invent the radio after watching a programme about AIDS in Africa.

3   (p.157) Set a 12-minute time limit. Students work individually. Warn them when five minutes remain. They check their answers in pairs, and then open-class. Insist on justifications for answers.

ANSWERS

1 C (lines 2–6)   2 C (lines 25–29)
3 A (lines 34–41)   4 D (lines 60–64)
5 D (lines 81–85)   6 B (lines 90–98)
7 C (lines 8–9 and 11, as well as the fact that the direct quotations are presented without criticism or comment)

4   (p.158) Students discuss the questions in groups, appointing a representative to report their discussion to the rest of the class.

BACKGROUND INFORMATION: Students might like to look at the following website: http://www.theelectricshoeco.com. It provides information on one of Trevor Baylis's latest ventures – shoes that will power batteries by using the energy generated when walking.

5   Students work individually before checking their answers with a partner, and then open–class.

ANSWERS

2 descriptive   3 performance   4 depth   5 coverage
6 expense   7 metallic   8 humiliation   9 logically
10 disabilities   11 heroic   12 literature   13 translators

6   Students work individually before reading their descriptions to a partner.

ALTERNATIVE PROCEDURE: tell students not to indicate what their relationship to the person described is, i.e. they should not say 'My boyfriend is quite tall … ' but 'He/This person is … '. Their partner should try and to work out what relationship the writer has to the person described.

EXTRA ACTIVITY: Ask students to bring photographs of the people they have described to a subsequent class. Display the photographs in random order, labelling them a, b, c, etc. Display the descriptions next to the photographs, also in random order and labelled 1, 2, 3, etc. Students try to match the descriptions to the photographs.

POSSIBLE DESCRIPTION OF A THIN PERSON

People were always asking how he had managed to keep his figure, because even at 56 he was enviably lean. In fact there had been no effort whatsoever involved. He had inherited his father's wiry frame along with what amounted to a passion for astronomy. Long, cold nights had been spent in the cage of the Mount Palomar telescope gazing up at the starry firmament. For these vigils he decked himself out in an ancient aviator's helmet, complete with ear-muffs, a huge sheep-skin jacket, a fisherman's sweater, track-pants and the most enormous pair of fur-lined boots. All of this transformed the finely-formed almost delicate man into something resembling a yeti.

Grammar plus: participle clauses p.158

1   Read the information on participle clauses aloud to the class. Look at the sentences with the class and elicit the differences in form.

ANSWERS

1   The relative pronoun 'who' and the auxiliary 'were' are omitted.
2   The relative pronoun 'who' is omitted and the present simple verb is changed into a present participle.
3   The relative pronoun 'which' and the auxiliary 'was' are omitted.
4   The relative pronoun 'who' and the auxiliary 'is' are omitted.

2   Students work in pairs before checking their answers open-class.

ANSWERS

1   We all noticed his sister standing next to the exit.
2   The students finishing first should get on with their homework.
3   Not all the people asked to come actually turned up.
4   The piece of wood keeping the window open has disappeared.
5   There's the Indian tiger sleeping as always.
6   You should apply for the job paying the most.

3   (p.159) Look at the sentences with the class and elicit the answers.

ANSWERS

a)   **because** > as, since
b)   **so** > Therefore, As a result, Consequently
     In consequence (These alternatives would all be used at the beginning of a separate sentence.)
c)   **Once** > When, As soon as

4   Students work in pairs before checking their answers open-class.

ANSWERS

1   Being so late, we decided to catch a taxi.
2   Having received a large salary rise earlier this year, Sarah is thinking of getting a new car.
3   Having more time, I'm going to start going swimming again.
4   Rushing out of his office, he shouted to his PA that he'd be back soon. OR Shouting to his PA that he'd be back soon, he rushed out of the office.
5   Enjoying a long Sunday morning lie-in, I was not pleased to hear a loud banging on the front door.
6   Their children having all left home, they are thinking of moving somewhere smaller.

7 Having shown them what the problem was, he expected some thanks.

8 Being under so much pressure at the moment, shouldn't you get someone to help you?

Refer students to the **Grammar reference** on p.195 of the *Advanced Gold Coursebook*.

5 Students work individually before reading their improved texts to a partner. Monitor, and get a couple of students who have used particularly interesting vocabulary and participle clauses to read their texts to the rest of the class.

POSSIBLE IMPROVED TEXT

To say that Jeremy and Sue's holiday wasn't going well would be putting it mildly. They were more than a little taken aback **on arriving at the Youth Hostel** to be told to leave their valuable items at reception. They duly left their passports, over $1000 in traveller's cheques, and Jeremy's brand new digital camera as well as Sue's battered but trusty Leica. The rather shifty-looking receptionist seemed slightly too anxious to accept all this, **promising effusively to store it in the safe. Looking forward to thoroughly exploring the picturesque town the next day,** they decided to go to bed early and get a really decent night's sleep. Despite the snoring and snuffling of the other hostelers, clearly audible through the paper-thin walls, they eventually drifted off. At seven the next morning, they were abruptly woken by the most ungodly row coming from the reception area. **Unconcerned about appearing in pyjamas,** they rushed down to see what was going on. The desk was surrounded by a crowd of furious hostel guests **all shouting at once in their various languages.** It turned out that during the night there had been a burglary and that all the valuables in the reception safe had been stolen … or at least this was the story the shifty-looking receptionist was sticking to. Jeremy and Sue were there in this remote town at the very beginning of what was to have been their dream trip and their passports, cameras and traveller's cheques were … who knows where. They stood there aghast and bewildered, the full enormity of the disaster only just beginning to dawn on them … .

---

*FURTHER PRACTICE: **Advanced Gold Exam Maximiser** p.100.*

Exam focus p.160

▶ Paper 3 English in Use: Part 2 (open cloze)

Read the exam information aloud to the class. Tell students to read the Suggested procedure silently. Set a ten-minute time limit for the task. Students work individually before checking their answers open-class.

ANSWERS

1 to   2 this   3 that   4 about   5 for   6 unlike   7 of
8 a   9 the   10 be   11 so   12 do   13 against   14 such
15 be

---

*FURTHER PRACTICE: **Advanced Gold Exam Maximiser** pp.100–101.*

Vocabulary: language of business p.160

1 Allow a few moments for students to look at the words and think about their meaning. Play the cassette. Students work individually before comparing their answers with a partner, and then open-class.

ANSWERS

a) turnover > Number 2
f) to go bankrupt > Number 3
b) get the sack > Number 4
d) be laid off > Number 5
c) to take maternity leave > Number 6
g) to work flexitime > Number 7
e) to take early retirement > Number 8

---

2 Students work in pairs before checking their answers open-class.

ANSWERS

1 maternity leave   2 gone bankrupt
3 taking early retirement   4 laid off   5 shareholders
6 got the sack   7 flexitime   8 turnover

---

3 (p.161) Students work in pairs before checking their answers open-class.

ANSWERS (suggested sentences)

a competitor: *One of our competitors has brought out a product that has captured over half our market share.*
compete (verb), competing (adj), competition (noun), competitive (adj), competitiveness (noun)
monopoly: *The US government claims that Microsoft has tried to create a monopoly.*
monopolistic (adj), monopolise (verb), monopolisation (noun)
production: *Production at our Morwell plant has increased by 15% in the last six months.*

---

produce (verb), produce (noun), producer (noun), product (noun), productive (adj), productively (adv), productiveness (noun), productivity (noun)

personnel: *Some of the senior personnel in the company are to be asked to take early retirement.*

manufacture: *We're hoping to begin manufacturing the shoes before the end of the year.*

manufacture (noun), manufacturer (noun), manufacturing (noun)

subsidiary: *The company have set up several wholly owned subsidiaries in Asia and the Pacific.*

subsidiarity (noun), subsidiary (adj)

promotion: *She hopes to get a promotion to Senior Branch Officer.*

promo (noun), promote (verb), promoter (noun), promotional (adj)

efficient: *He's the most efficient administrative assistant we've ever had.*

efficiency (noun), efficiently (adv), inefficient (adj)

economical: *Wouldn't it be more economical to buy paper in bulk?*

economic (adj), economically (adv), economics (noun), economist (noun), economise (verb), economy (noun), uneconomic (adj), uneconomical (adj)

investment: *Investment in microcredit schemes is on the increase.*

invest (verb), investor (noun)

viable: *I'm sorry to say that the company is no longer economically viable and will have to be wound up.*

viably (adv), viability (noun)

4   Students discuss the questions in groups, appointing a representative to report to the rest of the class.

*FURTHER PRACTICE: **Advanced Gold Exam Maximiser p.101.***

Speaking: starting your own business p.161

1 & 2   Divide the class into two groups. Two-thirds of the class should be 'business partners' and should work in pairs or groups of three. They should begin by choosing a business venture and then go on to discuss the questions in Exercise 2. The other third of the class are bank managers. They should work in pairs, planning questions to put to potential loan-seekers.

3   Put one 'bank manager' with each group of business partners. Monitor the role-plays and ask a good group to perform for the rest of the class. The others should listen and suggest improved strategies to the business partners and tougher questions for the bank managers.

4   The writing can be done in class or for homework.

English in Use p.162

▶ Paper 3, Part 1 (multiple-choice cloze)

1   Students discuss the questions in pairs, and then open-class.

2   Set a two-minute time limit for this.

> **ANSWERS**
>
> Pros:
> friendship with colleagues and opportunities to flirt with them;
> having an office phone to use for long-distance telephone calls to friends abroad;
> 'free' stationery and 'free time' to play computer games.
> Cons:
> stressful atmosphere;
> pressure to meet deadlines;
> poor salaries and career prospects;
> rigid working hours, boring tasks and lack of job security;
> old-fashioned equipment, poor lighting and uncomfortable chairs.

3   Set a ten-minute time limit. Students work individually before checking their answers with a partner, and then open-class.

> **ANSWERS**
>
> 1 D   2 A   3 C   4 D   5 A   6 B   7 D   8 B   9 A
> 10 D   11 C   12 C   13 D   14 A   15 C

*FURTHER PRACTICE: **Advanced Gold Exam Maximiser p.103.***

Writing: job application p.162

1   Students read the advertisement and discuss it in pairs before comparing their reactions with the rest of the class.

2   (p.163) Students work individually before checking their answers open-class.

> **ANSWERS**
>
> 1 in   2 for   3 from   4 of   5 in   6 about   7 of
> 8 with   9 to   10 at   11 to   12 to

3   Students work in pairs before sharing their answers with the rest of the class.

ANSWERS

'I am writing … '
'… in reply to your advertisement in the … of … .'
'… from my enclosed CV … '
'… have some experience of … ,'
'I feel very enthusiastic about the possibility of working
    with … '
'… I am available to attend an interview at any time which
    might be convenient.'
'Please don't hesitate to contact me at the above address if
    you need any further information.'
'I look forward to hearing from you.'

4   Students close their books and write the letters
individually. They should then compare letters with a partner,
and then check their work against the original.

5   Students work individually before comparing key words
and phrases with the rest of the class.

POSSIBLE KEY WORDS

on our farm   join in   various activities   fruit picking
working with animals   looking after the children
chance to improve your English
accommodation and food provided
small weekly allowance

6   (p.164) Students work individually.

7   Students work in pairs.

8   Students work individually. This can be done in class or
as homework.

FURTHER PRACTICE: **Advanced Gold Exam Maximiser
    pp.104–105.**

Vocabulary: phrasal verbs with *up/down* p.164

1   Students work with a partner before checking their
answers open-class.

ANSWERS

2 = meaning b
3 = meaning e
4 = meaning a
5 = meaning c

2 . Students work individually before checking their
answers open-class.

ANSWERS

1 up   2 down   3 up   4 down   5 up   6 up
7 up   8 down   9 up   10 down

3   Students work in pairs.

MEANINGS

catch up to come from behind and reach someone in front
    by going faster
keep up with to manage to go or learn as fast as
    someone
run up to to move closer to while running
wind up to turn something such as a handle or part of a
    machine around and around, especially in order to make
    something move or start working
freshen up to wash your hands and face in order to feel
    clean and comfortable
tidy up to make a place look tidy
liven up to become more exciting, or to make an event
    become more exciting
speed up to move or happen faster or make something
    move or happen faster
speak up used to ask someone to speak louder
narrow down to become less or make something less in
    range, difference, etc.
cut down on to reduce the amount of something that you
    eat, buy, use, etc.
calm down to become quiet after strong emotion or
    nervous activity, or make someone or something
    become quiet
settle down to stop talking or behaving in an excited way,
    or to make someone do this
close down if a company, shop etc. closes down or is
    closed down, it stops operating permanently
track down to find someone or something that is difficult
    to find by searching or making inquiries in several
    different places
sidle up to walk towards something or someone slowly
    and quietly, as if you do not want to be noticed
melt down to heat a metal object until it becomes a
    liquid, especially so that you can use the metal again
cool down to become cool or cooler, or make something
    do this
blaze up to burn with a brighter flame
creep up on to surprise someone by walking up behind
    them silently
touch up to improve something by changing it or adding
    to it slightly
mount up to gradually increase in size or amount

water down to make a statement, report etc less forceful by removing parts that may offend people; to add water to a liquid, especially for dishonest reasons; dilute

fix up to improve something or make it suitable

hunt down to catch someone in order to kill, hurt, or punish them, after chasing them or trying very hard to catch them

FURTHER PRACTICE: Advanced Gold Exam Maximiser p.102.

Unit 13 review p.165

ANSWERS

1 1 I'd like to freshen up before we eat.
2 This place needs to be livened up. …
3 We've narrowed down the number of possible candidates for the job to five. OR We've narrowed the number of possible candidates for the job down to five.
4 They settled down to watch the film.
5 The number of reports I have to write before the end of the month is mounting up.
6 I was sure some kind of animal was creeping up on me.

7 We are going to fix up the spare room so that … OR We are going to fix the spare room up so that …
8 He was furious because he was sure the orange juice had been watered down.

2 1 competitive   2 inefficient   3 manufacturing
4 viability   5 economist   6 productive   7 monopolises

3 1 ✓
2 ✓
3 ~~there~~ ➞ their
4 12, months ➞ 12 months (no comma)
5 university-degree ➞ university degree (no hyphen)
6 ~~possibilitys~~ ➞ possibilities
7 skills). ➞ skills. (no bracket)
8 ✓
9 ~~extremly~~ ➞ extremely
10 ~~Company~~ ➞ company (lower-case 'c')
11 ✓
12 more, than ➞ more than (no comma)
13 ~~british~~ ➞ British (capital 'B')
14 ~~headquaters~~ ➞ headquarters
15 ✓
16 lives' ➞ lives (no apostrophe)

UNIT
14 It's only natural

Listening p.166

1 Students work in groups, appointing a representative to tell the rest of the class about their words and phrases.

2 Play the cassette while students read the poem. Discuss the question open-class.

ANSWER

He is in awe of them. Evidence: 'Tiger and devil and bard'; 'And he sings to the stars of the jungle nights, Ere cities were, or laws.'

3 (p.167) Play the cassette. Students work individually. Check stress marking open-class. Students then work in pairs, reading the poem to each other. Get a good reader to read to the whole class.

STRESSED WORDS/SYLLABLES

At <u>mid</u>night in the <u>alley</u>
A <u>Tom-cat comes to</u> wail,
And he <u>chants</u> the <u>hate</u> of a <u>million years</u>
As he <u>swings</u> his <u>snaky tail</u>.

<u>Male</u>volent, <u>bony</u>, <u>brindled</u>,
<u>Tiger</u> and <u>devil</u> and <u>bard</u>,
His <u>eyes</u> are <u>coals</u> from the <u>middle</u> of <u>Hell</u>
And his <u>heart</u> is <u>black</u> and <u>hard</u>.

He <u>twists</u> and <u>crouches</u> and <u>capers</u>
And <u>bares</u> his <u>curved sharp claws</u>,
And he <u>sings</u> to the <u>stars</u> of the <u>jungle nights</u>,
Ere <u>cities</u> were, or <u>laws</u>.

<u>Beast</u> from a <u>world</u> primeval,
<u>He</u> and his <u>leaping clan</u>,
When the <u>blotched red moon leers</u> over the <u>roofs</u>
Give <u>voice</u> to their <u>scorn</u> of <u>man</u>.

He will <u>lie</u> on a <u>rug</u> tomorrow
And <u>lick</u> his <u>silky fur</u>,
And <u>veil</u> the <u>brute</u> in his <u>yellow eyes</u>
And <u>play</u> he's <u>tame</u>, and <u>purr</u>.

But at <u>mid</u>night in the <u>alley</u>
He will <u>crouch again</u> and <u>wail</u>,
And <u>beat</u> the <u>time</u> for his <u>demon's song</u>
With a <u>swing</u> of his <u>demon's tail</u>.

BACKGROUND INFORMATION: The poem is by Don Marquis (1878–1937), an American newspaper columnist and poet. He is famous for his two characters, Archy, a poet reincarnated as a cockroach who types messages on Marquis's typewriter all in lower case, and Mehitabel, the cat with whom Archy has an intense rivalry. Students can read further examples of Don Marquis's work on: www.halcyon.com/jim/donmarquis.

Exam focus p.167

▶ Paper 3 English in Use: Part 4 (word formation)

Read the exam information aloud to the class. Students read the Suggested procedure silently. Set a ten-minute time limit for the task. Check answers open-class.

ANSWERS

1 talkative   2 unimaginable   3 similarities   4 knowing
5 scientific   6 consciousness   7 definition   8 exhibition
9 activity   10 visible   11 unpredictable   12 sensational
13 unrivalled   14 composition   15 strength

FURTHER PRACTICE: Advanced Gold Exam Maximiser p.107.

Reading p.168

▶ Paper 1, Part 3 (multiple choice)

1 Students discuss the questions in groups, appointing a representative to report their discussion to the rest of the class. Explain that the title contains a pun on the word 'tale', which means 'story', and is a homophone of 'tail', i.e. 'the moveable part at the back of an animal's body'.

POSSIBLE ANSWERS

Pandas, orang-utans. Like tigers, both these animals are gradually having their habitat encroached upon by humans.

2 Enforce the seventeen to eighteen-minute time limit. Students work individually before checking their answers with a partner, and then open-class. Insist on justifications for answers.

ANSWERS

1 C (lines 2–6) 2 A (line 18) 3 D (lines 43–44)
4 D (lines 55–56) 5 B (lines 63–64) 6 A (line 76)

3 (p.169) Students discuss the questions in groups, appointing a representative to report their discussion to the rest of the class.

FURTHER PRACTICE: *Advanced Gold Exam Maximiser*
pp.108–109.

Grammar plus: reported speech (advanced features) p.170

1 Students work in pairs before checking their answers open-class.

ANSWERS

1 'From my observations, the tiger is cruel.' (lines 54–55)
2 'Sita is not at all comfortable with humans on foot,' (lines 59–60)
3 'but if you want to watch her properly, the best thing is to get up on an elephant.' (lines 60–62)
4 'We put seven cameras around the park.' (lines 65–66)
5 'I want to get more photos of Sita's cubs though.' (lines 69–70)
6 'She might have a year or so left …' (lines 74–75)

2 Students work in pairs before checking their answers open-class.

ANSWERS

Rule 1 - Reported speech sentence 6
Rule 2 - Reported speech sentence 4
Rule 3 - Reported speech sentence 5
Rule 4 - Reported speech sentence 2
Rule 5 - Reported speech sentence 3
Rule 6 - Reported speech sentence 1

Refer students to the **Grammar reference** on p.196 of the *Advanced Gold Coursebook*.

3 Students work individually before checking their answers with a partner, and then open-class.

ANSWERS

1 We agreed that we **would/should/could/might** all spend the night at Jim's house.
2 It **is** believed that the poachers responsible for the recent killings all live locally.
3 ✓
4 He disagreed with my view **that** it was wrong to put animals in zoos.
5 ✓
6 ✓
7 It has **been** announced that the government will raise interest rates next week.
8 ✓

4 Play the cassette. Students note what they hear. They should then work with a partner to choose a reporting verb and write their sentences. Check answers open-class.

ANSWERS

2 She reminded me/us/him etc. not to forget to get my/our/his etc. grandmother a birthday card.
3 He advised me/her/them etc. to make sure that I/she/they etc. talked it over with my/her/their parents/mum and dad.
4 She warned me/us/him not to make the same stupid mistake that she had made.
5 She congratulated us/them etc. on our/their etc. engagement.
6 He/I etc. introduced Sarah and Michael to each other.
7 He has decided not to go back to college next year. OR … that he won't go back to college next year.
8 He/She complained about the food./that the food was not hot.
9 She admitted that she had been/to going out with Matthew for the evening.
(See **Tapescript** on p.130.)

5 Students work in pairs before listening to the cassette and checking their answers open-class.

POSSIBLE ANSWERS (as on recording)

1 It's true. I know I was wrong to get angry.
2 Well, far be it from me to brag, but you know I did earn over £100,000 last year.
3 No, I've certainly never met him before.
4 Well at least I know how to keep a secret!
5 You really ought to think very carefully about what you are doing.
6 You do realise this will be your last chance.

7 … so, really, I need to change things completely, once and for all …
8 Rebecca, Rebecca, Rebecca …

6 Students work individually before comparing versions with a partner, and then open-class.

POSSIBLE SUMMARY

The man said that he and his girlfriend had been getting on really well, but the woman had a different view. She thought that it had never really been right for her and that he had then started to take her for granted and to order her around. Unfortunately, according to the woman, when she tried to talk to him about it he refused to listen. She felt she had no option but to end the relationship. His perspective, however, was that it was the woman who had suddenly changed and had begun to criticise him for no apparent reason. He claims that he still does not understand why she broke off the relationship.
(See **Tapescript** on p.130.)

FURTHER PRACTICE: **Advanced Gold Exam Maximiser p.110.**

Vocabulary: text-referring words p.171

1 Focus attention on the extract. Elicit the words open-class.

ANSWERS

drowned   was savaged   have been lost

2 Students work in pairs before checking their answers open-class.

ANSWERS

1 question   2 problem   3 topic   4 situation
5 aspect   6 view   7 trend   8 issue

3 Students work in pairs before checking their answers open-class.

ANSWERS

1 situation/state of affairs   2 key/solution

FURTHER PRACTICE: **Advanced Gold Exam Maximiser p.111.**

Listening p.172

▶ **Paper 4, Part 2** (note taking)

1 Students work in groups, appointing a representative to report their discussion to the rest of the class.

POSSIBLE ANSWERS

1 They are both volcanoes that have had famous eruptions. Vesuvius is in Italy; Krakatoa (Krakatau) is in Indonesia. When Vesuvius erupted in 79 AD, the towns of Pompeii and Herculaneum (near present-day Naples) were completely buried. Krakatoa erupted in 1883 enveloping the surrounding islands and much of the rest of the southern hemisphere in a dense cloud of smoke. The eruption destroyed most of the island of Krakatau and only a remnant remains today.

2 Tsunamis (or tidal waves): The villages of Sissano, Warapu, Arop and Malol in Papua New Guinea were hit by a tsunami on 17 July, 1998. 2000 people died.

Earthquakes: San Francisco 1906. Statistics vary but one estimate puts the number of deaths caused directly or indirectly by the earthquake at 3000. 225,000 people were made homeless and 28,000 buildings were destroyed. The 'cost' of the earthquake is estimated at $400 million. An earthquake in Lisbon in 1755 caused the deaths of 60,000 people. The following are some more recent major earthquakes with human casualties and devastating damage to property: Chile 1960; Kobe (Japan) 1995; Taiwan, Turkey and Athens 1999; El Salvador 2000; India 2001.

Floods: Poland 1998, Venezuela 1999.
Epidemics: The pneumonic flu pandemic of 1918, which killed an estimated 40 million people.

2 Allow a minute for students to read through the questions. Play the cassette. Check answers open-class, replaying the cassette where necessary.

ALTERNATIVE PROCEDURE distribute copies of the **Tapescript** on p.130, so that students can correct their own work.

ANSWERS

1 sun turned blue   2 1,511   3 Turkey
4 500 million   5 sun and moon   6 carbon dioxide
7 7 days   8 people to move

BACKGROUND INFORMATION: Students might enjoy looking at the following website, which is dedicated to volcanoes: http://volcano.und.nodak.edu/vw.html. It includes images of volcanoes as well as excellent geological and historical information. There are links to the Vesuvius homepage with more detailed information about a possible eruption.

FURTHER PRACTICE: *Advanced Gold Exam Maximiser* **p.111.**

Vocabulary: word + prepositions p.172

1 Students work individually before checking their answers with a partner, and then open-class.

> **ANSWERS**
>
> 1 for 2 about 3 by 4 of 5 to 6 for 7 of

2 Students work individually before checking their answers with a partner, and then open-class.

> **ANSWERS**
>
> 2 i 3 a 4 h 5 b 6 c 7 d 8 e 9 g

3 (p.173) Students work individually before checking the prepositions open-class.

> **ANSWERS**
>
> due **for**   concerned **about**   shocked **by**   critical **of**
> indifferent **to**   responsible **for**   capable **of**
> eligible **for**   immune **to**   irrespective **of**   baffled **by**
> absent **from**   addicted **to**   anxious **about**   wrong **with**

4 Students work individually completing the sentences before getting up and mingling and reading their sentences to as many people as possible. How many people completed the sentences in a similar way?

FURTHER PRACTICE: *Advanced Gold Exam Maximiser* **p.106.**

English in Use p.173

▶ **Paper 3, Part 5** (register transfer)

Read the exam information aloud to the class. Students work individually before checking their answers with a partner, and then open-class.

> **ANSWERS**
>
> 1 cared   2 responsibility   3 important/vital/necessary
> 4 bills/treatment   5 arrangements   6 condition/shape
> 7 acceptable   8 balance/combination   9 basis/foundation
> 10 dictate   11 elimination   12 emphasised/stressed
> 13 avoid

Speaking: sounding interested p.174

1 Focus attention on the questions. Play the cassette. Elicit answers to the questions open-class.

> **ANSWERS**
>
> 1 the third speaker
> 2 the first speaker
> 3 Lack of interest has a negative effect on the listener, whereas sounding involved involves the listener too and therefore creates a positive impression.

2 Students work in pairs. Monitor, and get a good pair to perform for the rest of the class.

3 Students work in pairs but with different partners to those in Exercise 2. Choose a good pair to repeat their discussion for the rest of the class. Do the other students agree with what they say?

Writing: report (2) p.174

1 Students work in pairs before comparing their answers with the rest of the class.

> **ANSWERS**
>
> Plan C is the best of the three as sections 2, 3 and 4 cover the main points in the task input. The other plans omit some points and add other irrelevant points.

2 (p.175) Students work in pairs before discussing their answers with the rest of the class.

> **ANSWER**
>
> The one point that should not be there is point 8.

3 Students work individually before checking their answers open-class.

> **ANSWERS**
>
> 1 Plan C
> 2 All the Dos and Don'ts are covered.

4, 5, 6 These can be done in class or for homework.

FURTHER PRACTICE: *Advanced Gold Exam Maximiser* **p.112.**

Listening: weather p.176

▶ **Paper 4, Part 4** (multiple matching)

Tell the students to read the instructions and the questions. Play the cassette. Pause for thirty seconds. Play the cassette again. Check answers open-class, replaying the cassette where necessary.

ALTERNATIVE PROCEDURE: distribute copies of the **Tapescript** on p.131, so that students can correct their own work.

ANSWERS

D 1   H 2   G 3   C 4   B 5   G 6   B 7   F 8   A 9   H 10

Grammar check: countable/uncountable nouns p.176

1   Students work in pairs before checking their answers open-class.

ANSWERS

1 **advice** ('advice' is an uncountable noun)
2 **iron** (the uncountable noun 'iron' is the metal, while 'an iron' is an electrical appliance used for making cloth and clothes smooth)
3 **much news** ('news' is uncountable, therefore 'many news' is impossible)
4 **a very interesting time** ('an occasion' = the count noun; the uncountable noun would not be possible here)
5 **space** (meaning = what is outside the Earth's air, where the stars and planets are; 'the space' (the countable noun = area) would be unlikely here)
6 **information** ('information' is an uncountable noun, therefore 'an information' is impossible)
7 **research** ('research' is uncountable, therefore 'a research' is impossible here)
8 **a hair** (it is unlikely that there would be more than one, therefore the uncountable noun is unlikely)
9 **Travel** ('travel' is uncountable, therefore 'a travel' is impossible)
10 both are possible though 'a coffee' (meaning a cup of coffee) is more likely; 'coffee' (meaning perhaps several cups of coffee) is also possible.

2   Students work in groups, appointing a representative to report to the rest of the class.

POSSIBLE ANSWERS

Common uncountable nouns: accommodation, advice, behaviour, bread, copper (and all other metals), English (and all other languages), furniture, health, knowledge, luggage, news, progress, research, rice (and all other grains and cereals), salt (and all other condiments, e.g. pepper), scenery, spaghetti, traffic, travel, trouble, water (and all other liquids), weather, work.

Nouns which can be countable and uncountable: egg ('Would you like a boiled egg?' 'You've spilt egg on your tie.'); chicken ('I bought a chicken to have for Sunday lunch.' 'There was a choice between chicken and fish on the plane.'); glass ('Pass me a glass and I'll pour you a drink.' 'What did people use for windows before they invented glass?').

Normally uncountable nouns that are used to refer to particular varieties: wine ('Would you like wine with your meal?' 'They produce a very good white wine on that island.'); coffee, tea, beer, etc. (the countable noun means 'a glass, cup, can or bottle of'); time, space, room ('There's room for one more in this compartment.' 'Have you got a single room for the night?'); paper ('We need to get some more paper for the printer.' 'Have you read the headlines in today's paper?'); experience ('Have you had much experience of this kind of work?' 'My summer in France was one of the most positive experiences I've ever had.'); pity ('What a pity Marie couldn't be here.' 'Feeling pity is not the same as feeling genuine compassion.'); abstract nouns such as 'difference', 'point', 'reason', 'right', 'difficulty', 'chance', 'question' after 'little', 'much' and other determiners ('He's got as much right to be here as you have.' 'Freedom of speech is a fundamental right.')

3   Students work in groups, appointing a representative to report their discussion to the rest of the class.

ANSWERS

1 advice   2 right   happiness   wealth   3 love   bread

BACKGROUND INFORMATION: **Lord Chesterfield** (1694–1773) wrote letters to his son which are full of little gems of wisdom. The letters were never intended for publication but remain in print.

George Bernard Shaw was born in 1856 in Dublin. He moved to London at the age of 20 and began to write. He was a member of the socialist Fabian Society, which campaigned for improved conditions for industrial workers. He is the author of *Pygmalion*, the play on which the film *My Fair Lady* was based. He wrote a large number of other plays, among them *Candida*, which was written in 1897.

He won the Nobel Prize for Literature in 1925. He lived to the age of 94.

Ursula Le Guin (b.1929, Berkeley, California) is a science fiction and fantasy writer. She also writes poetry, short stories, essays on science fiction and children's fiction. Apart from *The Lathe of Heaven* (1971), she is well known for her novels *The Dispossessed* (1974) and *The Left Hand of Darkness* (1969).

FURTHER PRACTICE: **Advanced Gold Exam Maximiser p.106.**

Unit 14 review p.177

ANSWERS

1 1 congratulated   2 urged   3 boasted   4 conceded
  5 warned   6 remind   7 whispered   8 complained

2 (possible answers)
  1 situation   2 solution   3 aspect (of)   4 response
  5 topic   6 view   7 trend   8 issue

3 1 D   2 G   3 I   4 A   5 C   6 H

15 It's all in the past

Reading p.178

▶ **Paper 1, Part 2** (gapped text)

1 Students discuss the photographs in groups.

2 Set a two-minute time limit for this.

ANSWERS

1 That they were human sacrifices of deserters and cowards to the Mother Goddess.
2 They will disappear as developers exploit the bogs more and more.

3 (p.179) Set a twelve-minute time limit. Students work individually before checking their answers open-class. Insist on justifications for answers.

ANSWERS

1 D
Rick <u>Turner</u> ... (line 10);
What Rick <u>Turner</u> was to <u>unearth</u> ... would become known as <u>Lindlow Man</u> ... (lines 13–15);
<u>Turner's</u> life ... (line 18); Today, <u>he</u> still feels great affection for <u>the man whose remains he saved then</u> (Para D);
... it soon became <u>obvious to Turner</u> that he had stumbled on an extremely rare and important find (para D);
In the end, <u>it was not just Turner</u> ... (line 22).
2 G
... <u>multi-disciplinary project</u> ... <u>the best of modern archaeology</u> (lines 30–31);
Many things came of <u>this work</u>. (Para G);
<u>The contents of his stomach</u> were well-preserved ... they consisted largely of <u>a chapati-like bread made from two varieties of wheat and barley</u> (Para G);
Hi-tech scientific analysis of the remnants of <u>this last meal</u> (lines 32–33).
3 A
... a hole in the top of his head ... a neat cut in his throat ... (lines 43–45);
In addition to <u>these</u>, the forensic report on the body identified <u>two further injuries</u> (Para A).

4 F
... why are they <u>preserved</u> so well? (lines 55–56);
skin ... exceptionally <u>well-preserved</u> ... (Para F);
It used to be thought that the key to <u>preservation</u> ... (lines 57–58).
5 B
But ... (Para B);
The Danish archaeologist, P.V. Glob ... (Para B);
<u>He</u> noted ... (line 69).
6 E
... <u>it seems</u>, were spring sacrifices of such people to the Mother Goddess. (lines 74–76);
<u>This, however</u> ... (Para E);
... <u>industrial peat quarrying</u> ... has all but <u>removed the bogs</u> ... (Para E);
With <u>the loss</u> of unique <u>environments and ecosystems</u> ... (lines 77–78).

*FURTHER PRACTICE: **Advanced Gold Exam Maximiser** pp.114–115.*

Grammar plus: passives (advanced features) p.180

1 Students work individually before checking their answers open-class.

ANSWERS

1 He has been besieged by local reporters.
2 Funding for archaeological research was to be significantly reduced.

2 Students work in pairs before checking their answers open-class.

ANSWERS

It is believed: Use 2
... was called: Use 1
... has been besieged ...: Use 4
... would be significantly reduced: Use 3

3 Students work individually before checking their answers with a partner, and then open-class.

ANSWERS

1 Unfortunately over 20% of the workforce is going to be made redundant.
2 (no transformation possible)
3 It is said that archaeologists …
4 (no transformation possible)
5 It is believed that …
6 … she was sent a large cheque …
7 Your room must be cleaned up …

4   Students listen to the cassette.

1 Either let students practise reading the report in pairs or get them to 'read along' with the recording.

2 Students work in pairs.

3 They read their reports to another pair. Monitor and get good pairs to read their reports to the whole class.

Refer students to the **Grammar reference** on p.195 of the *Advanced Gold Coursebook*.

FURTHER PRACTICE: **Advanced Gold Exam Maximiser p.116.**

Listening: a world language p.181

▶ **Paper 4, Part 1** (sentence completion)

1   Students discuss the questions in groups, appointing a representative to report their discussion to the rest of the class.

POSSIBLE ANSWERS

Esperanto is probably the best example. It is still spoken and used by hundreds of thousands of people, though it is yet to achieve status as a world language. Students can find an enormous amount of information on Esperanto (in no less than 41 languages including Middle English) at: http://www.esperanto.net. If they want to try their hands at learning Esperanto, they can do so at: http://www.tios.cs.utwente.nl/esperanto/hypercourse/index.html. There is a webring (a collection of related websites) called Scattered Tongues at: http://www.idi.ntnu.no/~hannemo/sc/index.html. This has information on a wide number of constructed languages, including languages constructed for science fiction films, and books and information about how to go about constructing a language.

2   Allow a minute for students to study the questions. Play the cassette. Pause for thirty seconds. Play the cassette again. Check answers open-class, replaying sections of the cassette as required.

ALTERNATIVE PROCEDURE: distribute copies of the **Tapescript** on p.132, so that students can correct their own work.

ANSWERS

1 alphabet   2 existing languages   3 learning to speak
4 German grammar   5 linguistic confusion
6 international understanding   7 European
8 radio programmes

3   Students discuss the questions in groups, appointing a representative to report their discussion to the rest of the class.

English in Use p.181

▶ **Paper 3, Part 3** (error correction, extra word)

1   Students discuss the questions in groups, appointing a representative to report their discussion to the rest of the class.

2   (p.182) Set a twelve-minute time limit. Students work individually before checking their answers open-class.

ANSWERS

1 out   2 ✓   3 up   4 ✓   5 of   6 ✓   7 those
8 himself   9 made   10 were   11 up   12 ✓   13 the
14 which   15 ✓   16 to

3   Students work with a partner deciding on the word class of the items in 2. Check answers open-class. Refer students to the **Exam focus** section on Part 3, Error correction on page 28. They work with a partner noting further word classes that occur in this task type.

ANSWERS

Word classes in 2: 1 preposition/adverb
3 preposition/adverb   5 preposition
7 determiner/pronoun   8 pronoun   9 verb   10 verb
11 preposition/adverb   13 article   14 pronoun
16 preposition
Other word classes tested: conjunctions (so, because, because of), qualifiers (quite)

FURTHER PRACTICE: **Advanced Gold Exam Maximiser p.117.**

Speaking p.182

Students discuss the questions in groups, appointing a representative to report their discussion to the rest of the class.

Grammar check: *have/get something done* p.183

1   Students work individually before checking their answers in pairs, and then open-class.

ANSWERS

1 I'm having my car repaired at the moment.
2 'Get your hair cut!' he shouted/said/ordered.
3 I'll have you arrested if you do that again.
4 I eventually got my computer fixed.
5 I won't have you use/using my house as a hotel.
6 I won't get my homework done until 9 p.m.

2   Students work in pairs before checking their answers open-class.

ANSWERS

1 True (1, 3 and 4 from Exercise 1)
2 True (example sentence from Exercise 1)
3 True (6 from Exercise 1)
4 True (2 from Exercise 1)
5 False ('have something done' is used in more formal contexts than 'get something done')

3   Students work individually before getting up and mingling. They should tell other students what they would do and make a note of anyone who had the same ideas. Find out how many people would have the same things done.

*FURTHER PRACTICE: **Advanced Gold Exam Maximiser** p.118.*

Vocabulary: idiomatic language of talking/communication p.183

1   Students work in pairs before comparing their answers with the rest of the class.

ANSWERS

1 **to say the least** used to say that you could have described something, criticized someone etc a lot more severely than you have
2 **(making) small talk** (having) polite friendly conversation about unimportant subjects
3 **give someone a talking-to** to talk to someone angrily because you are annoyed about something they have done
4 **get to the point** (used to tell someone) to reach the most important part of what they want to say

5 **talk shop** to talk about things that are connected to your work, especially in a way that other people find boring
6 **can't make head or tail of** to be completely unable to understand something
7 **get the wrong end of the stick** to misunderstand one small thing that makes you misunderstand everything about a particular situation
8 **get a word in edgeways** to get a chance to speak
9 **(talk) at cross-purposes** two people who are at cross-purposes do not understand each other, because they are talking about different things but do not realize it
10 **talk down to** to talk to someone as if they were stupid when in fact they are not

2   Students work in pairs. Get each pair to demonstrate one of the expressions for the rest of the class.

POSSIBLE DIALOGUES

1 A: To be quite frank with you, she's never been what you'd call an ideal neighbour.
  B: To say the least!
  A: Yes, you're right. She's really been a complete disaster.
2 A: I thought they were talking about something interesting so I went in to listen, but it turned out he was telling her about a new washing powder and then she went on to talk about a football match she'd seen on TV.
  B: So, they were just making small talk then.
3 A: Well, I finally decided I would tell him we were all pretty fed up with his playing loud music so late at night and that he shouldn't leave his rubbish on the stairs in such hot weather but that he should wait until just before the bins are collected to put it out and that his dog often barks when he goes out.
  B: It sounds like you gave him a really good talking-to.
4 A: Well, first he said that he'd always really liked me and that he'd often wanted to get to know me a bit better, and then he said how interesting he thought I was and that he'd really like to know more about what I did, but that sometimes it was difficult for him to express his feelings and that he worried that he might embarrass me or upset me even …
  B: You must have been wishing he'd get to the point!
5 A: Well, then he started asking me about the report I'd been working on and whether or not I'd be willing to lend him the software package I used to analyse the statistics.
  B: Oh no! So he started talking shop.

6 A: Yes, he went on and on about all sorts of different computer programmes you could use to produce these really elaborate graphs to display the results of the survey and how if you applied this or that formula you could get a very different result.

B: I'm sure I wouldn't have been able to <u>make head or tail</u> of it.

7 A: I'm sure I told her we'd be meeting outside the entrance to the cinema and then going to Don Simon's to have dinner before the film. I can't understand why she isn't here yet.

B: Perhaps she <u>got the wrong end of the stick</u> and thought we were all meeting at the restaurant.

8 a: Well, in fact I didn't speak to her. I left a message with her boyfriend Nigel and you know how he is. He started telling me about the restaurant they took his parents to for their wedding anniversary and how delicious the food was and how cheap it was, all things considered.

B: I can imagine. I bet you could hardly <u>get a word in edgeways</u>.

9 A: It turned out that she was referring to the meeting we had on the 10th of January and I was looking at the minutes of the meeting of the 10th of February.

B: Oh no! So you'd been <u>talking at cross-purposes</u>.

10 A: He's so patronising! He started off by actually telling me how to switch on the computer and then he said 'I'll show you how to use this fantastic word processing package called 'Word' though it will probably be a bit sophisticated for you.'

B: Unbelievable! He always <u>talks down to</u> me too.

3 Students discuss the questions in groups, appointing a representative to report their discussion to the rest of the class.

FURTHER PRACTICE: **Advanced Gold Exam Maximiser p.116.**

Exam focus p.184

▶ Paper 4 Listening: Part 4 (multiple choice)

Read the exam information aloud to the class. Students study the Suggested procedure silently. Allow a minute for students to look through the questions. Play the cassette. Pause for thirty seconds. Play the cassette again. Check answers open-class.

ALTERNATIVE PROCEDURE: distribute copies of the **Tapescript** on p.132. Students correct their own work.

ANSWERS

1 A 2 B 3 C 4 C 5 C 6 A 7 A 8 B 9 B 10 A
(See **Tapescript** on p.132.)

FURTHER PRACTICE: **Advanced Gold Exam Maximiser p.113.**

Vocabulary: revision p.185

Students work in groups.

EXTRA ACTIVITY: Each group chooses ten questions to put to the other groups. Play a revision game where groups ask each other their revision questions.

FURTHER PRACTICE: **Advanced Gold Exam Maximiser p.119.**

Speaking p.185

1 Students work in groups, appointing a representative to report their discussion to the rest of the class.

2 Students work individually, reading the idea, and then with a partner, before comparing ideas with the rest of the class.

Writing: Paper 2 overview p.186

1 Read the exam information aloud to the class.

2 Students work in pairs before reporting their discussion to the rest of the class.

3 Students work individually.

4 Students work individually before comparing answers with a partner, and then with the rest of the class.

ANSWER

Band 3

5 (p.187) Students work with a partner.

POSSIBLE IMPROVED ANSWER

The most thrilling, exhilarating and inspiring holiday I've ever had was when I rode my Harley Davidson 500cc with a group of friends to the south of Sinai.

We'd all been slaving away in Cairo for six months and this was to be our well-earned reward for so much hard work. The mere idea of escaping the constant barrage of noise and the ever-present pollution in this, one of the biggest cities in the world, was absolutely blissful.

We set off from Cairo on three bikes: my Harley, Tina's Honda Gold Wing and Nigel's Triumph. After much debate we decided on the coast road as it would give us the best views. We shoved our snorkels, masks, cameras and a couple of clean T-shirts each into our panniers and we were off.

I don't think there's anything that really compares to the feeling of freedom you get on a bike on the open road. The scenery was amazing. It was incredibly rocky and sometimes quite lonely and desolate. About halfway down the coast we stopped to see St. Catherine's monastery. It's a really magical place and you can even stay overnight and fully soak up the atmosphere. In fact we decided to walk up nearby Mt. St. Catherine so that we could see the sun rise. We sat in silence together and savoured the moment. It was extraordinarily beautiful.

We continued our journey down to Sharm el Sheikh in the south, staying at a cheap but cheerful hotel and spending our days snorkelling or scuba diving. There's an incredible range of fish and coral and the colours are out of this world. In the evenings we'd sit out sipping cups of mint tea under the stars and talking to the other travellers who'd chanced upon this wonderful spot. Among them were some Australians. Somehow one guy and I really took to one another. We still keep in touch even after all these years and we often reminisce about that very special time we had together in Egypt.

6   1 Students work individually. 2 Students work with a partner. 3 Students work individually. This can be done in class or for homework.

7   Students exchange work with a partner.

8   Students work individually. This can be done in class or for homework.

FURTHER PRACTICE: Advanced Gold Exam Maximiser p.118.

Certificate in Advanced English quiz
p.188

Students work individually before checking their answers open class.

ANSWERS

1 Five: Paper 1 Reading, Paper 2 Writing, Paper 3 English in Use, Paper 4 Listening, Paper 5 Speaking.

2 40 marks.

3 No. The grade is based on the total score for all five papers.

4 Reading 1 hour 15 minutes; Writing 2 hours; English in Use 1hour 30 minutes; Listening 45 minutes (approximately); Speaking 15 minutes.

5 Yes, though the question papers are collected at the end of each test for security reasons. It is essential to transfer your answer to the answer sheets.

6 No.

7 Newspaper and magazine articles, contributions to leaflets and brochures, notices, announcements, personal notes and messages, formal and informal letters, reports, reviews, competition entries, information sheets and memos.

8 In pen.

9 Nothing if you only write a few too many, If your answer is a long way over the word limit you will lose marks.

10 Part 1 Multiple-choice cloze, Part 2 Open cloze, Part 3 Error correction (extra word OR spelling and punctuation), Part 4 Word formation, Part 5 Register transfer, Part 6 Gapped text.

11 If both answers are correct the candidate is awarded the mark(s); if one answer is incorrect no marks are awarded (this is the same in Paper 4).

12 All spellings must be correct.

13 In part 2 only.

14 There may be sound effects to set the scene but not while there is speech.

15 Common words and words that are easy to spell are expected to be correct.

16 Yes.

17 It doesn't make any difference.

18 The examiners are trained to make sure that both candidates have plenty of opportunity to speak.

19 You get the results by post about six weeks after taking the exam.

20 You get a slip of paper telling you what grade you got overall (A, B, C, D and E). D and E are fail grades. If you pass, the slip indicates which papers you did particularly well in and if you fail, it tells you which papers were weakest. About a month after getting your results you will receive a certificate if you passed CAE.

Units 11–15 progress check p.189

The Progress check can be treated as an open-book exam in which students do the exercises, looking back to relevant sections of the units as necessary. It can be done in class or for homework. Alternately, students can revise the **Vocabulary**, **Grammar** and **English in Use** sections of the previous five units before tackling the Progress check, once again either in class or for homework.

Check answers open-class or provide students with copies of this key so that they can correct their own work.

ANSWERS

1   See Unit 11 Grammar plus: relative clauses

ANSWERS

1   What are the names of the three students who have just arrived from Cyprus? (no comma before 'who')
2   Saint Michel en Grève, where my friend Gillian lives, really took my breath away.
3   Most people are really taken with the islands, which are all very different from one another.
4   My letter, to which I have received no reply, was sent on 1st December.
5   In 1975 she published her theory, which met with immediate derision from other psychologists.
6   Is that your cousin who's standing next to you in the photo? (no comma before 'who's')
7   ✓
8   ✓

2   See Unit 11 Vocabulary: expressive descriptions

ANSWER

2 Actually   3 Presumably   4 clearly/obviously
5 naturally/frankly   6 Surely   7 Personally   8 Basically
9 obviously/clearly/presumably   10 Obviously/Naturally

3   See Unit 13 Training.

ANSWER

1 one   2 also   3 no   4 until   5 against   6 where
7 from   8 had   9 by   10 majority   11 including   12 of
13 whose   14 from   15 more

4   See Unit 12 Grammar plus: emphasis with inversion

ANSWERS

1   Never before had I set out on such a long journey alone.
2   Not only is he intelligent and kind-hearted, he's also really good-looking.
3   Rarely have I met such a rude man as Carl.
4   At no time should you let the cats out.
5   Hardly had I got back from my holiday when I heard the news.

5   See Unit 12 Vocabulary: expressions with *take*

ANSWERS

1 out   2 for   3 on   4 away   5 upon   6 up   7 in
8 to   9 for   10 as

6

ANSWERS

a 9   b 7   c 8   d 3   e 10   f 2   g 4   h 5   i 1   j 6

7   See Unit 15 Training.

ANSWERS

1 ✓   2 it   3 on   4 the   5 who   6 to   7 ✓   8 are
9 it   10 for   11 of   12 a   13 is   14 ✓   15 ✓

8   See Unit 13 Vocabulary: language of business

ANSWERS

1 cool   2 speak   3 Calm   4 liven   5 narrowed
6 catch   7 track   8 speed   9 creep   10 cut

9   See Unit 13 Grammar plus: participle clauses.

ANSWERS

1 b   2 c   3 a   4 f   5 g   6 d   7 e

10   See Unit 13 Vocabulary: language of business

ANSWERS

1 to **go** bankrupt   2 to **go** on strike
3 to **take** early retirement   4 to **work** flexitime
5 to **get** the sack   6 to **be** laid off
7 to **take** maternity leave

11   See Unit 11: Exam focus: Paper 3 English in Use: Part 5 (register transfer).

1 take off   2 everyone   3 be/seem   4 give you   5 to eat
6 and see   7 anyone does   8 take   9 get there
10 you leave   11 bit before   12 very important
13 have to

Tapescripts

UNIT 1

page 9, Listening, Exercises 2, 3 and 4

Presenter: Hello, welcome to Fabulous Families, the programme where we get to meet families with a difference. Today we have with us a mother and daughter both firmly rooted in the circus tradition.

Elena Lev, 16, is one of the youngest performers in the internationally acclaimed Cirque du Soleil. Born in Moscow, she began training at the age of six as a rhythmic gymnast, with her mother. Her act, which involves spinning large numbers of golden metal hoops around herself, combines the grace and agility of a gymnast with the flexibility of a contortionist and the dexterity of a juggler.

Elena, not many people share their working lives with their parents. Tell us a little about what it's like to actually live and work with your mother.

Elena (Junior): Well, my mother is definitely the biggest part of my life. I mean, although it's me who gets the applause after a performance, in my heart I know that if she hadn't been pushing me since I was three years old, I wouldn't be a centre of attention.

Really, since I was little, my memories are of having a mother and a coach who are the same person. Apart from my few hours of school each day, we're always together.

And I suppose it's because I trust her completely that I always try my best to do whatever she asks.

P: Many people will be wondering how you feel about leading such a unique lifestyle. Do you ever feel that you're missing out on some of the things that other young people enjoy?

E (Jr): Well, really my life isn't so different. I mean, like other teenagers, I do have to do school work of course. And I have lots of friends in Cirque du Soleil, so how I live feels pretty normal to me. It's a really very rich life, with lots of opportunities to travel and learn different languages, but, I guess, it's also a life of restrictions because of the training schedule. But, you know, this is something I totally accept, because, after all, it's what I choose to do.

P: And what about the constant moving around. Does that ever bother you?

E (Jr): Well, for 11 years I lived in Moscow, but then, after we joined Cirque du Soleil and started travelling, I suppose, 'home' really became whatever city we were working in. And that's been fine.

P: Now perhaps we could turn to the senior member of this partnership for a moment. Elena, perhaps you could tell us a little about your daughter's early years. Was it obvious she was going to follow the family circus tradition?

Elena (Senior): Well I think it was from the time that Elena was barely three years old … she seemed to love movement, music, dancing and gymnastics – everything we were involved in. I remember one day she turned to me and said, 'Mamma, I want to be like you.' And as soon as she started to learn the basic movements, my husband and I knew she had the potential to be very good. By her sixth birthday, when she was ready to go to school, I decided I wanted to spend all my time with her, so I could start to really coach her seriously in rhythmic gymnastics.

Watching her after we started working together always reminded me of what I looked like at her age. Now I feel I am like a kind of mirror for her. All I have to say is 'Elena, watch me,' and she knows instinctively what she has to do. I am her strongest critic, but she can take it from me because we have this, well, this, this fantastic trust in each other.

P: Right. But even so it must have been strange to be her mother and her trainer?

E (Sr): No, no. When Elena started with Cirque du Soleil, my role well it did change quite fundamentally. As well as being her mother and her coach, I also became her baby-sitter and bodyguard. We actually really look forward to her days off or holidays because that means we have a chance to do, well, very ordinary things, like cooking a meal together. In fact, for us, something ordinary becomes very special.

Sometimes we go to parties together and people think we're, well, we're like sisters. Elena has always been very mature. She hasn't had any of the problems some teenage girls have with their parents. She knows that if she's working, she can't stay up late at night with her friends. And she doesn't think about boyfriends yet.

I know there'll come a time when Elena will have to work without me but even when we do have to separate, I won't be far away. I'll still make sure that I am there to help any time she needs me.

page 11, Exam focus, Paper 5 Speaking: Part 1 (Introduction), Exercise 3

Interlocutor: Good morning. My name is Susan Jenkins and this is my colleague, Brian Wilcox. And your names are … ?

Fine, Well, first of all, we'd like to know a little about you. Do you know each other?

Well, now's the chance to get to know each other! Ask each other about your homes and families, where you're from, what you're interested in, how you like to spend your free time, why you're learning English, your plans for the future, and so on.

page 12, Listening, Exercises 2, 3 and 4

Sue: … and how about you, how was your weekend, Pete?

Pete: Well, amazingly enough, I did finally make it to that exhibition at the Serpentine that I've been meaning to go to for ages!

Ellie: What … the one that was reviewed in all the papers?

P: That's it. The thing was that … You know my friend Clare … well, she doesn't often come up to London and every time she does, she likes to go and see the latest exhibition of this or that. Anyway, we always meet up for lunch first, have a chat and then go off to see whatever.

S: So, what was it you actually ended up seeing?

P: Would you believe I can't exactly remember the name of the exhibition but basically it was a kind of retrospective of some of the most important bits of so-called 'modern' art of recent years. It was actually really interesting.

E: So, what kind of stuff was in it?

P: Well, quite a few things I'm sure you've either seen or read about it. For example, you remember that whole fuss when the Tate Gallery paid thousands of pounds for that pile of bricks … well, that was there …

E: Yes, I remember that. In fact I just can't understand how people can consider that kind of thing to be 'art'. I mean, where's the beauty, where's the skill, where's the 'genius'? I just don't get it.

P: Hmmm … I know what you mean but it certainly did provoke people and made them think, which I guess is a good thing. Anyway, the one that really got me was where they had a plain white kitchen stool and, sort of attached to it, on top, was a bicycle wheel. That wouldn't have been so bad except for the way it was described in the catalogue … something about it representing the infinite divide between man and God or something. Honestly, it amazes me how people can write such pretentious rubbish and be taken seriously.

E: And I bet that half the time the artist never imagined anything like that.

P: I sometimes wonder if the artist thought anything at all … maybe it's just an enormous practical joke! Maybe the whole thing's being done tongue in cheek!

S: Oh come on now, be fair. There are lots of young artists out there trying out new things, you know, experimenting and so on. If people never tried anything different we'd still be stuck in the Middle Ages!

P: Yeah, yeah, I guess you're right …

S: But anyway, I was meaning to ask … was there that actress … you know the one who slept in a glass cabinet for 24 hours or something! I thought that was quite an interesting idea …

P: Oh I know what you mean … no, she wasn't, but there was that horrible piece by what's his name … you know, who cut the cow in half …

E: Oh good grief … I remember, that was grotesque! Don't you think it's incredible that people can come up with such vile notions and call them 'art'. I always thought that art was there to, you know, lift the soul … like poetry … but some of these things, just unbelievable …

UNIT 2

page 18, Listening, Exercises 2 and 3

Arthur Dent had exactly no suspicion that one of his closest friends was not descended from an ape, but was in fact from a small planet somewhere in the vicinity of Betelgeuse and not from south London as he usually claimed. Arthur had never, ever suspected this.

This friend of his had first arrived on the planet Earth some fifteen Earth years previously, and he had worked hard to blend himself into Earth society – with, it must be said, some success. For instance, he had spent those fifteen years pretending to be an out-of-work actor, which was plausible enough.

He had made one careless blunder though, because he had skimped a bit on his preparatory research. The information he had gathered had led him to choose the name 'Ford Prefect' as being nicely inconspicuous.

He was not conspicuously tall, his features were striking but not particularly handsome. His hair was wiry and gingerish and brushed backwards from the temples. His skin seemed to be pulled backwards from the nose. There was something very slightly odd about him, but it was difficult to say what it was. Perhaps it was that his eyes didn't seem to blink often enough and when you talked to him for any length of time your eyes began involuntarily to water on his behalf. Perhaps it was that he smiled slightly too broadly and gave people the unnerving impression that he was about to go for their neck.

He struck most of the friends that he had made on Earth as an eccentric, but a harmless one. For instance, he would often gatecrash university parties, drink too much and start making fun of any astrophysicists he could find till he got thrown out.

Sometimes he would get seized with oddly distracted moods and stare into the sky as if hypnotised until someone asked him what he was doing. And, then he would start guiltily for a moment, relax and grin. 'Oh, just looking for flying saucers,' he would joke, and everyone would laugh and ask him what sort of flying saucers he was looking for. 'Green ones,' he would reply with a wicked grin and laugh wildly for a moment.

In fact what he was really looking for when he stared distractedly into the sky was any kind of flying saucer at all. The reason he said green was that green was the traditional livery of the Betelgeuse space fleet. Ford Prefect was desperate that any flying saucer at all would arrive soon because fifteen years was a long time to get stranded anywhere, particularly somewhere as mindbogglingly dull as Earth.

Later that day Ford Prefect popped round to see Arthur, who was currently lying on the ground in front of his house trying to prevent it being demolished by men with bulldozers from the local town council. The sun was just beginning to dry out the mud that Arthur lay in. A shadow moved across him.

'Hello Arthur,' said the shadow.

Arthur looked up and squinting into the sun was startled to see Ford Prefect standing above him.

'Ford! Hello, how are you?'

'Fine,' said Ford, 'look, are you busy?'

'Am I busy?' exclaimed Arthur. 'Well, I just have to lie in front of all these bulldozers and things because they'll knock down my house if I don't, but other than that … well, no, not especially, why?'

They don't have sarcasm on Betelgeuse, and Ford Prefect often failed to notice it unless he was concentrating. He said, 'Good, is there anywhere we can talk?'

page 25, Listening, Exercise 4

2: It was my first job and I was just out of university so it was all quite a big adventure in lots of ways. I suppose the thing that struck me first … and this may sound a bit silly … was the way that I couldn't actually make head nor tail of any of the signs in the streets. I mean everything was in Arabic script so I didn't know what any of the shops were without physically going inside. That was a small thing I guess but then the other thing, and everyone always says this, was how friendly people were. They just wanted to chat and say 'hello' and invite me to go and have tea. I mean, generally, there was a real generosity of spirit which I thought was wonderful.

3: I decided I wanted to spend a year off in Paris before going to college. My French wasn't bad and I had these romantic visions of sitting in cafés and watching the world go by. Anyway, I got this job with a family helping out looking after the kids and so on. The dad had some kind of work connection with my dad, and it all worked out pretty well. They were really nice and my French certainly improved. One thing that I hadn't really expected though was the way that everything was built around 'the family'. Every weekend seemed to be filled with visits to various family members. There was a definite feeling that family comes first and friends second. That was pretty strange for me.

4: My girlfriend and I had decided we wanted to take a break and do something a bit different so we signed up to do a year's voluntary teaching in China in a small university. It was an amazing experience in lots of different ways … but often it was quite small things which took us by surprise at the start. One thing I remember was the way, when people came round to your house, you always had to offer them things like drinks at least three or four times before they would accept them. Something else which led to a couple of quite embarrassing situations was that you really couldn't openly admire somebody's things. I did it once about someone's watch and they immediately took it off and insisted that I have it as a present. I felt terrible!

5: One of the things I really like about Portuguese people is the custom of kissing as well as saying hello. Except in extremely formal situations, it makes no difference whether or not you know them, if you are a girl or woman, they'll give you a kiss on both cheeks – the right cheek first and then the left. Of course this is quite different to English people, who generally just say 'hello', or kiss a close member of the family on the cheek – just the once – or shake hands. Imagine how embarrassing I found it when I first moved here and didn't know whether to shake hands or not, kiss or not and if I did kiss, I'd kiss the wrong cheek first and we'd end up banging noses instead!

UNIT 3

page 30, Listening, Exercise 5

Presenter: Hello and welcome to this week's edition of 'The People's Programme'. Today we have in the studio Max Valentin, a man who has managed to turn France upside down. Four years ago he buried a golden, jewel-encrusted owl worth £100,000 somewhere in France and started one of the most frantic treasure hunts in the history of the sport. Today, it would seem that thousands of frustrated treasure hunters are no nearer to solving the riddle – and the creator of it all has had his life turned into an endless cycle of questions, love letters, bribes and crank phone calls.

Welcome to the programme Max.

Max: Thank you.

P: Well perhaps we could begin by your telling us a little about how it all started …

M: Well, I suppose it all began one day twenty years ago when my boss asked me to organise a treasure hunt for some clients. During 1978 I wrote the eleven clues that would eventually comprise my book *Sur La Trace De La Chouette D'Or*, which means 'On The Path Of The Golden Owl'. In fact, for more than ten years what actually happened was that they sat in the drawer of my bureau, until 1997 when I met the sculptor Michel Becker. We talked about it all and eventually decided that I would provide the clues for the book and he would paint pictures to go with them. Er, but as well as that Michel also agreed to provide the prize. He sculpted an owl, the symbol of the dispossessed French court during the French revolution.

After that, then, basically, I went out and buried the owl with a pickaxe and a spade and two days later we launched the book which contained the clues.

P: And the book then shot into the bestseller lists with its tantalising promise of hidden riches. But then you started to get a little more than you bargained for …

M: Well, yes, people started to get really carried away. There was one guy who rang up my solicitor. He was very excited and he said he knew that the owl was buried in a cemetery. I don't normally tell people if they are right or wrong, but sometimes I have to. We had to stop him digging up the cemetery.

P: But really it is all supposed to be just a game, isn't it?

M: That's right. Essentially, the object is to solve each of the eleven clues in turn. Together they reveal an area of France, and hidden in each of these clues is part of a twelfth clue which pinpoints the exact location of the treasure. That's about all I can say really.

P: And isn't it right that at one point you found that it was all beginning to take over your life?

M: Well, yes. When it started I had my own Minitel site … Minitel was something in France a bit like a primitive version of the Internet. Anyway, so far I have received over one million messages and during the first couple of years I replied to a hundred thousand messages personally. I couldn't go away, or take a holiday for two years. I was spending fifteen hours a day in front of the Minitel. It was actually beginning to destroy my health.

P: So, why don't you just put an end to it and tell everyone where it is?

M: No, no I couldn't do that. Well, not yet anyway. It would be a betrayal of all the people who have spent so much time looking. Eventually, though, I suppose I will wake up one morning and say 'enough is enough'. It might be tomorrow or next month or next year. Then I will publish a clue that will turn the hunt into a race for the six or seven people who are closest to finding it.

P: Well I'm sure a lot of people would really like …

page 35, Speaking, Exercises 2 and 3

Female: So, what would you put first? What would you say is most important to you?

Male: Well, I suppose for me, I'd have to go for 'friends' as number one.

F: Really? Not family?

M: No. Well, well you see, as far as I'm concerned, you choose your friends and so I'm much closer to them. I mean my family's OK, but when I'm in trouble I always go to my friends first.

F: Yes, I guess you're right. And how do you feel about what would go next?

M: Yes, that's tricky. I'm not entirely sure. 'Work' certainly takes up a lot of time but it's not really that important to me. In terms of quality of life, my leisure time is very important to me. There's nothing I like more than to settle down on a sofa with a cup of tea and a good book.

F: So leisure would be your number two, would it?

M: Yes, I think so, but, on the other hand, I really love travel too. I mean, I'd be really unhappy if I had to stay in one place all the time. I like to get away for some kind of trip to somewhere interesting at least once a year.

F: Yes, that's the same for me too, but you do need money to do that.

M: I'm not sure I'd totally go along with that. I mean of course you need some money but I tend to travel really cheaply and often stay with friends … so money's not important.

UNIT 4

page 46, Speaking, Exercises 2 and 3

Female: Well, <u>it looks to me like</u> the young couple are probably boyfriend and girlfriend. <u>My guess is that it's</u> quite a new relationship and he must have done something to upset her. Now he's trying to talk her round – typical guy!

Male: OK, that's possible but I also think there is a good chance that they are brother and sister. <u>I get the impression</u> that she's about to do something stupid, and he is trying to give her some sensible advice. There is no way that she's going to take any notice of what he says though!

F: Hmm maybe. But whatever their relationship is, <u>I bet it's pretty up and down</u> most of the time. Uh, anyway, what about the couple in the street then?

M: Well, I did think they were work colleagues at first, but <u>on second thoughts I reckon it's pretty unlikely that they are only work colleagues</u> because of the way she's kind of leaning into him.

F: Yes, <u>I wouldn't be at all surprised if they were</u> in some kind of serious relationship and had just met for lunch, or something. I must say, he looks pretty sure of himself … even arrogant, but she seems to be taking what he's saying quite seriously.

M: And the last picture is pretty obvious, isn't it?

F: Why do you say that?

M: Well, he's got to be her grandfather or maybe great-grandfather, don't you think?

F: Yeah maybe but … not necessarily.

M: What else do you think he could be?

F: A friend of the family perhaps …

M: <u>I suppose it's just possible but</u>, to be honest, it does seem pretty unlikely …

page 47, Exam focus, Paper 4 Listening: Part 3 (sentence completion)

Interviewer: Hello. In today's programme we're going to be focussing on the great bard, William Shakespeare, largely acknowledged to be the greatest of all English playwrights. However, a problem we're facing today is that <u>fewer and fewer young people appear to have any knowledge or enthusiasm for him and his work, because it's perceived as 'difficult' and inaccessible.</u> Having said that, steps appear to be in hand to address this problem. I have with me two people both active in this regard – film critic Angela Rathbone and Cambridge college lecturer Simon Fenshaw.

I'd like to begin by asking you Angela first for a few comments on Australian director Baz Luhrmann's now highly acclaimed screen version of *Romeo and Juliet* …

Angela: Yes, well … for those who haven't seen the film … this is basically a streetwise account of *Romeo and Juliet* set in modern-day Verona Beach, where the streets play host to riots, car-chases and gunfights. In the midst of this chaos are Claire Danes' lilting Juliet, and <u>DiCaprio's Romeo, who is chiefly characterised by his moodiness and self-absorption.</u> And really it is their scenes together which give the film the weight that is crucial to its success. The picture is a roller-coaster experience, and perhaps the most radical element of all is that the play's language remains intact beneath the various elaborate embellishments. In essence, it's hard, it's fast, it's dazzlingly inventive and it's doing a very good job of <u>persuading today's teenagers that the bard, almost 400 years after his death, is cool.</u>

I: Yes, yes, I for one was somewhat astounded to hear stories of hordes of youngsters clamouring to see Shakespeare.

A: Yes, well, I'm sure the charms of Leonardo DiCaprio, and Claire Danes as the star-crossed lovers, have contributed something to this current Shakespeare frenzy, but it's also true <u>I think that this surge of interest reflects a continuing revolution in the way the bard is taught in the classroom.</u>

Simon: <u>Exactly</u> … no longer are bored pupils presented with a dog-eared copy of *A Midsummer Night's Dream* with the rude jokes cut out and told to mumble their way through the acts line by line. <u>In fact I even recognised some of my own teaching techniques in Luhrmann's film.</u> During the opening scene between Montagues and Capulets <u>where the dialogue is split into short segments to add pace, I wanted to stop the projectionist and say 'I've taught that!'</u>

I: Now, now, Simon you're actually sharing some of your ideas for making Shakespeare more accessible to young people in a new series of 'Shakespeare for Schools' …

S: Yes, I believe that everyone can understand and be moved by Shakespeare's work. And you see, that's why it's still performed and why it's worth doing. I mean, Shakespeare had an amazing genius for capturing who we are and revealing it to us. Our job, as teachers, is to re-reveal it and that's what these books are about. Each book in the series contains the play's unabridged text, a short synopsis of events, a glossary of obscure words and a host of ideas for pupil activities which will help them understand both the language and the subtext of the plays. Well, I'll give you an example, pupils might be encouraged to skip while quoting 'To be or not to be', to feel the rhythm of the verse, or to actually <u>mime a scene merely described by a character.</u>

I: And is this new approach to teaching Shakespeare reflected in the way pupils are assessed in schools?

S: Oh, yes, yes, and that's another really exciting thing. Even the National Schools Authority, which sets a compulsory Shakespeare paper for 14-year-olds, has taken note of the trend. Pupils might be asked, for example, to explain <u>how, as a director, they would direct Juliet in a particular scene</u>.

I: Now, Angela, I understand you are also …

page 51, Listening, Exercises 2 and 3

1: Hi, it's Debbie … just to say how much I enjoyed last night. I didn't realise there were going to be quite so many people there but it really was great fun. Really good idea to get all the men changing places after every course. I got to speak to loads of people … <u>There was actually one guy … I think he works with</u> Peter. I can't actually remember his name, he was wearing a blue <u>jacket and a black polo neck …</u> <u>anyway … I was sort of wondering if you … you know … had his number … anyway … if it's a hassle don't worry about it</u> … so … anyway … thanks a lot again. We must fix up for you to come round here soon. Bye for now …

2: Hello. This is the Barton Health Clinic. You previously had an appointment with <u>Dr Sengupta for this Thursday at 3.30 p.m. Unfortunately, Dr Sengupta is off sick and the next available appointment is not until next week, unless of course you wouldn't mind seeing another doctor.</u> Could you please ring and tell us what you would prefer in terms of arranging another appointment. Thank you.

3: <u>Hi dad. It's Sara. Just arrived at mum's. The flight was fine … everyone was really nice</u> … and we got to see the latest Brad Pitt movie which was really cool. Anyway, mum says 'hi' and she'll give you a ring later. Ooh … yes … don't forget to feed Pickles … Remember? You promised! OK … gotta go … don't work too hard. Bye. Lots of love.

4: Hello. My name is Simon McLoughlin, that's M-C-L-O-U-G-H-L-I-N. I am ringing in response to your ad in the *Hornsey Chronicle*. I understand you have a second-hand mountain bike for sale. <u>I would very much like to come round and have a look at it</u> at some point if that were possible. Could you possibly ring me some time and let me know when it would be convenient? My number is 01324 971 883. Thanks very much.

5: Hi there, it's me … I can't believe it. I've just heard. I got it. Isn't that amazing! I still can't really get my head round it. The letter was in the post this morning … I keep re-reading it. And after the interview was such a disaster too. The other people must have been really desperate! Anyway, <u>I'm going to have to go out and do some serious clothes shopping to prepare my new high-flying executive image … why don't you come along too?</u> But … where are you? … Listen, I'm probably going out around 2 p.m. so if you're interested and get home in time … give me a call and we can meet up in town … OK … this is so exciting! … See you soon.

UNIT 5

page 54, Listening, Exercises 2 and 3

Presenter: Hello and welcome to this week's edition of 'Future Fantastic'. Now, it may well sound like the stuff of science fiction but a certain Manchester family, the Michaels, are currently paying £65 a month … for the future privilege of being … deep frozen.

In fact, they are just one of ten British families who have signed up with the London branch of <u>the Cryonics Institute, whose main office is based in the United States</u>.

Now I actually have with me in the studio today, Paul Michaels … So Paul as I understand it, this is a case where you and your wife Maureen have not only vowed to stay together in this life, but you are also investing money to ensure you'll be together in the next one, too.

Paul: Well, that's the idea, yes. Perhaps I can explain … Essentially what'll happen is that when we die, we'll be drained of blood, which will be replaced by a kind of anti-freeze. After that we'll be sent off to America to be frozen in liquid nitrogen. There, we'll stay in deep freeze until the day science finds a way of bringing us back to life and curing us of whatever was wrong with us.

P: And, as I understand it, to complete the family, you've even arranged for your 15-year-old son, Alex, to follow you.

Paul: Yes, yes, that's right. He's very keen on the idea! My wife and I talked about it for years before we finally decided to go ahead and, when the time came to sign, we asked Alex to join us and he said 'yes'. <u>Of course, if he changes his mind, that's his decision</u> but it won't stop us. On the other hand, I don't think I would ever have gone ahead without Maureen. You see, for us marriage will hopefully be until life us do reunite, rather than death do us part.

P: Now without wishing to sound overly sceptical, I must say that this will seem to many listeners like something out of a rather far-fetched science-fiction movie.

Paul: Well, yes, I do realise that's that how it may appear to those who don't really understand much about it. <u>But to those of us who are involved … this is absolutely serious.</u>

You see, as I see it, with the possibility of freezing at least there's a chance you'll be able to come back. To me it's only logical. <u>Paying out for this treatment is really a kind of life insurance policy.</u>

In fact, the idea of suspended animation or 'cryonics' as it's known, has been around for a long time. Well, <u>pop star Michael Jackson has signed up for it</u>. And rumour has it that Walt Disney is also in deep freeze storage somewhere.

P: Now you pay around £65 a month into an insurance policy which will pay to freeze your family.

Paul: That's right.

P: But some people would regard that as quite a significant amount of money to put towards such an eccentric kind of scheme.

Paul: <u>Well, you see, ever since I was seven, the idea of death has horrified me.</u> OK, I mean, maybe ultimately I'll get bored of life after another thousand years and I'll want to die but the thing is that I want it to be my choice when I die. And I'm quite prepared to pay whatever it takes to make that possible.

P: Is it right that your wife, Maureen, is rather less optimistic than you that science will ever be able to reunite you both.

Paul: Well, yes and no. I suppose, as she's said, <u>she looks on the whole thing as emigrating, in a way</u>. When you emigrate fundamentally you've no idea what the new country will be like. It's a kind of step in the dark. For us, instead of going abroad we're going to the future, and perhaps that not a bad way of looking at it.

page 59, Vocabulary, Exercise 4.2

1: You know people say it's wrong, we mustn't, it's dangerous. I don't think nature is a fixed thing. Who are we to say that it's nature and it begins here and it ends there?

2: Well, I can just imagine all these people walking around looking the same.

3: I can understand it if someone was so desperate for a child and they could get one that way.

4: You could never recreate a person unless they've gone through the same experiences. It's not nature, it's nurture. We're talking about character, personality, whatever it is one loves about someone. You're never going to reproduce that.

5: I don't mind if it's really for research. It'd be wonderful if it could help produce skin for burns victims, cure cancer and understand the ageing process.

6: I think you accept things, things do progress and there's nothing you can do about it.

UNIT 6

page 68, Listening, Exercises 2 and 3

Presenter: And in today's edition of 'Future Thoughts' we've asked Mary Fitzroy of the National Sports Council to peer into her crystal ball and give us her views of the world of sport and the extent to which it may or may not be changing over the next 50 years or so.

Mary Fitzroy: Well, to be perfectly honest, I do have my doubts as to whether the world of sport will change in the next half century. Yes, there are new rules, events and legends that will come along, but sport is essentially conservative by nature and tends to lag behind wider developments in society. I mean, if we think about the great sporting events, for instance the Cup Final, Wimbledon, and so on, they're great because of their long history … Um, I think that, fundamentally, this is what imbues victory with a real sense of achievement. Traditions are protected and innovation, anything new, is, is treated sceptically.

In fact, I believe that we will, broadly speaking, love the same mainstream sports in 2050 as we do today. But, the need for most people to live in urban areas will continue to have an influence. Any game that works well in confined spaces – such as basketball or five-a-side football – starts at an advantage for the modern city dweller. But then other games like, er, cricket or baseball, may well be suffering by 2050 because fewer people will be able to play these games because of the space that the ground takes up.

Now alongside this, um, we will probably also see the emergence of new and different kinds of sports such as 'Bar Fly Flying' – now this is a, this is a game where you wear a sticky kind of Velcro™ suit and you jump from a small trampoline against a sticky Velcro™-covered wall – and 'Bungee Running' – where you stretch a piece of elastic until you're 'pinged' into a safety net – and also 'Bouncy Boxing' – where you hit a friend with giant inflatable gloves.

One of the problems that will emerge from this, though, is the growing gap between rich and poor. So that while the 'haves' are having fun, bouncing around on trampolines and the like, the 'have-nots' will be left playing low-cost, traditional sports, such as football, in the street. And despite this, people will still have their sporting heroes. Television has made sport big business in the last thirty years and by 2050 the sporting elite will have been elevated further – to the status now enjoyed by music and film icons. This means they'll be paid more, and will do fewer performances.

Ironically though, um, while the rewards for excellence will increase stratospherically, it's unlikely that the same will be true for performance times. Jessie Owens set a 100-metre world record of 10.2 seconds during the 1936 Berlin Olympics. More than fifty years of improvements in training regimes, sports nutrition and track construction have still only managed to shave less than half a second off his time. So there's clearly a limit to what humans can do. I don't believe we'll ever run 100 metres in nine seconds. What will happen in 2050 is that they won't be measuring in hundredths of seconds, but thousandths.

page 73, Speaking, Exercise 2

Male: So … what do you think of this one, I mean the idea of holiday athletics clubs for young people?

Female: Well, as far as I'm concerned, I would say that getting young people interested in and doing different sports is probably the key to it all. I mean, it's so much easier to instill good habits and attitudes in people when they're young. And on top of that, it's a time when kids can take part in a wide range of activities so they can find out which ones they really enjoy. What's more, like I said, if people get into the habit of doing regular exercise early enough, they'll just carry on with it through their adult lives.

M: But, having said that though, plenty of people – including me! – did lots of sports as a teenager and then kind of gave up on it when they left school. That's partly because of the effort it needs to get to places to do the kind of exercise you enjoy. So, I think, this suggestion of putting money into building more leisure centres is a good one. I mean, if I had one nearer me, I'm sure I'd be more likely to go along. Not only that but I'd probably get interested in trying out new kinds of things if there were classes being run and so on.

F: We do need to remember that places like this cost a fortune to set up so it may not be a very practical idea financially.

M: OK … well, what about the occasional reminder, then, like putting leaflets through doors once in a while, just to jog people's memories that they should be doing some kind of regular exercise?

F: That's all very well but do you want to know what I do with leaflets through the door? … Well, the first thing I do …

page 73, Listening, Exercises 2 and 3

Presenter: Every sports star knows the feeling – that nightmare moment when you have to retire because you are just too old. Well, maybe that's fair enough when you are in your late 30s. But spare a thought for Harriet Slynn, one of our top sportswomen. She's had to quit a promising football career – at the age of nine. Her mother, Sue, battled with the Football Association, invoked the Equal Opportunities Commission and wrote countless letters but all to no avail.

The Football Association was immovable. No mixed football after nine years old.

Harriet's mother: They had no right to say what they were saying. They just came up with feeble excuses like problems with the changing rooms.

P: Harriet herself was disappointed but not distraught. She has, after all, plenty of other options. She is national triathlon champion for her age group, she ran in last month's London mini-marathon, finishing 148th, and she's in the England under-elevens girls' chess squad. She's in the school netball team and fancies her chances at shot putt and long jump. Quite simply, whatever she turns her hand to turns into trophies, medals and badges.

Taking all of this into account, it's a bit of a shock to discover that Harriet is just 1 metre 30. So, how come she more than holds her own with boys who may be a head taller? The secret may be that she is wonderfully self-assured without being arrogant or precocious. Here is an eleven-year-old who can discuss training programmes, motivation and ambitions … and that is rare indeed. Her parents have such confidence in her ability to handle a press interview that they are quite happy to leave her on her own.

Harriet Slynn's sporting career started at the phenomenally early age of just three years old, when she entered a fun run. A year later, she showed an aptitude for gymnastics and started winning trophies. At school, she proved so good at football that she was an automatic choice for the team. She played midfield, scored goals and never had any problems about being a girl in a field of boys. When her younger brother Adam went for a trial with a regional junior rugby team, she tagged along, liked the game and got involved. Bumps and bruises don't seem to worry her, but her mother is less sanguine.

Hm: Her legs get covered in bruises and she has had some heavy falls recently, but it doesn't worry her. Personally, I would be devastated if she came home with a broken nose or a cauliflower ear.

P: Then came triathlons. When her dad took part, she joined in, liked that too and last year won six of the seven races in her age group to become national champion. And as her dad says …

Harriet's father: She is naturally very competitive in everything she does. She doesn't need to be pushed. She even keeps a training diary.

P: Almost every evening of Harriet's week involves athletics, swimming, cycling, running or rugby training, though on Fridays she is involved in drama, and some Saturdays there is a chess match.

Hm: We're glad that she's got a balance between the physical and the cerebral. But ultimately, it's her decision about what she does.

P: Harriet hasn't settled on one sport yet. She enjoys them all. Ask her what sports she doesn't like and she can't think of one. She is also remarkably mature about the future. No vows of Olympic medals or being the first woman to play for England in the World Cup: she likes the idea of physiotherapy and wouldn't mind being a woman referee. A laudable ambition, but you feel she may be underselling herself. Anyway, I made sure and got her autograph – for my daughters you understand …

UNIT 7

page 81, Exam focus, Paper 4 Listening: Part 2 (note taking)

The physical resemblance to his father is alarmingly striking. The deep-set, dark, almost haunted eyes. The nervous twitch of his lips when he smiles. There is no doubting that actor Chris Chaplin is the son of the world's first great film star.

In fact, he is the youngest of Chaplin's eight children from his fourth marriage to Oona O'Neill, who was 37 years younger than him. When Chris was born, his father was 74. Now, Chris, at 35, could pass for Charlie Chaplin at the same age but the young actor has no difficulty in resisting the temptation to cash in on his father's name.

When Sir Richard Attenborough made his biographical film, *Chaplin*, Chris refused point-blank to be in it, even though he would have been perfectly cast for the title role and was only two years older than the American actor, Robert Downey Jnr., who did play his father

Unlike his father, who revelled in his fame and fortune, Chris actually has far more in common with his mother, Oona, in that he is shy and self-effacing. Most of Chris's work has been for Eastern European film-makers or in obscure theatre productions.

Because Charlie Chaplin's family were extremely poor during his childhood in London, Chaplin was acutely conscious of the value of money, and when he died in 1977 he was insistent that none of his children would inherit their share of his vast fortune – estimated at £40 million – until their 35th birthdays. Chris is the last of the children to come into his inheritance but he seems to shy away from outward displays of personal wealth.

Since his mother's death, Chris and his siblings have been entrusted with running the Chaplin estate and protecting the Chaplin name. Continuing the Chaplin tradition weighs on Chris as a heavy responsibility. He believes he inherited a sense of humanity from his father and a sense of duty from his mother and has said that, while, ultimately, Chaplin is a great name to have, the responsibilities that come with it can be quite a burden.

page 85, Speaking, Exercise 1

There aren't really very many of us in our family now. My dad died a few years ago and my mum doesn't have any brothers or sisters. Both my parents were quite old when I was born so I never knew any grandparents. I've only got one brother, Matthew – he's quite a bit older than me, 13 years actually. I suppose that's a bit unusual. He left home when I was 6, so growing up was a bit like being an only child. I've got to know Matthew more recently … adult to adult. We spend a lot of time swapping stories about our respective childhoods, which were similar in some ways but very different in others.

I do have a couple of aunts, Margaret and Jessica – my dad's sisters, but they live quite a long way away so I don't get to see them all that often. I really should make more of an effort to visit them but it's hard to get the time.

Matthew is married to Sofía. They've been married for years. She's Spanish. He met her on holiday one year and they had a kind of whirlwind romance and got married soon after. She came over to live here which was I suppose hard for her family but it's worked out well in the long run all things considered. There's always been a bit of tension between my mum and Sofía … I've never really understood why. I wish they got on a bit better but it never seems to change. Probably just one of those things.

They have three lovely kids – my nieces, Isabella, Cristina and Natalia. The two eldest are at university now, but Natalia's still at school. They're all very different but at the same time very obviously sisters!

And that's about it I guess. I don't have any cousins because my uncles and aunts never had kids … so really we're quite a compact little family. Sometimes I wonder what it would be like to have a huge, sprawling extended family like some of my friends. Hard to imagine really.

UNIT 8

page 95, Vocabulary, Exercise 2

1: The new advertising campaign is intended to **boost** sales.

2: It's an interesting book about the future but some of the ideas are rather **far-fetched**.

3: I'm afraid that is a **typically** male response to this kind of problem.

4: I've told her **countless** times not to accept lifts from people she doesn't know.

5: We must remember that the main purpose of this company is to **maximise** profit without compromising standards.

6: By the most amazing **coincidence** my new boss is someone I used to be at school with.

7: A few years ago a car fuelled by solar energy would have been **inconceivable**.

8: Jonathan says he **generally** gets in to work by around 8.30 a.m.

9: They've had a lot of bad **luck** with their neighbours. They're always having problems.

10: **Numerous** attempts were made to hide the truth, but it had to come out sooner or later.

page 96, Listening, Exercises 1 and 2

1/6: I'll never forget the day I had this strange feeling that I should phone my grandad.

I was relaxing on the sofa when suddenly I felt compelled to telephone him. I never usually phone him unless I have something to tell him, but I dashed to the phone. It rang and rang, and I kept thinking, 'Come on Grandad, pick up the phone' – somehow I knew he was there. It felt like forever before he finally came to the phone, coughing and spluttering. He said: 'I'll call you back,' and slammed down the phone. Who'd have thought it but when he eventually called back, from a mobile phone, he said: 'I'd fallen asleep and left the chip pan on. The kitchen was on fire and the house is full of black smoke. It was the phone that woke me.'

2/7: I was actually on holiday in Greece. It was the first decent break we'd had in ages. Anyway, we found accommodation in a small town in the Peloponnese and, while Jim, that's my husband, went off to cut some cactus fruit, I went to the restaurant downstairs and started to chat to a family of Australians on their grand tour of Greece. When Jim returned, they realised they were all of Cypriot origin. Well, imagine my surprise when we discovered that they were his first cousins, whom he'd never met before. After that, the holiday was one long party. We had a great time.

3/8: I remember this occasion where I was going to a dinner where I'd never met anyone in the room before. It was something I had to do for work. I sat at a table for six. The lady opposite started chatting to me and said how much she admired my gold bracelet which was set with tiny diamonds forming the number thirteen. I told her that this was my date of birth and then it transpired that we were both born on September 13th, 1956. Somehow the conversation turned to brothers and then to my amazement it turned out that our brothers were both born on July 5th, 1960.

4/9: I suppose one of the strangest examples I ever had of that kind of thing was one day when I was working on a surgical ward, I got talking to the anaesthetist … I'd seen her around once or twice before. Anyway, after a while we discovered that we'd both been at the same secondary school. She was about two years younger than me. At home, I rooted out our old school photograph and took it in to see if she was in it. Well, the hairs stood up on the back of my neck. She had been too tall to stand with the fourth-years, and had been put in the back row. Would you believe it? She was standing right next to me.

5/10: My youngest, Emma, was writing an essay on a Dutch artist, Vermeer, for a school project. One evening she came down from her room with a copy of a museum brochure which mentioned an article in the *Gazette Des Beaux Arts* of May 1866. I remember her asking: 'What are the chances of getting hold of a copy of this article quickly?' 'Remote,' I said. 'Forget it.' The next day as it happened, my wife and I were going to a house-clearance sale in a nearby town. Well, you'll never guess what happened next! In a passageway were two large tea chests filled with very old, torn magazines. The second one I picked up was *Gazette Des Beaux Arts* of May 1866, with the full article on Vermeer.

UNIT 9

page 108, Grammar plus, Exercises 1 and 2

John: So … who is this friend of yours … Amanda?
Hilary: Oh Amanda … she's great. What can I tell you? … Well, she's really nice and so on but <u>what I really like about her</u> is her wicked sense of humour. She always makes me laugh!
J: Go on … so give me an example …
H: Well … take last Saturday. She was having a party at her flat and invited all her friends, including a guy who works in her office, called Sam. Sam is quite nice but he's a bit pompous and arrogant at times. Anyway, <u>what Amanda did was to tell Sam</u> that it was a 'Roman toga' party and that everyone was coming dressed as a Roman. Sam tends to take these things very seriously and so he went to a professional costume-maker and got one specially made. So, of course <u>what happened was that he</u> arrived at the party in this elaborate costume and everyone else was in ordinary casual clothes. He couldn't believe it. He went completely red! He was so embarrassed! It was hysterical!

page 108, Grammar plus, Exercise 6.1 Example

What I particularly need to do to improve my English is to listen to more examples of real English people speaking because often I find it difficult to understand different accents. I think I'll try and see more films in English and <u>try</u> not to read the subtitles!

page 109, Speaking, Exercise 2

In Picture A we can see someone who looks as if they're attempting to rollerblade for the first time. The young woman seems to be thoroughly enjoying herself. However, she's obviously not quite ready to go it alone! The girl in Picture C gives the impression of being slightly less sure of herself. She seems to be offering us one of the cakes she's just baked, but they look a little burnt. Maybe that's why she looks rather hesitant. Overall, the woman rollerblading appears a good deal more confident about what she is doing.

page 114, Exam focus, Paper 4 Listening: Part 4 (multiple matching)

1/6: A lot of people ask me what it's like, isn't it lonely and so on. I suppose I feel the hardest thing is <u>having the self-discipline to sit down and produce 1000 words every day</u>. It really isn't about inspiration. <u>It's more about sheer will.</u> I was lucky though, my husband was great … really supportive. <u>He'd read through the new material every night</u> and give me his comments … and in the end, I can hardly believe it, but it did get done and <u>it's selling quite well</u>.

2/7: There was a lot of preparation and we had to get money from <u>sponsors</u> to make the whole thing possible but finally everything was ready. We flew out and <u>managed to set up at the base camp site. But what we hadn't reckoned with was the weather. It turned really nasty</u> and just didn't improve. It was terribly frustrating after all we'd gone through to get that far. But, in the end we had no option but to give up. We are going to try again next year though.

3/8: I know it's stupid but it's just one of those things that I <u>never got taught properly at school</u> and ever since I've really just been a bit embarrassed about admitting it. As a result I've never really done anything about it, although I suppose I could have done. Anyway, <u>this year we're having a fantastic holiday in the Greek islands and I definitely don't want to spend the whole time sitting on the beach watching the rest of my family have all the fun in the sea. So, I've definitely decided to have some lessons.</u>

4/9: It's funny, everyone seems to have their own pet way to do it and, of course, <u>they're all really quick to tell you their 'foolproof' way.</u> I've tried lots of different things – I even went to a <u>hypnotist</u> – but none of them really seem to work for me. <u>I think I've been doing it for too long.</u> Still, I do want to try again as <u>I've got this cough now</u> which is really bad some of the time. As well as that, <u>my children keep nagging me about it</u> which is driving me mad!

5/10: It's all been <u>a bit off and on over the last few years</u>. I mean it was different when we were little but, you see, a big part of it was that I never particularly liked her husband. And then there was all that business over who should look after our parents when they weren't very well and that wasn't easy at all. <u>I do try and see things from her side but sometimes it's very hard.</u> I suppose <u>I could have made a bit more effort but she always seems to treat me like a little kid which really gets on my nerves.</u>

UNIT 10

page 119, Listening, Exercises 3 and 4

I wrote my first software program when I was 13 years old. It was for playing tick-tack-toe. The computer I was using was huge and cumbersome and slow and absolutely compelling.

Letting a bunch of teenagers loose on a computer was the idea of the Mothers' Club at Lakeside, the private school I attended. The mothers decided that the proceeds from a rummage sale should be used to install a terminal and buy computer time for students. Letting students use a computer in the late 1960s was a pretty amazing choice at the time in Seattle – and one I'll always be grateful for.

This computer terminal didn't have a screen. To play, we typed in our moves on a typewriter-style keyboard and then sat around until the results came chug-chugging out of a loud printing device on paper. Then we'd rush over and take a look and see who'd won or decide our next move. A game of tick-tack-toe, which would take thirty seconds with a pencil and paper, might consume most of a lunch period. But who cared? There was just something neat about the machine.

I realised later part of the appeal was that here was an enormous, expensive, grown-up machine and we, the kids, could control it. We were too young to drive or do any of the other fun-seeming adult activities, but we could give this big machine orders and it would always obey. Computers are great because when you're working with them you get immediate results that let you know if your program works. It's feedback you don't get from many other things. That was the beginning of my fascination with software. The feedback from simple programs is particularly unambiguous. And to this day it still thrills me to know that if I can get the program right it will always work perfectly, every time, just the way I told it to.

As my friends and I gained confidence, we began to mess around with the computer, speeding things up when we could or making the games more difficult. A friend at Lakeside developed a program in BASIC that simulated the play of Monopoly™. BASIC (which is 'Beginner's All-purpose Symbolic Instruction Code') is, as its name suggests, a relatively easy-to-learn programming language we used to develop increasingly complex programs. He figured out how to make the computer play hundreds of games really fast. We fed it instructions to test out various methods of play. We wanted to discover what strategies won most. And – chug-a-chug, chug-a-chug – the computer told us.

Like all kids, we not only fooled around with our toys, we changed them. If you've ever watched a child with a cardboard carton and a box of crayons create a spaceship with cool control panels, or listened to their improvised rules, such as 'Red cars can jump all others', then you know that this impulse to make a toy do more is at the heart of innovative childhood play. It is also the essence of creativity.

page 120, Speaking, Exercise 2

Male: Well it's obviously a photo of some astronauts floating about doing something in space.
Female: Yes, but, to start with, how many of them are there?
M: Well, there are definitely two on the right and then on the left, as far as I can see, it looks like some kind of tube or machine or something.
F: Yes, I think you're right and then, I'm not exactly sure but it seems to have a sort of metal bar attached to the foot of one of the astronauts. I could be wrong but could that be to stop the astronaut floating away?
M: Maybe, I'm not sure. I can also just about make out a yellowy box-like thing on the left side of the tube.
F: Yes, I see what you mean. And there's also a white box of some kind, like a big dice, next to the feet of the horizontal astronaut. Any idea what that's doing there?
M: None whatsoever, maybe it's for keeping his packed lunch in!

page 121, Listening, Exercise 1

Andrew: Did either of you see this letter in the paper today about the 'cyber-widow'?
Cathy: What letter, Andrew? What do you mean 'cyber-widow'?
A: Well, it's quite hard to get your head round … but … this woman has written in to say that her husband of 15 years is leaving her to … wait for it … go and live with a woman in Australia who he met on the Internet eight weeks ago.
Ben: … and has he actually ever met her … face to face?
C: No, that's the amazing thing. They've spoken on the phone but never actually met in person. Anyway, apparently the Australian woman is trying to find him a job out there. And he's got his plane ticket and he's off to live in Paradise at the end of the week …
C: How can people do something like that … they must be completely nuts. Suppose it all goes wrong?
A: I think all this Internet stuff is awful. It's really sad that people have to resort to meeting each other by computer. Why can't they just go out and get a life for goodness' sake!
B: Hey, hang on a minute. That's really unfair. You know Andrew you can be incredibly narrow-minded sometimes! What's wrong with chatting to people on the Internet? You'd be surprised. You get to meet people from all over the world.

C: So, you actually have first-hand experience of this, do you Ben?

B: Well, as it happens …

A: You've got to be kidding! …

B: What? I just don't understand what your problem is. I've got to know some really interesting people …

A: Oh, yeah, right … but what I've heard is that loads of people just go on and pretend to be all sorts and so you never really know who you're talking to.

B: Oh what rubbish! It's very easy to work out if someone is genuine or not. Actually, I'm going to be meeting up with someone from the States who's coming over for work next week.

C: What, meet up … in the flesh?

B: Sure, why not?

C: Listen you've really got to be careful about that kind of thing. If I was you …

page 123, Speaking, Exercise 4

Student 1:   OK Bjorn, you have 60 seconds to talk about 'the use of computers for learning English' from … now!

Student 2:   I personally think that <u>computers can be very useful for learning English</u>. There are many different types of program that a student can use to improve their grammar or vocabulary or … umm …

Student 3:   <u>Challenge. Hesitation!</u>

S2:   OK … OK …

S1:   <u>Well done Maria.</u> 50 seconds remains. Are you ready? Go!

S3:   Although it is definitely true that, erm, …

UNIT 11

page 130, Speaking, Exercises 2 and 3

Female: Well, I think we must keep the one of the Changing of the Guard in front of Buckingham Palace. I mean, tourists love it – it's what lots of them come to Britain for, isn't it?

Male: That's probably very true for a lot of people but I do wonder if it's a rather old-fashioned image of Britain and a bit out of date now?

F: OK … so would you prefer something like this new modern sculpture, er, the 'Angel of the North'?

M: Yes, I think I would … I mean, it's a bit different and not the same old boring cliché about Britain you always get …

F: Hmm, that's certainly an interesting point but I still feel people are more likely to buy postcards of things which are more familiar and well-known.

M: So, I suppose you want the one of the Scottish guy playing the bagpipes?

F: Hmm, well, I'm not sure about that. Perhaps that's a bit specific. How about we have the one with the four mini-pictures – isn't one of them Shakespeare's birthplace? That gives a good overview of different parts of Britain and different types of things that might interest foreign visitors.

M: Fine, but if we have that, we can't really have the village pub one, can we? It's a bit too similar to the picture of Shakespeare's birthplace.

F: In that case, we're just left with the one of the Nottinghill Carnival and I'm not sure that it's really very typical of 'Britain' …

M: Well, I can see what you mean but, having said that, I do think it would be really good to have a postcard showing a different side to the UK. You know … giving a bit of, a bit of a sense of the diversity and vibrancy that you can get. And the Brazilian tourists should love it!

F: OK … so, as a compromise then, why don't we go for the Angel of the North, the one with the four mini-pictures from around Britain and the one of the Nottinghill Carnival.

M: Sounds good to me!

page131, Listening, Exercise 3

On September 30th, 1968, the first Boeing 747 rolled out of the production plant. Since then, these planes have carried a number of passengers equivalent to one quarter of the world's population. Despite this, nobody has produced a guide to knowing your way around one of these giants of the sky – until now. Here then, are some essential pointers for the wary air traveller.

Seat 30C is definitely the best seat to get sick in: mainly because the first-aid kit is located in the galley between business and economy. However, on a British Airways 747 flight, sit as near to the flight deck as possible. In a medical emergency, the crew get remote back-up from MedAir, a company based in Phoenix, Arizona. One of MedAir's doctors, who are on 24-hour standby, will relay advice.

If you're in a hurry, try seats 30AB and C and 31HJ and K. Passengers sitting here will be the first economy class travellers to be let off the plane. If you are familiar with the disembarkation procedure at your destination, you could chance it and get a seat at the back: they might allow passengers to exit both ways.

Since the cabin crew begin to serve meals at either end of the section in economy, you'll be served last if you book a seat in the middle block, that is seats 46 to 52DEF and G.

The best seats for the video screens are definitely 55ABCHJ and K and 45ABCHJ and K – close enough, but you don't get a crick in your neck. Unfortunately, as the world's most popular in-flight entertainment appears to be *Bean: The Ultimate Disaster Movie*, you may wish to hide in the toilet instead.

Those with first-flight nerves or delicate stomachs should avoid the end of the plane (for example seats 68ACDEFGH and K) as this is where turbulence makes itself felt most strongly.

Seats 30C, 31C and H, 32C and H are probably the noisiest parts of the aircraft. Don't sit here if you want peace and quiet as you'll be right in the middle of the plane's catering operation, and subject to a cacophony of clattering trays and rumbling trolleys.

Because of their extra leg room, 54AB and C and HJ and K are the most popular seats on the plane. For safety reasons, airlines will not allow passengers with mobility problems to sit in them.

page 135, Listening, Exercises 2 and 3; Vocabulary, Exercise 1

Presenter: Michael Palin, one of the original Monty Python team, went on an extraordinary adventure in the early 1990s. He set out to travel from the North Pole to the South Pole, following the 30 degree east line of longitude. Palin and his team, using aircraft only as a last resort, endured extremes of heat and cold, as they crossed seventeen countries on trains, trucks, ships, rafts, ski-doos, buses, barges, bicycles and balloons. The journey took 141 days. Here we hear an extract from his diary. It is the 64th day and they have recently arrived in the Sudan.

Michael Palin: Day 64 Wadi Halfa to Atbara. At four o'clock we cross the sand to the station. Crowds are already milling around the long train, which is made up of three open service wagons at the front, eighteen passenger coaches and eight freight cars at the back, a total of twenty-nine vehicles behind one American-built diesel.

The Governor arrives to see us off. He presents me with a box of dates for the journey, and smiles and shakes hands with us all most warmly. 'When the train leaves you will see a sight,' he chuckles, and indeed as the whistle wails across the desert at five o'clock sharp and this huge, unwieldy combination begins to move, the low embankment is filled with a mass of running figures, hurtling towards the train, leaping onto the coaches and eventually clambering up onto the roof.

Apart from the Roof Class travellers who, if they are prepared to risk extremes of heat and cold and blowing sand, are not officially discouraged, there are three Classes on the train. Although we are in First it's quite basic – we are four to a compartment, few of the lights or fans work and the washbasin in the WC has disappeared. The train superintendent, another big, friendly man, reckons there could be 4000 passengers altogether, though he doesn't know for sure. A milepost in the sand indicates 899 kilometres to Khartoum.

Once a source of great pride, the Nile Valley Express is now much reduced. Nearly all the coaches are in need of repair, and the wooden struts of their frames can often be seen through the rotten panelling. Delays are almost obligatory, sometimes extending to days. But, for all its inadequacies, riding this train is an exhilarating experience. As night falls on the Nubian Desert and a pale half moon lends a ghostly glow to a landscape of silver sand and occasional low, jagged peaks, I sit at the open door of our coach, with a little Van Morrison on my personal stereo, and marvel at the sheer beauty of it all.

Twice we come to an unscheduled halt – once for a broken vacuum pipe, and once for 'engine failure'. As soon as the train stops, passengers on the roof jump down and curl up to sleep on the sand, usually in groups of three or four, with one person on watch in case the train should start. Some get out to pray, others to stretch their legs and cool off in the light desert breeze.

Then miraculously, the train rumbles into motion and they all rush back as we continue into the night, shadows from lighted compartments forming an abstract pattern of cubes and squares on the floor of the desert and spent cigarettes flashing from windows like fireflies.

UNIT 12

page 146, Grammar plus, Exercises 6, 7 and 8

Extract 1

Male 1: … and when you think … when you think … what a mess this lot have made of things since they got in … well, well, I mean … it's absolutely …

Male 2: You're absolutely right … I mean … umm … The first thing they do, the first thing they do is … they do in the health service. I mean … if you look at it … I mean, what have we got now: no nurses, and then … you have to, you have to wait ages to get anything seen to, and then, of course, well then they haven't got the money for the machines they need.

M1: … Yeah, and what about the old folks, like my old mum? My old mum, you know, you know it's so bad now, she has to choose between having the fire on and having a bite to eat. Can you believe it? It's shocking. That's what it is, shocking. I mean, you know, it's no good trying to tell me there are too many old people. There's plenty of money, plenty of money … they just spend it on their own stupid nonsense.

M2: Oh yeah, well ummm … I know which way I'm going to be voting …

M1: You can say that again!

Extract 2

… and, to conclude, it falls upon me to highlight just a few of the catastrophic decisions that this government has made since the last election.

In fact, no sooner had they got into power than they began dismantling the framework of our National Health Service. And now look at the results: a shortage of nurses, lengthy waiting times for patients, not to mention totally inadequate equipment and resources.

As well as that, at no time in living memory have we had such poor provision for our elderly. We should all be appalled at the current situation where many of our older citizens are having to choose between heating and food during the winter months. This surely cannot be right. They put this all down to the growing numbers of pensioners but, frankly, never have I heard such a lame excuse. The reality of course is that they have diverted this money to finance their own political propaganda machine.

Under no circumstances can we allow this government to be re-elected. If we do, we have only ourselves to blame for the chaos that will surely follow.

page 149, Listening, Exercise 1

Well, here we are at the Koestler Parapsychology Unit, the UK's leading ESP [Extra Sensory Perception] research centre, deep in the heart of Edinburgh University. This is Britain's very own X-Files laboratory. The Institute enjoys an international reputation and the team here have devised a range of rigorous tests for ESP ability since they began back in the late 1980s. They're the toughest ever administered and yet they've produced some startling results. The key test, known as the 'ganzfeld' experiment, takes place in a small, soundproof, windowless room deep within the unit, which contains a set of hissing headphones, a red light – and a big comfy armchair.

Once settled into the armchair, the subject's eyes are covered with halves of ping-pong balls, through which the red light creates a warm glow – an effect similar to the experience of gently dozing on a summer's day. Then on go the headphones, through which comes a gentle hissing sound. After half an hour, the subject feels totally calm and relaxed. And then the experiment can begin. Outside the room, a computer randomly selects what will be 'transmitted' from an image library and projects it onto a TV screen. Watching it is the 'sender' – who focuses on the screen and attempts to telepathically beam the message over to the person in the sealed room.

Then comes the crucial part of the experiment. The computer picks another three images, mixes them up, and shows all four to the person in the sealed room. The person then has to pick out the one that was 'beamed over' to them, something they only have a one-in-four chance of doing by fluke.

The evidence that something spooky occurs during these tests is now starting to mount up, according to Morris: 'Since I came here, 10 years ago, I've come to the conclusion that the probability that something is going on has gone from around 80 per cent to around 90 to 95 per cent.

The latest and most impressive evidence comes from a series of 128 ganzfeld tests carried out at the Koestler Parapsychology Unit. Results show that the proportion of people able to pick out the picture being beamed to them was 48 per cent – almost twice the rate expected. The chances of doing this by fluke alone are less than one in 39 million. Impressive? Well, scientists should certainly think so; they get excited by any result with odds of just one in 20. By those standards, the latest results are a million times more 'significant' than many scientific findings. In short, by any scientific research standards, the results could be taken as proof that ESP exists.

UNIT 13

page 154, Listening, Exercises 2 and 3

Interviewer: Welcome to this week's edition of 'Making A Difference' and today we are very fortunate to have with us Muhammad Yunus … a banker with a plan to end world poverty with £17 and a lot of trust. Muhammad tell us more …

Muhammad Yunus: Hello. Well … in the early days I remember getting very excited, teaching my students in Bangladesh how economic theories provided answers to economic problems of all types. Yet, all of a sudden, I started having an empty feeling. What good were all these elegant theories when people were dying of starvation around me? So, I and some of my students went to the neighbouring village of Jobra.

In Jobra, one day, I came across a young woman constructing a stool out of bamboo. She was squatting on the dirt floor of her veranda. She wore a red sari and could have been any one of a million women who labour every day from morning to night in utter destitution. Her name was Sufia Begum.

I asked her if she owned the bamboo she was working with. She told me that she did and explained that it cost five taka (13 pence) to buy. However, she doesn't have five taka, so she has to borrow this from 'paikars' who are a kind of middlemen. The arrangement is that she must sell her bamboo stools back to them at the end of the day, to repay her loan. Then, what is left over is her profit.

I asked her how much she actually sold the bamboo stools for. Apparently, it turns out to be five taka and 50 paisa. So, at the end of her day's work she makes 50 paisa profit. That's just over one penny! I was horrified. Surely there was a better way.

The next day we started making a list of how many in Jobra, like Sufia, were borrowing from traders and missing out on what they should have been earning from the fruits of their labours. The list finally named 42 people who in total had borrowed 856 taka, a total of less than £17. I couldn't believe that all this misery was purely because of the lack of £17.

So, I decided to lend them the £17 and I said that they could repay me whenever they could afford to. That was the beginning of it all. Our clients do not need to show how much wealth they have. On the contrary, they need to prove how poor they are.

Now, our staff meet more than 2,300,000 borrowers face to face each week, on their doorstep. Each month we lend out more than $35 million in tiny loans. At the same time, almost a similar amount comes back to us in repayments.

UNIT 14

page 170, Grammar plus, Exercise 4

1:   You are both more than welcome to spend the night at my house.

2:   Whatever you do, don't forget to get your grandmother a birthday card.

3:   If I were in your position, I would make sure that you talked this over with your mum and dad.

4:   It's really important that you don't make the same stupid mistake that I did.

5:   Marvellous news about the engagement! It's absolutely wonderful.

6:   Sarah, this is Michael, my best friend. Michael, this is Sarah.

7:   I'm definitely not going to go back to college next year.

8:   I'm sorry but this really isn't good enough. The food is barely lukewarm.

9:   OK, so it's true. I did go out with Matthew for the evening.

page 170, Grammar plus, Exercise 5

1:   It's true. I know I was wrong to get angry.

2:   Well, far be it from me to brag, but you know I did earn over £100,000 last year.

3:   No, I've certainly never met him before.

4:   Well at least I know how to keep a secret.

5:   You really ought to think very carefully about what you're doing.

6:   You do realise this'll be your last chance.

7:   … so, really, I need to change things completely, once and for all …

8:   Rebecca, Rebecca, Rebecca …

page 170, Grammar plus, Exercise 6

The man's view

We'd been going out for ages more than three years. I thought we were getting on really well. We'd talked about maybe getting a place together and so on. My family all really liked her and I think her family liked me. Then suddenly one day she seemed to change. Nothing I did was good enough. She was always criticising me. And then one day she announced that it was all over. I still don't understand how it happened.

The woman's view

It was never really right. I suppose we didn't really want the same things. Still, it was OK, until at some point he just started taking me completely for granted. He started kind of ordering me around. It was awful. I tried to talk to him about it but he just wouldn't listen. In the end I had no choice. I had to finish it.

page 172, Listening, Exercise 2

On 27th August 1883 the volcanic eruption on Krakatoa blocked out the sun until 11 a.m. the following day, poured ash over ships 6000 kilometres away, and created a tidal wave so powerful it wiped out 165 coastal villages. The after-effects of that explosion were almost as staggering: the world's temperature dropped for five years and the sun turned blue as ash and aerosol from the volcano circled the equator for 13 days.

No eruption since has matched Krakatoa for sheer destructive power and some believe that this means that the planet is due for another massive explosion from one of the 1,511 volcanoes which have erupted in the past 10,000 years, and could do so again.

Considering mankind first recorded a volcanic eruption in a wall painting in Turkey way back in 6200 BC, we continue to treat them with an astonishing blend of ignorance and complacency. And while we now understand how many of the different types of volcanoes work, we still don't really understand all the factors which may make a volcano erupt.

And the dangers are very real. The US Geological Survey, for example, believes that 500 million people are at risk from volcanoes that might, at some point, erupt. So working out the causes is more than mere academic concern.

Many theories have been put forward, including sudden changes in sea level, specific alignments of the sun and moon, the pattern of underlying earthquakes, ground deformation and the escape of carbon dioxide. All these things have been cited as possible indicators of future activity, but even if they are, it's far from easy to read the signals. And, even so, the potentially devastating consequences of volcanic activity are still not taken as seriously as they might be by officialdom.

Dr. Flavio Dobran, who used to be professor of vulcanology at the universities of Rome and Turin, is highly critical of the official line on Vesuvius. This maintains that an emergency plan, foreseeing the evacuation of around 700,000 people from the high-risk areas within seven days of an eruption, is both safe and sensible.

The problem with this is that computer simulations suggest that once the rock plug in Vesuvius gives way, it will take just 200 seconds to reach the town of Torre del Greco (population 100,000) and only 100 seconds more to reach the outskirts of Naples and its three million inhabitants. And this is why Dobran thinks the Italian government should either persuade people to move or build thirty-metre high barriers a few miles from Vesuvius's central vent to stop the flow. Both suggestions have been ignored.

page 176, Listening

1/6: Now I know we all want to get out there and <u>enjoy the sunshine</u>. But we do have to remember we're not used to how hot it gets in the early afternoon. I mean we don't want to all end up with sunburn do we and spoil things for <u>the rest of the week? I think the best thing is</u> if we all go downstairs to the indoor pool for a while, and then, a bit later we can go and find a spot near the sea. Anyway, it'll be less crowded then too.

2/7: With a bit of luck they say it'll be raining tomorrow <u>which I think would be good for us</u>. I mean, that always means <u>a low turnout</u> and I'm sure our <u>supporters</u> believe in us and they really want the kind of change we're offering and they won't be put off by a bit of bad weather. On the other hand, I can feel a kind of complacency about the lot <u>in office</u>. Everyone assumes they're going to <u>get in again</u>. And that means people won't think that their particular <u>vote</u> matters. I think it's going <u>to give us a real chance</u>. Of course, the other side of the coin is if it's nice and sunny but that seems pretty unlikely at the moment.

3/8: I know it seems OK now but we've got to remember the way that storm clouds can spring up out of nowhere and visibility can go right down. I'll never forget the time when Ted and I were up in Scotland a couple of years ago. We suddenly got caught by this incredible cloudburst, in the most horrendous driving rain. We could hardly see what was going on. Fortunately we hadn't got too far and <u>made it back to the base camp OK. Some others weren't so lucky and got stuck up there until the rescue team could get to them. I don't want us to risk any chance of that happening.</u>

4/9: In fact, you know, this notion of SAD, that is 'seasonal affective disorder', is very real to many people. I mean <u>I have had a number of people come to see me feeling lethargic and suffering from symptoms of depression</u> and you know it very specifically relates to the winter months. You might find it hard to believe but something like 500,000 people in Britain suffer from SAD brought on by, by low cloud and the long dark winter nights, and these people become extremely depressed due to <u>changes in their biochemistry</u> you see, and they sleep for many hours but they never feel rested. They're irritable and feel incapable of work or socialising. A large percentage of <u>sufferers</u>, however, can be helped in the winter months, if they spend two or three hours under artificial lights.

5/10: <u>It was actually great.</u> I mean I know it was <u>incredibly muddy</u> and we were all slipping and sliding all over the place but that was <u>part of the fun</u> I guess. Mum's going to kill me when she sees <u>my kit</u>! I couldn't believe the number of <u>people who turned out to watch</u>, especially as there was nowhere to shelter. My sister came and <u>was shouting like mad</u>. It was such good fun! I mean, I know <u>we lost</u> and everything but <u>we had a brilliant time</u> and I'm sure <u>we'll win our next match</u>.

UNIT 15

page 181, Listening, Exercise 2

Wouldn't life be easier if the whole world spoke the same language? Many hundreds of men and women, not content to simply dream this dream, have actually sat down and created languages for the world to speak.

The idea of a universal language is known to have appealed to the ancient Greeks, and in twelfth-century Germany St Hildegard is said to have invented a language with a new alphabet and a vocabulary of 900 words.

In the seventeenth century, one of the most enthusiastic proponents of this idea was the English cleric and scientist John Wilkins. Wilkins's proposals, published in 1668, followed the fashion of the time for totally logical systems of communication that bore no relation to existing languages. But it was not until the late nineteenth century that the world really put artificial languages to the test by attempting to learn to speak them. The pace-setter was Volapük, launched in 1880 by Johann Schleyer, a German priest. Within a decade, it had about 200,000 supporters in Europe and the United States. But it soon became apparent that Volapük was far too complicated, largely because of its reliance on German grammar.

The next universal language to appear was Esperanto, in 1887. Esperanto was invented by Dr Ludwig Zamenhof, and it sprang from the linguistic confusion of his own upbringing. As a boy he had spoken Russian, Yiddish, Polish and Hebrew at home, and learnt another five languages at school, and this had convinced him of the need for a world language.

Esperanto has enjoyed greater success than any of its rivals, especially in the period after the First World War. Then, many people hoped that, in the interests of fostering international understanding, Esperanto would be adopted as the official world language. This was not to be, but Esperanto has nevertheless remained the world's best-known auxiliary language. It's especially popular with Japanese people, who find it easier to learn than French, German or English, even though the constructions and roots of Esperanto are totally European.

Today there are more than 100 periodicals published in Esperanto, and thousands of books. Several countries also broadcast Esperanto radio programmes. And while Esperanto may not have succeeded in becoming the medium of the world, who knows, maybe we will have found a new Esperanto before this century is over?

page 184, Exam focus, Paper 4 Listening: Part 4 (multiple choice)

1: It's weird because even now I get this recurring dream where I end up waking up in a real state. I usually find myself sitting bolt upright in bed. I'm panicking because I know I've got a really important history exam that morning and I haven't done nearly enough revision. I feel physically cold with the terror of it. Then I realise that that was something that happened years ago and I don't actually have a history exam and that it's all in the past. Still for a moment I'm right back there as a terrified 18-year-old. It's amazing that one bad experience like that can have such long-term, far-reaching effects.

2: I used to hate revising for exams. My parents were really strict about it. I remember long hot summer evenings when my friends would be out having fun and I would be stuck indoors with my books. I don't know how much good it did though, as my mind used to constantly wander off and I used to daydream about being somewhere else. I don't know if I will do the same with my kids if I have any. I mean, there's definitely more to life than doing well in exams. Still, I probably wouldn't have got where I am today without my parents pushing me … so maybe I should be grateful.

3: I was at this really progressive school where they didn't have exams as such. They didn't believe in them. We did work hard though and I felt I learnt a lot. We were given a lot more personal responsibility than most other kids my age. I mean we had to choose which classes we went to … or even if we went to classes at all. That meant though that we were pretty motivated in the classes we attended because we had actually chosen to go rather than being forced to go. We had to do lots of our own research for projects we were working on. We got really good at knowing how and where to look for information. That's helped me a lot since I left school.

4: I do feel that with exams a good part of it is to do with luck. I mean, I used to 'question spot' like mad, by which I mean that I'd look at old exam papers and make a calculated guess as to which questions would come up in the exam and revise those subjects well and just not touch the other areas. It was a risky strategy but most of the time, fortunately, it paid off. What it means now is that I know loads about some things and absolutely nothing about the rest. I think that might be defeating the object of being at school but it kind of worked for me.

5: What they say about school days being the best days of your life was definitely true for me. I remember that I used to be involved in everything: sports team, choir, orchestra, drama … you name it, I was in it. I had lots of good friends too … it was great. I think I kind of threw myself into all the school stuff as things weren't great at home. It became like a substitute kind of family. Anyway, I did pretty well academically too, but then after I left things took a bit of a downturn and since then I suppose I've never really found my niche as such. I've kind of drifted from one thing to another. I do miss that time.

Unit 1 test

Choose the best alternative to fill the gap in each of the following sentences.

1   I was completely ………… by the skill and daring of the trapeze artists.
    A awful   **B** awestruck   **C** awkward   **D** awesome

2   When she saw me nearly drop the priceless vase she ………… in horror.
    A grasped   **B** grunted   **C** grumbled   **D** gasped

3   My brother has always had a penchant ………… fast motorbikes.
    A to   **B** at   **C** for   **D** on

4   He could hear someone playing a ………… melody on a flute.
    A hunting   **B** haunting   **C** haunted   **D** hunted

5   The little girls were ………… brightly coloured hoops around their waists.
    A twirling   **B** curling   **C** swirling   **D** hurling

6   She ………… us how to get to the gallery where the exhibition was on.
    A explained   **B** told   **C** said   **D** described

7   Tim ………… some money from Simon to buy some art materials.
    A borrowed   **B** lent   **C** sent   **D** gave

8   The way he behaved at the party is ………… as far as I'm concerned
    A forgiving   **B** unforgiving   **C** forgivable   **D** unforgivable

9   The woman next to me marred my ………… of the performance by coughing and snuffling throughout the second act.
    A enjoying   **B** enjoyed   **C** enjoyable   **D** enjoyment

10 I ………… she is hoping to be able to work in a circus when she's a little older.
    A knew   **B** know   **C** was knowing   **D** am knowing

11 Where do you keep ………… knives and forks?
    A –   **B** some   **C** a   **D** the

12 The tickets for the play weren't nearly as expensive ………… we thought.
    A as   **B** than   **C** that   **D** so

13 I certainly feel a lot ………… since I started going swimming every day.
    A more fit   **B** fit   **C** fitter   **D** fittest

14 She's one of ………… talented performers I've even seen.
    A more   **B** a more   **C** most   **D** the most

15 If you ………… the chance, you should try and see Cirque du Soleil next time they're in town.
    A had   **B** would have   **C** had had   **D** have

16 ………… you already have some knowledge of rhythmic gymnastics, you'll need to find a trainer.
    A Unless   **B** Providing   **C** If   **D** Supposing

17 If you had told me you liked modern art, I ………… given you our invitations to the opening of his exhibition.
    A had   **B** would   **C** would have   **D** have

18 Let me give you ………… advice. Make sure you know how to do something else apart from acting.
    A an   **B** the   **C** –   **D** some

19 She's got ………… lovely thick shiny black hair.
    A a   **B** the   **C** –   **D** some

20 I'm considering ………… to one of those circus training schools to learn to walk a tightrope.
    A to go   **B** go   **C** going   **D** I go

21 My parents wouldn't let me ………… a rock band until I was fifteen.
    A joining   **B** to join   **C** join   **D** to joining

22 I wish I ………… time to see more exhibitions.
    A could have   **B** have   **C** had   **D** would have

23 ………… he's very talented, he's found it difficult to make a living from his art.
    A Despite   **B** In spite of   **C** However   **D** Although

24 She's ………… good pianist. I'm surprised she doesn't play professionally.
    A so   **B** such   **C** a so   **D** such a

25 Is that the artist ………… paintings were so controversial?
    A who's   **B** whose   **C** who   **D** that

Unit 2 test

Choose the best alternative to fill the gap in each of the following sentences.

1 She smiled rather too .... when they announced that the other actor had been given the role.
A bitterly B uneasily C broadly D sincerely

2 The waiter hovered .... all the time they were eating their meal.
A intimately B drastically C patiently D attentively

3 I .... regret having told her where I had hidden the money.
A abominably B bitterly C drastically D intuitively

4 I wouldn't say I know her .... , but we see each other from time to time.
A intimately B imperceptibly C sincerely D intuitively

5 The two little boys were lying on the floor giggling ....
A uneasily B irresponsibly C helplessly D intimately

6 They're erecting a statue in the town square to .... the wonderful work done by volunteers during the floods.
A celebrate B remember C commemorate D recall

7 I had a .... something terrible was going to happen that day.
A premonition B prediction C preview D precursor

8 The original design was .... by a team of architects working in close consultation with the gallery director.
A originated B initiated C started D conceived

9 The five Olympic rings are a .... of the five continents.
A logo B sign C symbol D emblem

10 I've lost my .... and I can't get into my e-mail account.
A sign B symbol C password D logo

11 When I was at school we were strictly .... to eat in the street.
A outlawed B prohibited C sanctioned D forbidden

12 Passengers are asked to .... their cigarettes and to refrain from smoking until they reach the terminal building.
A douse B smother C put D extinguish

13 There was a .... on board the Bounty and the crew put the captain in a lifeboat and set it adrift.
A rebellion B insurrection C mutiny D revolution

14 Everyone was .... with him after he missed the penalty in the last five minutes of the match.
A comforting B feeling C commiserating
D feeling sorry

15 There was the most fantastic .... during the opening ceremony.
A display of fireworks B firework display
C firework's display D display firework

16 They went on a .... holiday in South-East Asia.
A seven weeks' B seven week's C seven-week
D seven week

17 If we had a .... we could play a game to pass the time.
A pack cards B pack of cards C cards' pack
D card pack

18 She was wearing a .... that must have cost millions.
A necklace of diamonds B diamond's necklace
C diamonds' necklace D diamond necklace

19 She jammed her finger in the ....
A car's door B car door C cars' door D door car

20 My favourite kind of yoghurt is made from ....
A milk of the sheep B milk of sheep C sheep milk
D sheep's milk

21 You .... to open a window if you're too hot.
A should B must C ought D have

22 She said we .... come early if we didn't want to.
A hadn't B mustn't C couldn't D needn't

23 You .... have seen Jess in the street because he's in Formentera.
A mightn't B mustn't C shouldn't D couldn't

24 You .... come out to the airport to meet me. I could have taken a bus.
A needn't have B needn't C don't need
D didn't need

25 You really .... come and visit us next time you're in Paris.
A can B could C ought D must

Unit 3 test

Choose the best alternative to fill the gap in each of the following sentences.

1 Some of the people in the audience got completely carried ………… and tried to get up on the stage.
A out   B off   C away   D over

2 How much ………… do Jerry's opinions carry with the committee?
A weight   B value   C importance   D worth

3 Lots of people said their idea would never work, but they managed to carry it ………… .
A out   B off   C away   D over

4 Sometimes I wonder what it was that carried her ………… the years of poverty and suffering.
A over   B away from   C through   D out of

5 There was a vote and the ………… was carried, 33 to 12.
A premise   B motion   C movement   D suggestion

6 Don't take any notice of Justine. She never carries ………… her threats.
A out   B off   C through   D over

7 You look very red in the face. ………… or something?
A Have you been running   B Have you run
C Were you running   D Had you been running

8 By the time Cristina's youngest daughter turns 21, I ………… .
A am retiring   B have retired   C have been retiring
D will have retired

9 It's been a good year. I ………… two books and a couple of articles, all of which are now in print.
A 've written   B 've been writing   C 'll have written
D 'd written

10 My neighbour really gets on my nerves. She ………… the washing machine on late at night.
A has always put   B had always put   C is always putting
D has always been putting

11 He ………… over a million dollars before he turned eighteen.
A had earned   B has earned   C was earning
D had been earning

12 What ………… this time next year, do you think?
A will you be doing   B will you do   C are you doing
D do you do

13 ………… of spending a whole month in France next summer.
A I think   B I will think   C I will be thinking
D I am thinking

14 She really is a ………… woman. She's made a fortune but she started with nothing.
A self-sufficient   B self-centred   C self-made
D self-governing

15 I suppose she is a little absent-………… from time to time, but she's absolutely brilliant.
A brained   B consciousness   C minded   D spirited

16 Ours isn't a particularly long-………… friendship but it's certainly the one I value most.
A run   B standing   C winded   D lasting

17 Nigel's fantastic in a crisis. He's so calm and …………-headed.
A hard   B square   C level   D light

18 You need to take vitamins to stop yourself getting run ………… .
A over   B out   C through   D down

19 Patrick was quite well-………… before he won the lottery.
A out   B up   C on   D off

20 ………… reference to your letter of September 17, 2000, I wish to inform you that your application has been accepted.
A On   B At   C With   D By

21 I would be most ………… if you would return my manuscript to me in the enclosed stamped addressed envelope.
A gracious   B indebted   C grateful   D ingratiated

22 Can you tell me the year ………… Australia introduced decimal currency?
A when   B which   C what   D in which

23 The currency ………… value has declined most rapidly over the last year is the Euro.
A which   B that   C whose   D who's

24 I'm not sure I'd ………… along with what the Prime Minister said about education spending.
A get   B go   C be   D carry

25 As far as ………… , family are more important than friends.
A I concern   B I'm concerned   C I'm concerning
D I've concerned

Unit 4 test

Choose the best alternative to fill the gap in each of the following sentences.

1 Remember .... some spaghetti when you go to the supermarket.
   A getting   B to get   C get   D you get

2 I would never have expected .... the exam if she hadn't told me I was doing so well.
   A to pass   B passed   C pass   D passing

3 When did you start .... the piano?
   A to playing   B to play   C play   D played

4 We don't usually allow members of the public .... the library.
   A using   B used   C to use   D to using

5 I don't regret .... to live in France, but I do miss New Zealand sometimes.
   A have come   B to have come   C having come
   D had come

6 She admitted .... the anonymous letter.
   A to send   B that she sends   C to sending   D have sent

7 He suggested .... a break around three in the afternoon.
   A to take   B to taking   C should take   D we take

8 Mentioning anything to do with overpopulation in front of Bill is like a red .... to a bull.
   A cloth   B dress   C robe   D rag

9 Be careful what you say to John. He's like a bear with a sore .... this morning.
   A paw   B stomach   C head   D tooth

10 Let me help you with that heavy suitcase. I'm as strong as a(n) ....
   A buffalo   B bull   C yak   D ox

11 Nothing ever seems to ruffle Lucy. She stays as cool as a .... whatever is happening around her.
   A lettuce   B cucumber   C radish   D tomato

12 She turned as white as .... when you mentioned the night of 15th November. I'm sure she knows what happened.
   A a sheet   B ice   C snow   D a wall

13 You're like a bull in a .... shop sometimes. How could you have been so insensitive as to mention Bruce to Caroline?
   A hardware   B china   C haberdashery   D pet

14 She's always .... clichés like 'money doesn't grow on trees' and so on.
   A putting out   B giving out   C passing out
   D trotting out

15 A study that's just been published .... our theory completely.
   A puts up   B holds up   C backs up   D takes up

16 I suppose it might be the seven-year .... but sometimes I wish I hadn't married Carlos.
   A scratch   B itch   C bite   D sting

17 I'll have spaghetti bolognese. No, on second .... , perhaps I'll have the lasagne.
   A opinion   B ideas   C thoughts   D impression

18 I don't think there's so much as a .... of truth in that rumour.
   A grain   B speck   C crumb   D pebble

19 He calls her 'Funny Face', but she says it's a(n) .... of endearment.
   A expression   B phrase   C term   D sign

20 It was just a .... of the tongue, but she still gave me a lower mark for the speaking test.
   A mistake   B slip   C error   D lapse

21 He had a momentary .... of concentration and before he knew it the car had spun out of control.
   A mistake   B slip   C error   D lapse

22 I know I can speak without fear of .... when I say that George Wilson has always been a tremendous asset to the company.
   A difference   B correction   C argument
   D contradiction

23 They had a bit of a difference of .... and they don't really see much of each other any more.
   A view   B opinion   C idea   D perspective

24 I wonder what .... of wisdom good old Professor Maxwell will cast before us in this morning's lecture.
   A gems   B jewels   C pearls   D stones

25 It's only a(n) .... of time before the traffic in this city ceases to move altogether.
   A issue   B question   C problem   D query

Progress test 1 Units 1–5

1 Only one of these sentences with modal verbs is correct. Find the mistakes in the others and correct them.

1 He might gone out to the cinema.

2 You should tried to give up smoking. You must be spending a fortune on cigarettes.

3 You must have know the café I'm talking about. Everyone goes there.

4 They mustn't have forgotten about the party. I rang and reminded them yesterday.

5 I may go to Cyprus in April but I haven't decided yet.

6 Nothing might possibly stop me loving Anthony.

7 You only need saying the word and I'll come and help you.

8 You haven't to bring a bottle of wine or anything. There'll be more than enough to eat and drink.

2 Complete the compounds to fill in the gaps in these sentences.

1 I'm so …………-minded lately. Yesterday I found my wallet in the fridge!

2 The air-………… in the cinema was turned up so high we almost froze to death.

3 She's a …………-made Internet entrepreneur.

4 It was a last-………… decision to go on holiday so we didn't have much choice of resorts.

5 She was wearing a very …………-fitting jacket and trousers.

6 I'm not worried about Cindy travelling on her own. She's a very …………-headed girl.

7 Most people can't tell the difference between mass-………… furniture and something crafted by an individual carpenter.

8 Those so-………… 'super-models' don't strike me as being that special.

9 He wasn't badly injured because he was wearing a bullet-………… vest.

10 He's had a …………-standing disagreement with a neighbour over where the boundary lies between their gardens.

3 Rewrite these sentences beginning with the words given.

1 If you won the lottery, would you give up your job?
Supposing …

2 If she had known what negative reactions her book was to receive she would probably never have written it.
Had …

3 If you came to Holland again, would you come to visit me?
If you were …

4 If you take a seat, the doctor will see you in a few moments.
If you'll …

5 If you discovered it was possible to live for five hundred years, would you want to?
Imagine …

6 If you are going past the Odeon can you give me a call if *The Beach* is on.
If you happen …

4 Complete the collocations in these sentences.

1 How long can you ………… your breath under water?

2 He kept ………… his fingers on the table.

3 Why don't you answer me instead of just shrugging your …………?

4 Don't wrinkle your ………… like that. You used to love liver.

5 If you don't stop ………… your knuckles, I'm going to scream!

6 She pursed her ………… in annoyance.

7 She sat rigidly in the dentist's chair with her fists tightly ....

8 She slipped over on an icy pavement and .... her ankle.

9 I think I might have .... a muscle in my back. It's really sore.

10 Why are you raising your .... like that? The shop assistant said it really suited me.

11 I asked the boy where his parents were but he just .... his head.

12 The two cats were sitting staring at the goldfish bowl, really licking their ....

5   Paper 2, Part 1: notes and messages

1   In each of the following notes, one of the highlighted sentence elements cannot be left out. Which one?

1 Hi Tom,
I won't be back before 11.30. I have got a training session at the pool. Sorry! I forgot to mention it this morning. The lasagne is in the oven. There is stuff for a salad in the fridge. Can you record Ally McBeal for me? There's a video in the machine. I will see you later.
Love,
Mary

2 Clara,
Peter phoned. He won't be able to come to the concert tonight. He said something about having to finish a project. He says you can use his season ticket if you want to. You should phone him before five this afternoon and let him know.
Tina

3 Dear Alan,
Don't forget! It's Dad's birthday on 21st September. Do you fancy going in with me on a present for him? I thought a subscription to 'History Today' might be good. Let me know as soon as possible. I'll be at home all weekend.
Love,
Elisa

2   Rewrite the notes leaving out the other sentence elements and using abbreviations for the underlined words and phrases.

3   Write notes of no longer than 50 words for the following situations.

1 Your flatmate's mother phoned to remind her/him about her/his father's birthday. She said she wanted your flatmate to call her back soon.

2 You are having a flat-warming party next month. Send your friends an e-mail message telling them the necessary details, asking them to bring their own drinks and to tell you if they can come to the party.

Unit 6 test

Choose the best alternative to fill the gap in each of the following sentences.

1 By the end of the first half of the twenty-first century women .... against men in many sports.
   A are competing   B compete   C are going to compete
   D will be competing

2 The Olympic games are .... start tomorrow morning at 8.30 a.m. our time.
   A due to   B on the point of   C about to   D bound to

3 By the end of the games Australia .... almost as many medals as they did in Atlanta.
   A will be winning   B will win   C will have won
   D are winning

4 Don't tell Alice who won. She .... the results and she'll almost certainly want to see the race.
   A won't have heard   B won't hear   C isn't hearing
   D doesn't hear

5 .... anything this Friday evening? We're having a few people over for a drink and a light meal.
   A Will you do   B Do you do   C Have you done
   D Will you be doing

6 He's a bit of a(n) .... He never seems to win anything or even get a place.
   A ran-also   B no runner   C also-ran   D has-run

7 The Dutch team managed to .... out a winner in the last five minutes of play.
   A get   B pull   C take   D hold

8 She's had a lot of .... in her career but she has continued to train hard and win races, nevertheless.
   A set-ups   B set-tos   C set-offs   D setbacks

9 Ian Thorpe is the quintessence of an athlete .... glory.
   A after   B in pursuit of   C trailing   D chasing after

10 His injuries prevented him from .... training until only a few weeks before the championships.
    A resuming   B restarting   C rekindling   D recalling

11 He got married and almost gave up tennis completely but now I hear he's .... a comeback.
    A having   B getting   C taking   D making

12 She won a gold medal in the 200 metres freestyle, a silver in the medley and .... of that she broke two world records.
    A in top   B at top   C on top   D to top

13 It's all very .... saying you're going to train harder, but you've got to actually do it.
    A good   B well   C fine   D right

14 After the .... had called the meeting to order, we got down to business.
    A leader   B boss   C conductor   D chairperson

15 A number of the .... were injured in the blaze.
    A fire-battlers   B fire extinguishers   C fire-stoppers
    D fire-fighters

16 He wanted to travel and got a job as a .... with one of the major airlines.
    A flying aide   B flight assistant   C flying waiter
    D flight attendant

17 She's a woman of her .... You can trust her to do what she says she'll do.
    A promise   B oath   C word   D vow

18 My parents always taught me to be .... person and not to let others influence me too much.
    A my   B true to   C my own   D a real

19 What .... gets on my nerves is the way the commentators are always criticising the other team.
    A absolutely   B quite   C completely   D really

20 She's .... talented but she doesn't spend enough time on the practice courts.
    A totally   B completely   C very   D absolutely

21 They didn't play .... well in the first round and were lucky to get through.
    A quite   B rather   C terribly   D really

22 The new coach has really made an effort to .... team spirit.
    A foster   B advance   C further   D favour

23 She threatened to .... him from the team unless he improved his attitude.
    A quit   B take   C cut   D drop

24 Our team .... first in the local schools' championship.
    A had   B did   C made   D came

25 He's a bit inclined to lose his .... and shout at people if our team are losing the match.
    A temper   B mind   C nerve   D balance

Unit 7 test

Choose the best alternative to fill the gap in each of the following sentences.

1 A: Do you think Justine will get the job?
   B: She should ....
   A do   B get   C have   D have done

2 A: Are you going to get a taxi to the airport?
   B I think ....
   A yes   B it   C so   D to

3 We were going to take our holidays in September but now we can't afford ....
   A take   B to   C so   D them

4 A: I went to France for my holidays this year.
   B: ....
   A I too.   B I also went.   C So did I.   D I did so.

5 I don't seem to have as much energy as I used ....
   A –   B to   C have   D to having

6 Tim is always striving .... perfection but seldom achieving it.
   A at   B towards   C to   D for

7 Living in Singapore has had a great influence .... her work.
   A to   B on   C for   D at

8 I'm not convinced .... research into parapsychology.
   A by   B to   C with   D from

9 Some of the differences in the results were dictated .... factors such as age, social class, gender and country of origin.
   A from   B to   C from   D by

10 According .... Dr Brewster, diet plays a more important role than we might think.
   A with   B to   C from   D by

11 Withdrawal .... human contact can actually affect a child's physical development.
   A to   B at   C by   D of

12 There has been a significant reduction .... the number of fatalities since wearing a helmet became obligatory.
   A of   B to   C in   D from

13 Receiving the anonymous phone calls led directly .... her breakdown in my opinion.
   A up   B towards   C to   D in

14 I have a lot of respect .... the principal of our college.
   A to   B with   C for   D by

15 They congratulated us .... the birth of our twin daughters
   A on   B for   C to   D by

16 Unfortunately your party coincides exactly .... the date of an important meeting I've got in Madrid.
   A to   B at   C with   D on

17 Passengers are asked to refrain .... smoking until they are well inside the terminal building.
   A to   B from   C for   D at

18 The transport strike resulted .... complete traffic chaos in the centre of the city.
   A to   B for   C on   D in

19 She insisted .... paying for the meal.
   A to   B in   C on   D at

20 I wish I .... sold that chair my grandmother left me.
   A couldn't   B didn't   C wouldn't   D hadn't

21 Isn't it time you .... in bed?
   A are   B will be   C were   D would be

22 I'd rather you .... say anything to John about this conversation.
   A don't   B won't   C didn't   D hadn't

23 I wish I .... ride a bicycle.
   A would   B did   C could   D had

24 I wish you .... being so childish about what I said to you yesterday.
   A stop   B would stop   C will stop   D have stopped

25 If only it .... such a wet day. We could have had a picnic.
   A isn't   B couldn't be   C hadn't been   D wouldn't be

Unit 8 test

Choose the best alternative to fill the gap in each of the following sentences.

1 Can you imagine .... in another country?
   A living   B to live   C live   D you live

2 I really miss .... my dog Prince out for his walk every day.
   A taking   B to take   C take   D I take

3 She made .... my favourite pair of jeans.
   A me throwing out   B that I throw out
   C me to throw out   D me throw out

4 My parents encouraged .... a foreign language.
   A me study   B me to study   C me studying
   D that I study

5 He begged .... him.
   A her not to leave   B her not leaving
   C that she didn't leave   D her not leave

6 If you want to avoid .... caught in heavy traffic, leave home before 7 a.m.
   A get   B getting   C to get   D you get

7 She threatened .... him to the police.
   A report   B reporting   C to report   D she report

8 They neglected .... us that the flight would be delayed.
   A inform   B informing   C to inform   D they inform

9 I wouldn't risk .... any later than 5.30 a.m. if I were you.
   A leave   B leaving   C to leave   D you leave

10 I'm sure I locked the door. I remember .... out my keys.
   A get   B getting   C to get   D I have got

11 Something that's really .... her confidence is winning the 200 metres.
   A busted   B bested   C boasted   D boosted

12 She's got some rather .... ideas about extraterrestrials kidnapping people.
   A far-off   B far-flung   C far-removed   D far-fetched

13 She has published .... books and articles on a wide range of subjects.
   A numerous   B numbered   C abundant   D manifold

14 They decided to hold a .... ten years after they had finished school.
   A summit   B reunion   C meeting   D assembly

15 I couldn't remember her name. It was so frustrating because it was on ....
   A the end of my nose   B the top of my head
   C the tip of my tongue   D the point of my chin

16 It's quite a .... your having been born in Melbourne in March 1981 too.
   A chance   B casualty   C luck   D coincidence

17 The film was really .... We were all on the edge of our seats.
   A grasping   B gripping   C griping   D grinding

18 I managed to get to the airport without a .... , but then I realised I didn't have my passport.
   A hatch   B hunch   C hitch   D hotchpotch

19 He pleaded .... us not to take the boat out in such bad weather.
   A to   B for   C with   D at

20 She discouraged .... a motorbike.
   A him to buy   B him from buying
   C that he should not buy   D him buy

21 They warned us .... the old road.
   A against take   B not to take   C against to take
   D not taking

22 He denied .... the money.
   A to take   B to have taken   C he took   D having taken

23 Remind .... Maureen a message about the visa.
   A me to send   B me sending   C me send   D that I send

24 She asked the students to sit in a ....
   A half-circle   B demi-circle   C semicircle   D mini-circle

25 The garden had become rather ....
   A outgrown   B overgrown   C ingrown   D grown

Unit 9 test

Choose the best alternative to fill the gap in each of the following sentences.

1 I suppose it's .... possible but I just don't think it will work in practice.
A theory   B theoretical   C theoretically   D theoretician

2 She showed a lot of .... in the lead-up to the exams.
A determiner   B determinant   C determined
D determination

3 Don't give Pete the job. He's completely ....
A reliance   B reliable   C rely   D unreliable

4 She was .... to do anything about the date of the examination.
A empowered   B powerless   C powerful   D impotent

5 Many of his friends sent cards and messages. Sadly, ... of them were able to be there with him.
A few   B a few   C quite a few   D only few

6 Did you .... any New Year's resolutions this year?
A have   B do   C make   D get

7 The Russian team .... control of the situation in the second half of the match.
A won   B earned   C gained   D obtained

8 I wish you wouldn't .... on at me about throwing those books out. I'm planning to read them again.
A get   B make   C take   D keep

9 I gather he .... quite an impression on the committee.
A did   B made   C gained   D kept

10 I don't know why you want to .... even with Domingo. Just forget about it.
A get   B have   C make   D go

11 She .... across as really self-confident but she's actually very humble.
A gets   B goes   C makes   D comes

12 You won't be able to take a decent photo in this poor light without a(n) ....
A lens   B tripod   C easel   D darkroom

13 As soon as she slipped the .... over the horse's head, he went completely crazy.
A saddle   B bridle   C snorkel   D mask

14 Can you ....-read or do you have to hear the melody before you can play it?
A view   B vision   C sight   D see

15 She writes the music and he writes the ....
A chapter   B blurb   C letters   D lyrics

16 You really can't swim in the ocean here without a ....
A jumpsuit   B tracksuit   C wetsuit   D spacesuit

17 I .... in a lovely warm bubble bath when I heard someone banging on the front door.
A soaked   B had soaked   C have soaked
D was soaking

18 I hadn't realised Tom was Canadian until he .... that his parents lived in Ottawa.
A had mentioned   B mentioned   C has mentioned
D was mentioning

19 I .... Poland for the first time seven years ago.
A have visited   B was visiting   C visited   D visit

20 I .... a lot of things change in this town since I came to live here.
A saw   B am seeing   C see   D have seen

21 I .... only just put out the light when the telephone rang.
A have   B had   C did   D was

22 A: How long .... here? – B: Since 1984.
A do you live   B are you living   C did you live
D have you been living

23 My French teachers .... a lot of emphasis on pronunciation.
A gave   B made   C placed   D devoted

24 Classes are scheduled early in the morning. .... many working people cannot attend.
A As consequence   B In a consequence
C Consequently   D For consequence

25 First and .... I would like to thank everyone for coming along tonight.
A foremost   B forethought   C forearm   D forewarn

Progress test 2 Units 6–10

1 Complete these sentences with a non-sexist word or expression.

1 The chair............ called the meeting to order.

2 People used to regard the work of flight .... as glamorous.

3 Police ....took more than an hour to bring the situation under control.

4 School .... are increasingly critical of the government's new education policy.

5 A spokes............ for the students said they were demonstrating against a proposed increase in university fees.

6 Fire............ said the fire was probably lit deliberately.

2 Paper 3, Part 3: error correction (spelling and punctuation)

In most lines of the following text, there is either a spelling or a punctuation error. For each numbered line write the correctly spelled word or show the correct punctuation at the end of the line. Some lines are correct – indicate these lines with a tick (3) in the box. The exercise begins with three examples (0), (00) and (000).

0	Lucky numbers are certainly not ~~unniversal~~. While	*universal*
00	seven is the lucky number for most people in	✓
000	the ~~West. It~~ is either eight or nine in Asia and	*West, it*
1	the Pacific. The luckyest date in the last century was	
2	considerred to be August 8th 1988 or 8/8/88. It was	
3	the date when the largest number of chinese were	
4	married. In Asia many people would do anything	
5	to get car license plate numbers or street adresses	
6	that add up to nine, or better yet are all nines. Asian	
7	calendars indicate that life is divided into twelve year	
8	cicles, with each year being represented by an	
9	animal. The most important birthday is the 60th	
10	marking the end of the fivth of these. Although	
11	there is no comon unlucky number for Asians,	
12	four seems to be regarded negatively by many,	
13	especially in Northeast Asia. In Japan it is asociated with	
14	death and houshold items – chopsticks, teacups and so on	
15	– usually come in a set of five to avoid the dreaded four.	

3 Rewrite the second sentence so that it has a similar meaning to the first sentence using the word in bold and other words.

1 We decided not to look for another flat for a couple of months.   **put**
We decided to .... for another flat for a couple of months.

2 You should start training more seriously. You've got a good chance of getting on the team. **encouraged**
She .... training more seriously because she said I had a good chance of getting on the team.

3 'I'm going to send these photographs to the newspaper if you don't pay up,' she said. **threatened**
She .... the photographs to the newspaper if he didn't pay up.

4 I wish I hadn't said I'd help Manuel move house this weekend.   **regret**
I .... I'd help Manuel move house this weekend.

5 Treating her like that was very unfair.   **deserve**
She .... treated like that.

6 I hope he wasn't offended when I told him I thought he was putting on weight.   **mind**
I hope he didn't .... I thought he was putting on weight.

7 I missed my train because of the heavy traffic. **made**
The heavy traffic .... my train.

8 'Why don't we stay in Madrid overnight?' said Silvia.   **proposed**
Silvia .... in Madrid overnight.

9 The organising committee would be delighted if you would give the opening lecture at the conference.   **invite**
The organising committee are pleased .... the opening lecture at the conference.

10 You didn't tell me you were going to be away for a whole month.   **neglected**
You .... you were going to be away for a whole month.

4 Complete these sentences with the missing prepositions.

1 Most musicians spend their lives striving ………… perfection.

2 They are hardly ever completely satisfied ………… a performance.

3 Often it is a teacher they had as a child that has had an enormous influence ………… their career.

4 Even when the reviews in the newspaper are very positive they tend not to be convinced ………… them.

5 An orchestra's programme is usually dictated ………… public tastes and the conductor's preferences.

6 According ………… some experts musical ability is actually determined by a gene.

7 Withdrawal ………… government funding meant the South African National Orchestra had to disband.

8 There had been a gradual reduction ………… the number of people attending their concerts.

9 This lead ………… the criticism that the music they played was no longer relevant to today's South Africans.

10 Non-musicians are often surprised to discover that orchestra members do not always have very much respect ………… conductors.

5 Ten of these sentences are either incorrect or unnatural. Correct them. In some cases there is more than one way of correcting the sentence.

1 She asked me if I had watered the plants and I told her I had done it.

2 I haven't got a mobile phone but I'm considering getting it.

3 Bill loves travelling and I love too.

4 I'm not taking my computer because I can use Mary's.

5 Tony said he was going down to the beach and I said we'd see him down at the beach.

6 Aunt Lucy said she hoped I'd do well in my exams and I said I hoped it too.

7 He said he would come but he didn't come.

8 I travelled alone a lot in 1995 and I really enjoyed it in 1995.

9 My mother never learnt to drive and I haven't learnt to drive.

10 I don't play basketball now but I used.

11 Eli told me to take it easy and I said I'd try to take it easy.

12 Alex didn't pass the exam but José did.

6 Paper 3, Part 6: gapped text

Read the following text and then choose from the list A–J the best phrase given below it to fill each of the spaces. Each correct phrase may only be used once. Some of the suggested answers do not fit at all. The exercise begins with an example (0).

The enduring allure of the one-to-one challenge

In 1906 betting at British sports events was banned, ending a tradition which went back (**0**) ….J…… . In his diary of 1663, Samuel Pepys describes a race between the Duke of Richmond's footman and another runner. Aristocrats regularly pitted their servants against rivals from other households, and large wagers were placed on the results. (**1**) ………… individual challenges regularly attracted large crowds of spectators – and betters. The celebrated series of meetings between W. G. George of England and Scotland's William Cummings culminated in a world mile record for George of 4 min 12.75 seconds, (**2**) ………… . Twenty thousand spectators were present at London's Lillie Bridge stadium on 23 August 1886 (**3**) ………… . A gripping race saw Cummings lose an eight-yard lead on the final lap and collapse 60 yards from home.

George, as the winner, received £100. Additionally, the runners shared the gate receipts after expenses had been paid, a source of revenue that was extremely lucrative. (**4**) ………… in 1885, 30,000 had turned up to watch. George, who had to turn professional to take up Cummings's challenge, (**5**) ………… . But even those gains did not match the profit made by Captain Barclay Allardice in 1809. Allardice was a wealthy Scottish landowner who took part in a challenge of walking 1,000 miles in 1,000 hours for 1,000 guineas or £1,100. (**6**) ………… his stake went up to £16,000 – nearly £250,000 by today's reckoning and nearly enough to get some of today's sprinters off their starting blocks.

A for an event billed as 'The Mile of the Century'
B In 1844,
C a mark which stood for 29 years.
D estimated he made £5,000 in two years.
E For the first of their mile races,
F With side bets,
G By the 19th century,
H the stadium being burned to the ground.
I As a result of this early success
J at least 300 years

Unit 11 test

Choose the best alternative to fill the gap in each of the following sentences.

1 The man .... wife I met at the conference phoned earlier to ask us to dinner.
   A which B who C whom D whose

2 'Illes Pitiuses' is the name of the hotel .... we stay when we go to Formentera.
   A that B where C which D –

3 I was amazed by all the things .... he told me about his trip to India.
   A who B what C – D when

4 The person to .... I spoke insisted that I take out a yearly membership.
   A who B which C whose D whom

5 The book, ... illustrations were painted by a local artist, provides an interesting account of the history of the islands.
   A whose B which C where D that

6 A large group of teenagers were .... around the entrance to the discotheque.
   A mulling B milling C muddling D mauling

7 The president of the local chamber of commerce welcomed us most ....
   A hotly B heatedly C warmly D steamily

8 I could hear the train's whistle .... in the distance.
   A warbling B warping C whaling D wailing

9 She was carrying such an enormous .... suitcase that she could barely get it up the two steps to the hotel entrance.
   A unworthy B unwieldy C unwisely D unworldly

10 The football fans looked like a .... of red and white moving towards the stadium.
   A mess B mass C miss D moss

11 The moon lent a .... glow to the softly rolling hills.
   A ghastly B beastly C ghostly D vastly

12 Periodically she could see the .... of a spent cigarette tossed overboard into the ocean.
   A flutter B flap C flight D flash

13 .... I would like to say how happy I am to be here with you today.
   A In the beginning B Festival C First of all
   D Best of all

14 .... there are fewer tourists in October, the weather can be almost as warm as it is in September.
   A Despite B However C In spite of D Although

15 He decided to put off his journey .... the poor weather.
   A because B consequently C because of
   D in consequence

16 There are various pros and cons to travelling by boat. .... it can be much cheaper than air travel, though it can also be less comfortable and less convenient.
   A Although B On the one hand C In spite of
   D Despite

17 Despite .... an excellent holiday, I still felt quite tired.
   A I had had B to have had C having had D have had

18 Putting it quite .... , she really gets on my nerves.
   A obviously B frankly C basically D apparently

19 .... she planned to meet up with them in Barcelona, but something went wrong and she didn't turn up.
   A Apparently B Personally C Frankly D Obviously

20 I don't think redecorating the living room is such a good idea, ... It looks fine as it is.
   A apparently B actually C obviously D basically

21 .... I would have told you I was going to be late if I had known the plane would be delayed.
   A Obviously B Personally C Apparently D Basically

22 It was very .... of you to put clean sheets on the bed for us. We could have changed them ourselves.
   A thought-provoking B thoughtful C thoughtless
   D unthinking

23 I don't object to people being vegetarians, but it gets on my nerves when they're .... about it.
   A self-centred B self-righteous C self-deprecating
   D self-sufficient

24 She's extremely .... She doesn't seem to care what she looks like and is happy to live with almost no human contact for months at a time.
   A unconvincing B uncomplicated C unconventional
   D inconceivable

25 She's one of the .... people I know. If she can avoid it, she won't have so much as a glass of water when we go to the bar for coffee.
   A meanest B maddest C cruellest D hardest

Unit 12 test

Choose the best alternative to fill the gap in each of the following sentences.

1 He began to take total strangers .... long-lost friends.
A being   B be   C to be   D were

2 She seemed to be listening but she was not taking .... anything that the lecturer said.
A off   B on   C to   D in

3 I'm afraid I've never really taken .... Alex. He's just not my type.
A to   B for   C on   D at

4 I hear they're taking .... staff at that new hotel opposite the football stadium.
A to   B for   C on   D at

5 I really admire the way he takes even the most difficult circumstances .... his stride.
A off   B on   C to   D in

6 I'm not demanding. I try to take people pretty much the way I .... them.
A encounter   B know   C find   D meet

7 He tried to take .... of her kindness and hospitality.
A benefit   B advantage   C profit   D gain

8 I don't think you should take it for .... that you can stay with them when you go to Barcelona.
A given   B read   C accepted   D granted

9 When he announced that he was leaving at the end of the month it completely took my .... away.
A mind   B breath   C heart   D soul

10 She's taking too much responsibility .... herself. She should learn to delegate.
A to   B for   C upon   D in

11 Walking up the hill to the station really took it out .... me.
A to   B off   C of   D for

12 I'm afraid I'll have to take this issue up .... someone in authority.
A with   B to   C for   D at

13 .... had I found the departure gate than they announced that there would be a two-hour delay.
A Hardly   B No sooner   C Scarcely   D Only after

14 Only after .... the contract did I realise that I would have to wait a month before I was paid.
A had I signed   B signed   C having signed   D to have signed

15 At no time .... she was responsible for what happened.
A did I believe   B having believed   C I had believed   D I have believed

16 Who .... you I was there?
A did tell   B has told   C told   D does tell

17 Have you asked him where .... last night?
A he was   B was he   C he has been   D has he been

18 What's that tune you're .... ?
A thudding   B hissing   C humming   D screeching

19 She could just make out a faint .... of light at the end of the tunnel.
A flash   B sparkle   C twinkle   D beam

20 The engines of the plane let out a huge ....
A bang   B roar   C crash   D thud

21 The candle .... in the draft and then went out.
A twinkled   B sparkled   C flashed   D flickered

22 She could hear the wild monkeys .... at one another in the jungle.
A screeching   B banging   C thudding   D humming

23 There was a mighty .... as the mirror fell to the floor.
A thud   B bang   C crash   D hiss

24 The fluorescent face of his watch .... in the dark.
A beamed   B flickered   C sparkled   D glowed

25 I knew he was only teasing me because he said it with a real .... in his eye.
A beam   B twinkle   C flicker   D glow

Unit 13 test

Choose the best alternative to fill the gap in each of the following sentences.

1 I can't .... exactly what I don't like about that logo, but it really doesn't work for me.
   A get my tongue round   B put my finger on
   C put my mind to   D come to grips with

2 Thousands of Internet businesses .... over the last few years.
   A have been establishing   B being established
   C have been established   D been established

3 The flight might .... by the poor weather conditions.
   A have delayed   B have been delayed
   C have being delayed   D has been delayed

4 She is going to .... to Branch Manager.
   A promote   B have promoted   C have been promoted
   D be promoted

5 The Olympic games received huge media ....
   A cover   B covered   C coverage   D covering

6 When you travel for work purposes, does you company pay all your .... ?
   A expensive   B expenditure   C expense   D expenses

7 I find it .... to be criticised in public.
   A humiliation   B humiliated   C humiliating   D humiliate

8 She was praised for her .... in the aftermath of the recent disaster.
   A heroic   B heroine   C heroism   D hero

9 .... even something as apparently simple as a menu can require considerable skill.
   A Translation   B Translator   C Translating   D Translate

10 The .... of her understanding of his poetry grew the more she read.
   A deepen   B depth   C deep   D deepened

11 She provided a complete .... of the product for the patent application.
   A descriptive   B descriptor   C describe   D description

12 .... that it was very stormy to the west, we took waterproof jackets with us.
   A We have noticed   B Have we noticed
   C Having noticed   D Have noticed

13 .... to his feet in a rage, he shouted that he would never resign.

A He jumped   B Jumping   C He has jumped
D To jump

14 Cristina will be on maternity .... until the end of the year.
   A holiday   B vacation   C break   D leave

15 He's made enough money to take .... retirement.
   A early   B premature   C advance   D anticipated

16 The business they started in January 2000 had .... bankrupt only a year later.
   A had   B gone   C made   D done

17 They had to lay .... over 20% of the workforce because of the fall in profits.
   A over   B into   C off   D onto

18 Why do you think Simon .... the sack? He was always a good worker.
   A had   B got   C made   D took

19 Is there any possibility of .... flexitime rather than the normal nine-to-five schedule?
   A working   B doing   C making   D going

20 How many shares in that company do you currently .... ?
   A possess   B hold   C maintain   D keep

21 Buying a large bag of rice would be far more .... than buying small packets.
   A economic   B economising   C economist
   D economical

22 The .... officer in our company has a degree in psychology.
   A personal   B person   C personnel   D personage

23 The government are refusing to .... small businesses that have accumulated too many debts.
   A subsidiary   B subsidise   C subsidised   D subsidising

24 Improved .... at our West Moreland plant has led to an increase in production.
   A efficiently   B efficient   C efficiency   D inefficient

25 The latest .... figures show that there are fewer jobless people than there have been for the previous ten years.
   A employee   B employer   C employment   D employing

Unit 14 test

Choose the best alternative to fill the gap in each of the following sentences.

1 They agreed .... the meeting until the following week.
A we postpone   B postponing
C that we should postpone   D postpone

2 She claimed .... a wind-up CD player.
A she invents   B inventing   C having invented
D to have invented

3 The students urged .... for election as their representative.
A that he stand   B that he should stand
C that he would stand   D him to stand

4 It .... that the search for survivors will be abandoned tomorrow morning.
A has announced   B announces   C has been announced
D is announcing

5 She .... we take a canal trip to see the city from the water.
A told   B suggested   C said   D advised

6 He admitted .... office stationery for use at home.
A to take   B to taking   C he should take
D he would take

7 I think the most important .... of the problem is the potential for environmental damage.
A respect   B aspect   C prospect   D inspect

8 I'd like to have your .... on the situation in Fiji.
A vistas   B visions   C views   D visages

9 Do you really think the world is due .... another major volcanic eruption?
A to   B for   C from   D of

10 I assure you there is no need for you to concern yourself further .... the matter.
A about   B for   C by   D of

11 Journalists have been extremely critical .... the election procedures.
A about   B for   C by   D of

12 Everyone was shocked .... his violent reaction to the news.
A about   B for   C by   D of

13 The local population seem indifferent .... the suffering of these poor animals.
A to   B for   C from   D of

14 Which member of staff is to be responsible .... the new sales drive?
A to   B for   C from   D of

15 Cats are capable .... tremendous loyalty and affection.
A to   B for   C from   D of

16 People are eligible .... a pension at the age of 65.
A to   B for   C from   D of

17 You should be ashamed .... yourself.
A to   B for   C from   D of

18 What makes you think you are immune .... the flu virus?
A to   B for   C from   D of

19 Everyone is welcome to attend, irrespective .... previous experience.
A to   B for   C from   D of

20 I'm a bit anxious .... going to Hong Kong for Christmas.
A about   B for   C by   D of

21 I think there must be something wrong .... the satellite dish.
A for   B about   C with   D by

22 Did you read .... news about the volcanic eruption in the Pacific?
A a   B –   C some   D the

23 They won .... for two to French Polynesia.
A a trip   B a travel   C trip   D travel

24 A dog needs .... to run around.
A a space   B the space   C spaces   D space

25 She gave me an enormous .... of information about mobile phones.
A amount   B number   C lot   D bit

Progress test 3 Units 11–15

1 Paper 3, Part 4: word formation

For questions 1–15 use the word given in capitals at the end of each line to form a word that fits in each space in the same line.

EXTRACT FROM AN ARTICLE

Silicon Valley Millionaires	
Although the Internet is still probably only in (**0**) embryonic	(0) EMBRYO
form in (**1**) ………… to what it will be like in the future,	(1) COMPARE
there is no doubt that many Internet businesses have been	
extremely (**2**) ………… . San Francisco has the highest	(2) PROFIT
(**3**) ………… of self-made Internet millionaires. Some have	(3) CONCENTRATE
made their money from clever (**4**) ………… in Internet	(4) INVEST
businesses while others have used their skills to create	
(**5**) ………… Internet products. Regardless of how they	(5) INNOVATE
became (**6**) …………, one thing these people share is an	(6) WEALTH
almost (**7**) ………… dedication to their work. Many work	(7) OBSESS
at home in luxurious houses and flats. (**8**) ………… , this	(8) FORTUNATE
influx of very rich young people has pushed property values	
beyond the means of many others.	

EXTRACT FROM AN ENCYCLOPEDIA

How Sociable Are Cats?	
The cat is often characterised as a solitary, (**9**) …………	(9) SELF
animal, walking alone and coming together with other cats	
only to fight or mate. Wild cats fit this picture (**10**) …………	(10) REASON
well, but they are (**11**) ………… of changing their ways in	(11) ABLE
more crowded situations. Living in cities and towns, and in	
the homes of their human owners cats show a remarkable	
and (**12**) ………… degree of sociability. Anyone doubting	(12) EXPECT
this must remember that, to a pet cat, we ourselves are giant	
cats. The fact that domestic cats will share a home with a	
human family is, in itself (**13**) ………… of their social	(13) PROVE
flexibility. But this picture is (**14**) ………… . There are	(14) COMPLETE
many other ways in which cats demonstrate co-operation,	
mutual aid and (**15**) ………… .	(15) TOLERATE

2 In which of these sentences is it possible to omit *that*?

1 It has often been said that cats are less intelligent than dogs.

2 The company directors told the shareholders that they did not expect to be able to pay a dividend in the first year of trading.

3 The airline recommended that passengers suffering from fear of flying should take a course before booking a long-haul flight.

4 The financial adviser explained that more secure long-term investments would be better than short-term ones.

5 The tour guide said that we should be back at the coach by 2 p.m.

6 In Descartes' time almost no one believed that animals could think.

3 There are mistakes with prepositions in all but one of these sentences. Find the mistakes and correct them.

1 I'm beginning to feel a bit concerned with Bill. He should have phoned by now.

2 He's not actually due to a check up for another month but if his teeth are bothering him he should go to the dentist.

3 There's nothing wrong about feeling homesick. It's completely normal.

4 They were very critical for the bathroom facilities in the hotel.

5 I was completely baffled from his behaviour.

6 We're both feeling a bit anxious for the trip.

7 He's completely addicted by computer games.

8 Please phone us, irrespective to what time of day or night you arrive.

9 I thought I was immune of this winter's flu and colds, but I got quite ill at the end of term.

10 He'll be eligible to a full pension when he retires.

11 She was rather shocked for the way people treated animals there.

12 Jeremy has been absent of class six times this semester.

13 He had never believed he was capable for living on his own.

14 I think you should feel more than a little ashamed for yourself.

15 I'm going tomorrow evening and I haven't even started to get ready for the trip.

4 There is a missing word in each of these sentences. Work out which word is missing and insert it.

1 She took upon herself to visit her elderly aunt in hospital every day.

2 We've complained several times but as nothing has been done we'll have to take the matter with the authorities.

3 The flight back from Australia really took it out them.

4 I don't know why but I've never really taken Amanda. She's not my kind of person at all.

5 I wish you wouldn't always take it granted that I'll do the shopping.

6 The view of the Atlas Mountains at dawn completely took my breath.

7 Sam will take advantage you if you let him.

8 Sandra took the extra workload very much her stride.

9 It makes quite a change to see a company taking staff rather than making people redundant.

10 People kept taking me be my sister Mary, which was very embarrassing.

11 I'm not demanding. I take people very much the I find them.

12 He explained how to install the new program but he spoke so quickly I couldn't take it all.

5 Put in the missing word in each of the following sentences. In some cases two positions are possible.

1 I missed some classes at the beginning of the course and it took me ages to catch with the others.

2 Trying to cut on the number of cigarettes you smoke won't work. You should give up completely.

3 Would you like to use the bathroom to freshen before we go out?

4 I managed to track a copy of his first album in a second-hand record shop.

5 Would you mind speaking a bit? We can't hear you at the back of the room.

6 I was only away for a week but the work has really piled in my absence.

7 The pickpocket must have sneaked behind me and taken my wallet while I was waiting in the queue.

8 They're going to spend the money Tony inherited on having their house done.

9 Calm, will you! There's no point getting angry about it.

10 I can't keep with Anna. She's got so much energy she never seems to stop to draw breath.

11 I thought the film was a rather watered version of the story in the book. It wasn't nearly as powerful.

12 She's gone to the hairdresser to have her highlights touched.

13 They had to interview everyone on the list, but they've managed to narrow it to five applicants.

14 I wish you'd liven a bit. You seem so miserable lately.

15 When Andrew was younger it was impossible to imagine him ever getting married and settling.

16 The police have managed to pin the time of the murder to between ten and ten-thirty.

Work: the daily grind we can't do without

A man dies and finds himself in a sumptuous palace attended by servants and surrounded by every conceivable luxury. For a week he indulges in all the pleasures he never had the time, money or opportunity to enjoy when he was alive. Then one evening an angelic butler appears and asks him if everything is to his satisfaction.

'Perfect,' says the man, 'but tomorrow I'd like to do something different. Some work, perhaps.'

'Not possible,' says the angel.

'Why not?' says the man. 'This is heaven, isn't it?'

'No,' says the angel. 'Quite the reverse in fact.'

Work might seem like hell but however much we might think we loathe it, our psychological need for work is real. Everyone wants to be valued, and wages and salaries are the hard proof that we matter.

Not any old work qualifies however. No matter how worthwhile or demanding they might be, child-rearing, housework and voluntary employment tend to be regarded as non-jobs, hardly better than hobbies. In our work-centred culture, a 'proper job' means paid employment. Being paid for a job is our stake in society. It's good for our self-esteem.

Of course, we would also prefer work to be useful, interesting and congenial, as well as paid. But you don't have to enjoy your job to derive psychological benefits from it. In fact, our attitude to work is quite masochistic. According to psychologist Dr John Haworth, the constraints of a job, such as the need to overcome our own resistance to unenjoyable tasks, actually contribute to our sense of well-being.

The need to be in a particular place at a particular time, working as part of a team towards a common goal, gives us a sense of purpose and structure that we find difficult to impose on ourselves. Also, as the roles of the sexes become blurred, the modern workplace is an arena in which men can assert their identity and where women can create a new one. "I love my husband", says one female junior executive, "but I have to admit that the office is where I feel most fulfilled."

Although genuine workaholics are uncommon, many of us are 'job junkies' without knowing. When we are deprived of work we become irritable, unkempt, lethargic and unable to enjoy the expanse of leisure which, paradoxically, unemployment opens up for us. For people who are made redundant, the plunge into unemployment can be particularly cruel. At a stroke they have lost their livelihood and the foundation of their lives. To be told you are not needed is bad enough, but it does not end there: you still have to live in a work-driven culture that tends to regard the jobless as outsiders and victims of sloth or incompetence.

Information technology may end up making even the workplace itself redundant. Offices are extremely expensive, a drain not only on company profits but also on the time and energy of employees who spend large parts of the day commuting to and from them. Almost half the British workforce are now employed to process different kinds of information on computers. They don't in fact need an office in order to do their work. All that is necessary is a power outlet, a telephone line and a computer.

Already more than two million British employees are what have come to be known as 'teleworkers'. Some work from home full-time, keeping in touch with headquarters by electronic mail and phone. Others 'hot desk', logging on to a time-shared workstation for one or more days a week.

Many employees welcome the break with tradition, claiming that teleworking has improved their lives enormously. 'I used to spend two hours a day commuting,' says Bridget, an educational consultant with two children. 'Working from home not only gives me more time for work and for my family, but has allowed us to move out of town – something that was impossible when I was tied to the office.' But though commuting on the information highway may be preferable to sitting in a traffic jam, not everyone has the temperament for it.

A report from Swansea University psychology department came to the conclusion that the ideal teleworker is a self-sufficient and introverted individual. Steve, who works from home as a software designer for a bank, does not fit this profile. 'I liked the office culture,' he says 'the gossip and team spirit. Working from home can make you feel cut off.'

Various employers have reported that teleworking has improved productivity, in some cases by up to 50 per cent, but some of them are discovering the downside. The unsupervised worker may be an unseen ghost in the machine who causes irreparable damage but who goes undetected until it is too late.

Whatever the advantages and disadvantages of teleworking, it is a siren song that neither employers nor workers are likely to resist. After all, we were conditioned to the nine-to-five working day, a routine imposed by convention rather than the particular tasks in hand, and there is no reason we can't be conditioned out of it.

This article was written at home in the country during bursts of activity interspersed by periods of idleness. Perhaps that's the natural work rhythm to which we'll return in the world of virtual offices and video conferencing.

6   Paper 1, Part 3 (multiple choice)

Read the newspaper article opposite and then answer questions 1–7. Choose between the alternatives A, B, C or D, which one best answers each question.

1   What point does the story at the beginning of the article make about work?
   A To live without work would be unbearable.
   B Our working lives are hell.
   C People don't have to work in heaven.
   D Even angels have to work.

2   According to the text, what characteristic must work have to be psychologically beneficial?
   A It must be enjoyable.
   B It must be worthwhile.
   C It must be paid.
   D It must be boring.

3   What makes being made redundant worse than being unemployed for another reason?
   A You don't have any income.
   B You are treated as an outcast.
   C You know that you were not needed.
   D You are blamed for your situation.

4   How has information technology affected work?
   A Almost half the British population now work at home.
   B Offices are more expensive than they used to be.
   C People can get to work more quickly than before.
   D Offices have become unnecessary for many workers.

5   Why do some people dislike teleworking?
   A They feel isolated.
   B They become less sociable.
   C They become self-sufficient.
   D They miss driving to work.

6   What disadvantage does teleworking have for employers?
   A People don't work as hard as they do in offices.
   B They have less control over what the workers do.
   C Profits have fallen by almost 50 per cent.
   D Workers sometimes damage the equipment.

7   What is the attitude of the writer to the changes he describes?
   A He thinks they are positive.
   B He is not sure about them.
   C He thinks they are potentially harmful.
   D He thinks things were better before.

Unit tests keys

Key: Unit 1 test

1B 2D 3C 4B 5A 6B 7A
8D 9D 10B 11D 12A 13C
14D 15D 16A 17C 18D
19C 20C 21C 22C 23D
24D 25B

Key: Unit 2 test

1C 2D 3B 4A 5C 6C 7A
8D 9C 10C 11D 12D 13C
14C 15B 16C 17B 18D
19B 20D 21C 22D 23D
24A 25D

Key: Unit 3 test

1C 2A 3B 4C 5B 6A 7A
8D 9A 10C 11A 12A 13D
14C 15C 16B 17C 18D
19D 20C 21C 22D 23C
24B 25B

Key: Unit 4 test

1B 2A 3B 4C 5C 6C 7D
8D 9C 10D 11B 12A 13B
14D 15C 16B 17C 18A
19C 20B 21D 22D 23B
24C 25B

Key: Progress test 1 Units 1–5

1 1 He might **have** gone out to the cinema.
2 You should **try** to give up smoking. You must be spending a fortune on cigarettes.
3 You must know the café I'm talking about. Everyone goes there.
4 They **can't** have forgotten about the party. I rang and reminded them yesterday.
5 ✓
6 Nothing **can/could** possibly stop me loving Anthony.

7 You only need **say/to say** the word and I'll come and help you.
8 You **don't have** to bring a bottle of wine or anything. There'll be more than enough to eat and drink.

2 1 absent
2 conditioning
3 self
4 minute
5 tight
6 level
7 produced
8 called
9 proof
10 long

3 1 Supposing you won the lottery, would you give up your job?
2 Had she known what negative reactions her book would receive she would probably never have written it.
3 If you were to come to Holland again, would you come to visit me?
4 If you'll take a seat, the doctor will see you in a few moments.
5 Imagine it was possible to/you could live for five hundred years, would you want to?
6 If you happen to be going past the Odeon, can you give me a call if *The Beach* is on.

4 1 hold
2 drumming
3 shoulders
4 nose
5 cracking
6 lips
7 clenched
8 twisted
9 pulled
10 eyebrows

11 shook
12 lips

5 1 a) for (a salad)
    b) Peter
    c) Let me
  2 a) Won't be back before 11.30. Training session at the pool. Sorry! Forgot to mention it this a.m. Lasagne in oven. Stuff for a salad in fridge. Can you record Ally McBeal for me? Video in the machine. See you later. Love, Mary
    b) Clara, Peter phoned. Won't be able to come to the concert tonight. Something about having to finish a project. Says you can use his season ticket if you want to. Phone before 5 p.m. and let him know. Tina
    c) Dear Alan, Don't forget it's Dad's birthday on 21/9. Fancy going in with me on a present for him? Thought a subscription to *History Today* might be good. Let me know asap. Home all weekend. Love, Elisa
  3 (suggested answers)
    1 Your mum phoned to remind you about your dad's birthday. Phone her back asap.
    2 Hi. Just to let you know I'm having a party on 23/7 … from 9 p.m onwards. Flat 5, 23 Westfield Terrace, London, SW15. BYOB. RSVP. Rod

Key: Unit 6 test

1D 2A 3C 4A 5D 6C 7B
8D 9B 10A 11D 12C 13B
14D 15D 16D 17C 18C
19D 20C 21C 22A 23D
24D 25A

Key: Unit 7 test

1A 2C 3B 4C 5B 6D 7B
8A 9D 10B 11D 12C 13C
14C 15A 16C 17B 18D
19C 20D 21C 22C 23C
24B 25C

Key: Unit 8 test

1A 2A 3D 4B 5A 6B 7C
8C 9B 10B 11D 12D 13A
14B 15C 16D 17B 18C
19C 20B 21B 22D 23A
24C 25B

Key: Unit 9 test

1C 2D 3D 4B 5A 6C 7C
8D 9B 10A 11D 12B 13B
14C 15D 16C 17D 18B
19C 20D 21B 22D 23C
24C 25A

Key: Progress test 2 Units 6–10

1 a) person
   b) attendants
   c) officers
   d) teachers
   e) person
   f) fighters

2 1 luckiest
   2 considered
   3 Chinese
   4 ✓
   5 addresses
   6 ✓
   7 twelve-year
   8 cycles
   9 ✓
   10 fifth
   11 common
   12 ✓
   13 associated
   14 household
   15 ✓

3 1 put off looking
   2 encouraged me to start
   3 threatened to send
   4 regret saying/having said
   5 didn't deserve to be
   6 mind me/my telling him

7 made me miss
8 proposed staying/that we stay
9 to invite you to give
10 neglected to tell me

4 1 for
   2 with
   3 on
   4 by
   5 by
   6 to
   7 of
   8 in
   9 to
   10 for

5 1 She asked me if I had watered
   the plants and I told her I had/had
   done.
   2 I haven't got a mobile phone
   but I'm considering getting one.
   3 Bill loves travelling and I do
   too/so do I.
   4 ✓
   5 Tony said he was going down to
   the beach and I said we'd see him
   (down) there.
   6 Aunt Lucy said she hoped I'd do
   well in my exams and I said I hoped
   so too/I did too.
   7 He said he would come but he
   didn't.
   8 I travelled alone a lot in 1995
   and I really enjoyed it then.
   9 My mother never learnt to drive
   and I haven't either/neither have I.
   10 I don't play basketball now but I
   used to.
   11 Eli told me to take it easy and I
   said I'd try/try to.
   12 ✓

6 1G 2C 3A 4E 5D 6F

Key: Unit 11 test

1D 2B 3C 4D 5A 6B 7C
8D 9B 10B 11C 12D 13C
14D 15C 16B 17C 18B
19A 20B 21A 22B 23B
24C 25A

Key: Unit 12 test

1C 2D 3A 4C 5D 6C 7B
8D 9B 10C 11C 12A 13B
14C 15A 16C 17A 18C
19D 20B 21D 22A 23C
24D 25B

Key: Unit 13 test

1B 2C 3B 4D 5C 6D 7C
8C 9C 10B 11D 12C 13B
14D 15A 16B 17C 18B
19A 20B 21D 22C 23B
24C 25C

Key: Unit 14 test

1C 2D 3D 4C 5B 6B 7B
8C 9B 10A 11D 12C 13A
14B 15D 16B 17D 18A
19D 20A 21C 22D 23A
24D 25A

Key: Progress test 3 Units 11–15

1 1 comparison
   2 profitable
   3 concentration
   4 investment
   5 innovative
   6 wealthy
   7 obsessive
   8 unfortunately
   9 selfish
   10 reasonably
   11 capable
   12 unexpected
   13 proof
   14 incomplete
   15 tolerance

2 1 not possible
   2 possible
   3 not possible
   4 not possible
   5 possible
   6 possible

3 1 concerned **about**
   2 due **for**
   3 wrong **with**
   4 critical **of**
   5 baffled **by**
   6 anxious **about**

7 addicted **to**
8 irrespective **of**
9 immune **to**
10 eligible **for**
11 shocked **by**
12 absent **from**
13 capable **of**
14 ashamed **of**
15 ✓

4 1 She took **it** upon herself to visit her elderly aunt in hospital every day.
2 We've complained several times but as nothing has been done we'll have to take the matter **up** with the authorities.
3 The flight back from Australia really took it **out** of them.
4 I don't know why but I've never really taken **to** Amanda. She's not my kind of person at all.
5 I wish you wouldn't always take it **for** granted that I'll do the shopping.
6 The view of the Atlas Mountains at dawn completely took my breath **away**.
7 Sam will take advantage **of** you if you let him.
8 Sandra took the extra workload very much **in** her stride.
9 It makes quite a change to see a

company taking staff **on** rather than making people redundant.
10 People kept taking me **to** be my sister Mary, which was very embarrassing.
11 I'm not demanding. I take people very much the **way** I find them.
12 He explained how to install the new program but he spoke so quickly I couldn't take it all **in**.

5 1 I missed some classes at the beginning of the course and it took me ages to catch **up** with the others.
2 Trying to cut **down** on the number of cigarettes you smoke won't work. You should give up completely.
3 Would you like to use the bathroom to freshen **up** before we go out?
4 I managed to track (**down**) a copy of his first album (**down**) in a second-hand record shop.
5 Would you mind speaking **up** a bit? We can't hear you at the back of the room.
6 I was only away for a week but the work has really piled **up** in my absence.
7 The pickpocket must have

sneaked **up** behind me and taken my wallet while I was waiting in the queue.
8 They're going to spend the money Tony inherited on having their house done **up**.
9 Calm **down**, will you! There's no point getting angry about it.
10 I can't keep **up** with Anna. She's got so much energy she never seems to stop to draw breath.
11 I thought the film was a rather watered **down** version of the story in the book. It wasn't nearly as powerful.
12 She's gone to the hairdresser to have her highlights touched **up**.
13 They had to interview everyone on the list, but they've managed to narrow it **down** to five applicants.
14 I wish you'd liven **up** a bit. You seem so miserable lately.
15 When Andrew was younger it was impossible to imagine him ever getting married and settling **down**.
16 The police have managed to pin (**down**) the time of the murder (**down**) to between ten and ten-thirty.

6 1A 2C 3C 4D 5A 6B 7A

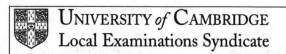
Candidate Name
If not already printed, write name in CAPITALS and complete the Candidate No. grid (in pencil).

Candidate's signature

Examination Title

Centre

Supervisor:

[X] If the candidate is ABSENT or has WITHDRAWN shade here ▭

Centre No.

Candidate No.

Examination Details

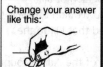

Multiple-choice Answer Sheet

Use a pencil Mark one letter for each question.

For example:

If you think C is the right answer to the question, mark your answer sheet like this:

| 0 | A B C |

Change your answer like this:

1	A B C D E F G H I
2	A B C D E F G H I
3	A B C D E F G H I
4	A B C D E F G H I
5	A B C D E F G H I
6	A B C D E F G H I
7	A B C D E F G H I
8	A B C D E F G H I
9	A B C D E F G H I
10	A B C D E F G H I
11	A B C D E F G H I
12	A B C D E F G H I
13	A B C D E F G H I
14	A B C D E F G H I
15	A B C D E F G H I
16	A B C D E F G H I
17	A B C D E F G H I
18	A B C D E F G H I
19	A B C D E F G H I
20	A B C D E F G H I

21	A B C D E F G H I
22	A B C D E F G H I
23	A B C D E F G H I
24	A B C D E F G H I
25	A B C D E F G H I
26	A B C D E F G H I
27	A B C D E F G H I
28	A B C D E F G H I
29	A B C D E F G H I
30	A B C D E F G H I
31	A B C D E F G H I
32	A B C D E F G H I
33	A B C D E F G H I
34	A B C D E F G H I
35	A B C D E F G H I
36	A B C D E F G H I
37	A B C D E F G H I
38	A B C D E F G H I
39	A B C D E F G H I
40	A B C D E F G H I

41	A B C D E F G H I
42	A B C D E F G H I
43	A B C D E F G H I
44	A B C D E F G H I
45	A B C D E F G H I
46	A B C D E F G H I
47	A B C D E F G H I
48	A B C D E F G H I
49	A B C D E F G H I
50	A B C D E F G H I
51	A B C D E F G H I
52	A B C D E F G H I
53	A B C D E F G H I
54	A B C D E F G H I
55	A B C D E F G H I
56	A B C D E F G H I
57	A B C D E F G H I
58	A B C D E F G H I
59	A B C D E F G H I
60	A B C D E F G H I

CAE1

DP306/80

UNIVERSITY *of* CAMBRIDGE
Local Examinations Syndicate

Candidate Name
If not already printed, write name
in CAPITALS and complete the
Candidate No. grid (in pencil).
Candidate's signature

Examination Title

Centre

Supervisor:
☒ If the candidate is ABSENT or has WITHDRAWN shade here ▭

Centre No.

Candidate No.

Examination Detail

0	0	0	0
1	1	1	1
2	2	2	2
3	3	3	3
4	4	4	4
5	5	5	5
6	6	6	6
7	7	7	7
8	8	8	8
9	9	9	9

Candidate Answer Sheet

Use a pencil

For **Parts 1** and **6**:
Mark ONE letter for each question.
For example, if you think **B** is the
right answer to the question,
mark your answer sheet like this:

0 | A [B] C D

For **Parts 2, 3, 4** and **5**:
Write your answers in the spaces
next to the numbers like this:

0 | *example*

Part 1				
1	A	B	C	D
2	A	B	C	D
3	A	B	C	D
4	A	B	C	D
5	A	B	C	D
6	A	B	C	D
7	A	B	C	D
8	A	B	C	D
9	A	B	C	D
10	A	B	C	D
11	A	B	C	D
12	A	B	C	D
13	A	B	C	D
14	A	B	C	D
15	A	B	C	D

Part 2	Do not write here
16	▭ 16 ▭
17	▭ 17 ▭
18	18 ▭
19	19 ▭
20	▭ 20 ▭
21	▭ 21 ▭
22	22 ▭
23	23 ▭
24	24 ▭
25	▭ 25 ▭
26	26 ▭
27	▭ 27 ▭
28	28 ▭
29	▭ 29 ▭
30	▭ 30 ▭

Turn
over for
parts
3 - 6 →

CAE-3

DP394/338

Part 3		Do not write here
31		31
32		32
33		33
34		34
35		35
36		36
37		37
38		38
39		39
40		40
41		41
42		42
43		43
44		44
45		45
46		46

Part 4		Do not write here
47		47
48		48
49		49
50		50
51		51
52		52
53		53
54		54
55		55
56		56
57		57
58		58
59		59
60		60
61		61

Part 5		Do not write here
62		62
63		63
64		64
65		65
66		66
67		67
68		68
69		69
70		70
71		71
72		72
73		73
74		74

Part 6								
75	A	B	C	D	E	F	G	H	I
76	A	B	C	D	E	F	G	H	I
77	A	B	C	D	E	F	G	H	I
78	A	B	C	D	E	F	G	H	I
79	A	B	C	D	E	F	G	H	I
80	A	B	C	D	E	F	G	H	I

SAMPLE

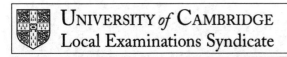

UNIVERSITY *of* CAMBRIDGE
Local Examinations Syndicate

Candidate Name
If not already printed, write name in CAPITALS and complete the Candidate No. grid (in pencil).

Candidate's signature

Examination Title

Centre

Supervisor:
[X] If the candidate is ABSENT or has WITHDRAWN shade here ▭

SAMPLE

Centre No.

Candidate No.

Examination Details

0	0	0	0
1	1	1	1
2	2	2	2
3	3	3	3
4	4	4	4
5	5	5	5
6	6	6	6
7	7	7	7
8	8	8	8
9	9	9	9

Listening Comprehension Answer Sheet

Enter the test number here ▭▭▭

For office use only ⌐3⌐ CPE ⌐5⌐ CAE ⌐0⌐⌐1⌐⌐2⌐⌐3⌐⌐4⌐⌐5⌐⌐6⌐⌐7⌐⌐8⌐⌐9⌐
⌐0⌐⌐1⌐⌐2⌐⌐3⌐⌐4⌐⌐5⌐⌐6⌐⌐7⌐⌐8⌐⌐9⌐

Write your answers below	Do not write here	Continue here	Do not write here
1	▭ 1 ▭	21	21
2	▭ 2 ▭	22	22
3	▭ 3 ▭	23	23
4	▭ 4 ▭	24	24
5	▭ 5 ▭	25	25
6	▭ 6 ▭	26	26
7	▭ 7 ▭	27	27
8	▭ 8 ▭	28	28
9	▭ 9 ▭	29	29
10	▭ 10 ▭	30	30
11	▭ 11 ▭	31	31
12	▭ 12 ▭	32	32
13	▭ 13 ▭	33	33
14	▭ 14 ▭	34	34
15	▭ 15 ▭	35	35
16	▭ 16 ▭	36	36
17	▭ 17 ▭	37	37
18	▭ 18 ▭	38	38
19	▭ 19 ▭	39	39
20	▭ 20 ▭	40	40

EFL 4

DP308/82